Religious Nationalism in Modern Europe

This volume examines the enduring nature of religious nationalism in modern Europe. Through a series of in-depth case studies covering Ireland, England, Poland, and Greece, the author argues that religious frontiers, or geographic lines of division between different and unique religions, are central to the formation of religiously based national identities.

Typically, as states develop economically and politically, religion plays a lesser role in both individual lives and national identity. However, at religious frontiers, religion becomes useful for differentiating and mobilizing groups of people. This is particularly true when the religious frontier also represents a threat or conflict. Although religion may not be the root of conflict in these instances, the conflict takes on religious tones because of its ability to unite an otherwise diverse population. Religion takes precedence over language, culture, or other national building blocks because the "other" can best be distinguished in religious terms. The in-depth case studies allow for a deep historical understanding of the processes that converge to create a modern religious nation.

Greatly expanding our current understanding of the conditions in which religious nationalism develops, this important book has implications for our understanding of religion and politics, secularization, European politics, and foreign policy.

Philip W. Barker is Assistant Professor of Political Science at Austin College in Sherman, Texas, USA.

Nationalism and Ethnicity/Routledge Studies in Nationalism and Ethnicity

Formerly known as Cass Series: Nationalism and Ethnicity, ISSN 1462–9755
Edited by William Safran
University of Colorado at Boulder, Colorado, USA
This new series draws attention to some of the most exciting issues in current world political debate: nation-building, autonomy and self-determination; ethnic identity, conflict and accommodation; pluralism, multiculturalism and the politics of language; ethnonationalism, irredentism and separatism; and immigration, naturalization and citizenship. The series will include monographs as well as edited volumes and, through the use of case studies and comparative analyses, will bring together some of the best work to be found in the field.

Nationalism and Ethnicity

Ethnicity and Citizenship
The Canadian case
Edited by Jean Laponce and William Safran

Nationalism and Ethnoregional Identities in China
Edited by William Safran

Identity and Territorial Autonomy in Plural Societies
Edited by William Safran and Ramon Maíz

Ideology, Legitimacy and the New State
Yugoslavia, Serbia and Croatia
Siniša Malešević

Diasporas and Ethnic Migrants
Germany, Israel and Russia in comparative perspective
Rainer Munz and Rainer Ohliger

Ethnic Groups in Motion
Economic competition and migration in multiethnic states
Milica Z. Bookman

Post-Cold War Identity Politics
Northern and Baltic experiences
Edited by Marko Lehti and David J. Smith

Welfare, Ethnicity and Altruism
New findings and evolutionary theory
Edited by Frank Salter

Routledge Studies in Nationalism and Ethnicity

Ethnic Violence and the Societal Security Dilemma
Paul Roe

Nationalism in a Global Era
The persistence of nations
Edited by Mitchell Young, Eric Zuelow and Andreas Sturm

Religious Nationalism in Modern Europe
If God be for us
Philip W. Barker

Religious Nationalism in Modern Europe

If God be for us

Philip W. Barker

Routledge
Taylor & Francis Group

LONDON AND NEW YORK

First published 2009
by Routledge
2 Park Square, Milton Park, Abingdon, Oxon OX14 4RN

Simultaneously published in the USA and Canada
by Routledge
270 Madison Avenue, New York, NY 10016

Routledge is an imprint of the Taylor & Francis Group, an informa business

© 2009 Philip W. Barker

Typeset in Times New Roman by
Taylor & Francis Books
Printed and bound in Great Britain by
CPI Antony Rowe, Chippenham, Wiltshire

British Library Cataloguing in Publication Data
A catalogue record for this book is available from the British Library

Library of Congress Cataloging in Publication Data
A catalog record for this book has been requested

ISBN 10: 0-415-77514-0 (hbk)
ISBN 10: 0-203-89284-4 (ebk)

ISBN 13: 978-0-415-77514-4 (hbk)
ISBN 13: 978-0-203-89284-8 (ebk)

To my wife, Kelly, who made all of this possible through her endless encouragement and patience.
And also to my parents, for always believing in me and introducing me to the love of learning.

Contents

List of tables

Acknowledgements

The sheer number of people who have contributed to this project in one way or another is overwhelming. However, there are some who stand out, and I would be remiss if I did not mention them. The most important is my wife, who was always supportive when I needed it most and always provided an ear when I needed to think out a new idea or unleash some built-up frustration. Her encouragement got me through the long weeks of typing, and this book is partly hers.

I would also like to thank Professor William Safran, who took me under his wing when I was a naïve young graduate student. I doubt that I will ever meet anyone who knows as much as he does, and I am grateful that he was willing to share a small bit of his knowledge and wisdom with me. This book would not be possible without the many things he taught me.

Similarly, a number of other colleagues have contributed invaluable suggestions and criticism, all of which resulted in a better book. As such, I want to thank William Muck, James Scarritt, and Roland Paris. Your time and thoughts were invaluable.

Finally, the rest of my family also share in my accomplishment. I am convinced that my love of learning is due to my parents and their overwhelming belief in me. I cannot imagine how much time and money was spent on my education – from the trips to the library through my college tuition. It is the greatest gift they have ever given me. My brother, my grandparents, my in-laws – they all thought I was crazy at least once, but they always supported me. Thank you.

Preface

This book is about the factor of religion in the nationalisms of Europe, a continent where—in contrast to Asia, the Middle East, and even North America—it was widely supposed to have disappeared as a consequence of modernization. Philip Barker's study is both concentrated and broadly based. While focusing on Greece, Ireland, and Poland—three countries where religious and national frontiers coincide—he provides a *tour d'horizon* of scholarly debates about the place of religion in modern nation-building processes.

Barker does not categorically dismiss the secularization thesis, but he is aware of its limits; and he acknowledges that the three countries that are examined in detail are less developed economically than their larger and more secular neighbors. But the substance of his argument is not relative development but rather the importance of boundaries, such as the Orthodox–Muslim divide between Greece and Turkey; the Anglican–Catholic divide between Britain and Ireland; the Catholic–Orthodox divide between Poland and Russia and, secondarily, the Catholic–Lutheran one with Prussia. Such boundaries, which are analogous to the Hindu–Muslim divide between India and Pakistan and the Jewish–Muslim divide between Israel and its Arab neighbors, have tended to be seen in largely religious terms and have defined the nature of external existential threats; and the efforts of ethnonational communities at freeing themselves from those threats have fused national and religious identities and sometimes trans-formed religious wars into political wars. Greekness was redefined in reli-gious terms: Greek nationalism was extended beyond language and ethnicity to embrace peoples in neighboring states who shared the Greek Orthodox religion. The fact that Russia, a "big brother" neighbor, was Eastern Orthodox strengthened the role of the majority religion in developing Bulgarian nationalism. To be Irish was to be Catholic because England was Anglican. To be Polish was to be Catholic because Russia was Orthodox. However, the author does not make an absolutely deterministic claim for the place of boundaries; he shows that the weakening and decline of Poland was due as well, and perhaps primarily, not to an external religious threat, but to internal institutional shortcomings, dynastic problems, and personal rivalries.

In any case, social identity is a matter of contrasts—it is determined by what we are in relation to others—in terms of how our language, race, ethnicity, historical memory and, above all, religion are different from those of our neighbors. Religion is seen as a weapon of collective definition by one categoric group in opposition to another—a neighboring country or another categoric group, such as a dominant or oppressive class.

Even in larger, more established, more advanced, and more secure states, religion has not been totally read out of court as an element of national identity. This is attested by the fact that, in avowedly secular countries such as Great Britain, France, Germany, and (more recently) Spain, adherents of minority religions are often not considered "genuine" members of the national community. As the author makes clear, religion is not to be confined to, or confounded with, "religiosity" in the customary sense—with theology or church attendance; for it relates to, and encompasses, culture, collective memory, family traditions, and forms of social community. The persistence of religion, or the reversal from secularism to selective desecularization, may be explained as a reaction to the excesses of industrialization; a protest against globalization; or a quest for a retrieval of authority structures or of *Gemeinschaft*.

The book leaves no doubt that religion was, and in many cases continues to be, a constitutive element of nationalism and an effective political mobilizing force. It may be instrumentalized to gain independence; to acquire political legitimacy; to create internal sociopolitical unity; to provide a political counter-ideology; and to fortify the cultural ramparts around a society. But the author raises a number of questions: when is national identity defined in terms of religion; as an extension of it; in opposition to it; or as a substitute for it; and when does it cease to be important? He poses the question whether a minor religion is more closely tied to an ethnonational matrix than a major religion—one with universalistic ambitions or pretentions. His study suggests that the distinction between an "ethnic" religion and a universal one with global ambition is not a rigid one; and he gets right into the middle of the controversy about which of the Christian religions with universal pretentions—Roman Catholicism or Protestantism—has been the more powerful tool for nation building.

This book represents a felicitous combination of theoretical analysis, cross-national comparison, and historical background. In summary, it is an important contribution to the study of nationalism.

William Safran
University of Colorado at Boulder

1 Modern religion

Religion is one of the most powerful social forces known to man. It can shape the way we view the world, frame our conceptions of right and wrong, and inform our sense of morality. It has the ability to drive people above and beyond themselves to thoughts of an afterlife, a higher calling, or even self-sacrifice. It has been a part of social movements from abolitionism and anti-colonialism to the civil rights movements of the 1960s. It has driven great thinkers and philosophers in an effort to prove the existence of a God – or to disprove it. It has led men and women to take up arms in a fight they see as righteous and steadfast. It has also contributed to or been used as justification for some of history's greatest tragedies – the Crusades, the Inquisition, and slavery. The events of 11 September 2001, the fighting in the former Yugoslavia, the ongoing debate about peace in the Middle East, the resurgence of the Religious Right in America, debates and confrontations about displays of the Ten Commandments – these events and others like them make it abundantly clear that religion continues to play an important part in the modern-day political arena.

And yet a case can be made that in Europe the story is somehow unique. Religion is undoubtedly still important in the continent of the Catholic Church, the Reformation, and the Crusades, but over time there has been a change. Church attendance and other indicators are at historic lows. The role of established churches in the political process has waned dramatically. A widespread push for secularism has become evident in many European states. Without a doubt, the nature of religion has changed in Europe, and quite possibly in irreversible ways. But not everyone agrees about the nature of this shift. There is an ongoing debate about the status of religion in today's Europe. The trend towards secularism has been accompanied by ethnoreligious fighting in the Balkans, increased concern over immigrant Muslim populations in France and Germany, and continued religious devotion in certain areas such as Poland. Clearly, our understanding of modern religion is far from complete.

There are countless reasons to study religion today. This book examines one small part of the religious puzzle – modern religious nationalism. Specifically, why are certain national identities intertwined with religion?

This chapter begins that exploration by looking at how much of a role religion plays in contemporary society. Is God truly dead, at least in the political world? How far has secularization gone? More importantly, interesting and pertinent questions arise in the process – questions that point in the direction of interesting observations and important lapses in our understanding of modern religion. For instance, if secularization is as complete as has been believed in the past, then how do we explain the religious nature of tensions in Northern Ireland or the former Yugoslavia? Exactly what role does religion play in these conflicts? What do we make of the religious resurgence in many of the former Soviet states? What are the reasons for the increase in new religious groups in many parts of the continent? Why do growing Islamic minorities present such a threat to supposedly secular states?

A brief history

Secularization and the death of God

Religion has always been an important force in the history of humankind. In Europe, specifically, religious divisions and wars have shaped the cultures, institutions, and maps of European states. The Reformation and Counter-Reformation, the Inquisition, the Treaty of Westphalia, and the Holocaust are all key events in the history of Europe and all intricately related to religion and its role in society. The map of Europe and the basic notion of the nation-state arose out of the Treaty of Westphalia and the notion of *cuius regio, eius religio* – that the religion of the King is the religion of the people. Throughout history, the ties between church and government in Europe have been strong – Henry VIII's separation from the Catholic Church and the French Revolution were both key events in history, and both were in response, at least partially, to church doctrine. For many centuries, religion was central to the nations of Europe – France, Spain, Italy, and Ireland were Catholic; England, the Netherlands, and much of Germany were Protestant; Greece was Orthodox.

Yet today we find ourselves in an era of secular states and declining church attendance. A shift has occurred, and modern Europe has a drastically different relationship with religion. Scholars of secularization, most notably in sociology, have claimed that there has been an undeniable and unchangeable drift away from traditional religion. As S. S. Acquaviva argues, "everywhere and in all departments, the dynamic of religious practice reveals a weakening of ecclesiastical religiosity and, within certain limits, of every type of religious belief, including the belief in God" (Acquaviva 1979: 83). In other words, every aspect of religion is withering away, from the institutional to the personal, the spiritual, and the societal.

This is by no means a new argument. Social scientists have been predicting the demise of religion for a hundred years or more. As Malcolm Hamilton explains, "The demise of religion in modern society has been predicted by many theorists, especially those writing in the nineteenth century" (Hamilton 1995: 185). Karl Marx, John Stuart Mill, Herbert Spencer, Max Weber, Emile Durkheim, Sigmund Freud, Auguste Comte, and others all predicted the weakening of religion in one form or another. Karl Marx famously said that "religion is the sigh of the oppressed creature, the heart of a heartless world and the soul of soulless conditions. It is the opium of the people" (Marx 1844). Freud compared religion to a "childhood neurosis" (Freud 1927). Acceptance of secularization became so widespread that "the consensus was such that not only did the theory [remain] uncontested but apparently it was not even necessary to test it, since everybody took it for granted" (Casanova 1994: 17).

This acceptance was reasonable, but it meant that the thesis went relatively unexamined. It is only in recent decades that secularization has been examined and questioned in a more thorough and scientific manner. Specifically, scholars such as Peter Berger, Steve Bruce, Bryan Wilson, and Sabino Acquaviva have put forth increasingly convincing accounts of the process and nature of secularization (Acquaviva 1979; Berger 1973, 1974; Bruce 1992; Wilson 1966, 1982). It is important to understand exactly what these arguments are and what is meant by the term "secularization" so that we can move forward in an informed and analytical way.

Defining secularization

The secularization thesis argues that religion loses its importance in nearly every way as countries become more modern (i.e., economically developed, scientifically advanced, and urbanized). Or as Steve Bruce states:

> the basic elements of what we conveniently refer to as "modernization" fundamentally altered the pace and nature of religious beliefs, practices, and organizations so as to reduce their relevance to the lives of nation-states, social groups, and individuals, in roughly that order.
> Bruce (1996a: 1), Gill (2001), Martin (1978), Moyser (1991)

This definition is, of course, a very strong one. Much weaker definitions and understandings of secularization have since been proposed, but each of them, at their core, argues that religion is in decline. The strong definition is a useful starting point for our discussion here.

Secularization occurs through a variety of processes, each of which contributes to the larger effect. For instance, Steve Bruce breaks the process of secularization down into three key factors or elements. The first is differentiation, which he describes as "the fragmentation of social life as specialized roles and institutions are created to handle specific features or functions previously embodied in or carried out by one role or institution" (Bruce 1999: 8). In other words, a single social institution may have carried out many different and varied functions in the past, but the process of modernization has meant that those functions are now carried out by a wide variety of diverse and specialized institutions. Family structure is used as an example. Historically, the family unit served an economic and social purpose – work, socialization, education, and many other dimensions of everyday life revolved around the home. Now, family members leave the home to go to work and school. Similarly, in terms of religion, the church has lost its grasp on its former strongholds of education, welfare, policy agendas, and moral leadership. Other institutions have taken over in these arenas, and religion as a whole has lost social significance as a result.

Second, Bruce points to "societalization" as a factor in secularization. The reference here is to Bryan Wilson, who states that "life is increasingly enmeshed and organized, not locally but societally (that society being most evidently, but not uniquely, the nation state)" (Wilson 1982: 154). In layman's terms, the local community has been weakened by the growth of large-scale society. As individuals focus more and more on national and regional identities, the heart of religion's strength is cut, as the church has traditionally found its strength at the local level. The rural life is in retreat, and with it, religion.

Rationalization is the final nail in religion's coffin, according to Bruce. Whereas the first two factors were essentially structural changes, rationalization is a shift in the way people think about the world. Modernization and the Enlightenment brought about a shift towards rationalism and the sciences. People sought scientific explanations for phenomena that had previously fallen squarely in the realm of the church (Bruce 1999: 13–14). Reason, not faith, became central to human thinking, and belief in ghosts, monsters, and angels withered away. The mysteriousness of the universe did not seem so mysterious, and once again religion suffered. The need for a god diminished with an increase in mankind's own power of exploration.

Bruce's analysis is by no means lacking in controversy. There is, and likely will continue to be for some time, an ongoing debate about exactly what secularization is. Hamilton indicates that there are at least six different definitions of secularization in the field of sociology (Hamilton 1995: 187). Jose Casanova argues that what we consider to be secularization is actually three entirely different, although intertwined, processes: differentiation, historical decline in religion, and privatization – meaning the separation of religion from the public sphere (Casanova 1994: 212–15).

The scope of secularization is also in dispute. Some, like Peter Berger, argue that secularization is a phenomenon unique to the Christian world. The very nature of Christianity (its organization, its focus on pluralism) was the trigger for the secularization of Europe (Berger 1973). Others, including Bryan Wilson, argue that the impetus for secularization came from outside the religious realm, instead focusing on the issues of modernization, science, technology, and urbanization (Wilson 1966, 1982). Still others point to the fact that an increase in science and rationality can no more be a cause of secularization than secularization itself. In other words, the two are opposite sides of the same coin. "[T]he growth of alternative interpretations of the world of a materialist and scientific kind is itself a part or aspect of the very process of change of which the decline of religion is also a part" (Hamilton 1995: 202).

Clearly, secularization itself is in need of clarification. What is important to understand is the fact that, for the latter half of the twentieth century, there was a shift in thinking – a shift that pointed to the rapid and inevitable decline of religion in the modern world, however defined. Such thinking shaped the way we viewed the world – in politics, sociology, theology, policy, and more. However, the undisputed explanatory power of secularization has not endured.

The return of God (Anderson 1983)

Beginning in the 1970s, the secularization thesis was subjected to renewed criticism. Social scientists such as Anthony Gill, Peter Berger, Callum Brown, and Jose Casanova began to point to the flaws in the secularization argument (Berger 1999; Brown 1992; Casanova 1994; Davie 2000; Gill 2001; Hastings 1997). Peter Berger, who had helped spawn the secularization thesis earlier in the century, now led the charge against it. "In the last few years I have come to believe that many observers of the religious scene (I among them) have over-estimated both the degree and irreversibility of secularization" (Berger 1974: 16). Berger later added, "[t]he big mistake, which I shared with everyone who worked in this area in the 1950s and 60s, was to believe that modernity necessarily leads to a decline in religion" (Berger 1998: 782). Social scientists were no longer so certain about their assumptions.

The reasons for the concerns were clear. The 1970s and 1980s saw a new resurgence of religiosity in many parts of the world: from the Iranian revolution, to the Troubles in Northern Ireland, to a vigorous emergence of charismatic churches in America. As Jose Casanova explains:

> From a global perspective, since World War II most religious traditions in most parts of the world have either experienced some growth or maintained their vitality. This has been the case despite the fact that throughout the world since World War II, there have been rapid increases in industrialization, urbanization, education, and so forth.
>
> The main exceptions to this apparently global trend are the rapid decline of primal religions, the sudden and dramatic decline of religion in communist countries following the establishment of communist states, and the continuous decline of religion throughout much of Western Europe …
>
> Casanova (1994: 26)

These observations led to a new wave of thought regarding modern religion. Some pointed to Europe as the exception and not the rule. Europe may have been secularizing, but the rest of the world was as religious as ever (Casanova 1994; Davie 2001a,b). At the same time, scholars made a point of showing that religious revival was not limited to Islamic fundamentalism. As Samuel Huntington points out, "The renewal of religion throughout the world far transcends the activities of fundamentalist extremists" (Huntington 1996: 96). Still others argued that religion had remained strong – we were simply looking in the wrong places. Religion was changing, but certainly not disappearing (Davie 2001b). "Religious sentiment does not simply wax and wane; it changes clothes and appears in garb to which we are sometimes unaccustomed. It may well be all around us, and yet we have not trained ourselves to recognize it" (Wuthnow 1992: 4).

In addition to the debate about the nature of secularization, there were growing arguments for desecularization (religion has returned) and/or non-secularization (religion never left), depending on your perspective. Regardless, it is now clear that the secularization thesis is no longer seen as a given. As Nicholas Demerath points out, "[I]n the eyes of its critics, secularization is a hypothesis that has been proved false and a term that should be expunged from proper usage" (Demerath 2001: 211). Samuel Huntington, in his now famous *Clash of Civilizations*, makes a similar point: "The Westphalian separation of religion and international politics, an idiosyncratic product of Western civilization, is coming to an end, and religion, as Edward Mortimer suggests, is 'increasingly likely to intrude into international affairs'" (Huntington 1996: 54).

So which is it? Is religion truly a dying force in the world of modern politics? Malcolm Hamilton describes the conundrum that we find ourselves in: "What is alleged to have been a fundamental change characterizing modern society is alleged by others not to have taken place at all. It is rather as if economic historians were in deep dispute as to whether the industrial revolution ever actually occurred" (Hamilton 1995: 186). And yet in spite of all the disagreement in the field, there is one area on which almost everyone agrees: Europe.

The European exception

Peter Berger, the one-time proponent of secularization turned critic, wrote in a recent book that:

> In Western Europe, if nowhere else, the old secularization theory would seem to hold. With increasing modernization, there has been an increase in key indicators of secularization, both on the level of expressed beliefs ... and, dramatically, on the level of church-related behavior ...
>
> Berger (1999: 9)

Grace Davie espouses a similar line of thought – that a shift has occurred and what was once seen as the rule (Europe) is now seen as the exception:

"European patterns of religion are no longer seen as a global prototype, but constitute an unusual case in a world in which vibrant religiosity becomes the norm" (Davie 2001b: 101). If there is a place in the world that demonstrates secularization, it is certainly Europe.

The evidence is everywhere. Polls show that the number of people who attend church at least once a month is incredibly low – less that 19 percent in England, 12 percent in France and the Czech Republic, under 10 percent in Sweden and Russia (http://www.europeanvalues.nl; 2007). When statistics for church attendance of once a week or more are examined, the results are even more striking. The number of monasteries and convents has decreased rapidly. When attendance figures are examined closely, it becomes clear that there is a large generation gap, with the older generations still attending regularly, but with younger generations generally separated from the church. Official separation of church and state is in principle formal and strict, most notably in places such as France, where there have been many disputes over the place of immigrant Muslims and their right to wear head scarves in schools. The list can go on and on. The point, however, is that Europe is different: different from the Middle East, different from Africa, Asia, even different from the United States and other "Western" countries. Secularization seems to be alive and well in Europe.

And yet, today's headlines still feature stories on talks in Cyprus that aim to ease tensions between Orthodox Greeks and Muslim Turks on the island; Slobodan Milosevic's war crimes in the former Yugoslavia; the ongoing and increasingly heated debate in France regarding Muslim head scarves in schools; and anti-Semitism in Europe. And all this in the most secular part of the world. As political scientists, we are all too often missing the bigger picture.

While the secular is the norm on the European continent, certain countries clearly defy the broader trend and cling closely to religion. Poland, Ireland, and Greece are prime examples. In spite of the wider secularism of Europe, these areas still maintain high attendance figures – nearly 70 percent in Ireland and just less than 80 percent in Poland – drastically higher than the numbers discussed earlier. In Greece, over 96 percent of the population still claim to be members of the Greek Orthodox Church; the same is true of the Catholic Church in Poland (http://www.europeanvalues.nl; 2007).

The exceptions do not stop at the level of attendance. In Ireland, divorce has only recently been made legal, and the conditions under which it is allowed are strict: legal separation for at least four of the last five years and "no reasonable prospect of reconciliation between the spouses." Abortion remains illegal. Three referenda in the last twenty years sought to liberalize the policy. All three failed. Very few other European states have restrictions as tight on abortion – among them are Poland and Portugal, which also has attendance figures of nearly 90 percent.

We are all familiar, of course, with the religious violence in Northern Ireland and the former Yugoslavia. Many are also familiar with the conflicts in Cyprus. All these cases have centered on political, economic, and social issues, but have found their strength in religious identities. Identity plays a role far beyond religious conflicts, too. It is widely accepted that "to be Polish is to be Catholic" (Safran 2003: 6). In addition, Greek Orthodoxy is a key component of Greek identity – so much so that a papal visit in 2001 caused a huge public stir. And it is certainly not a stretch to argue that the phrase "Irish Catholic" is redundant.

And so we see that, in the world's most secular forum, there are indubitable examples of the importance of religion. They are exceptions and, as such, they point us to the most interesting questions.

The question

Why are the Polish and the Irish nations so strongly associated with the Catholic Church, whereas the French and Spanish (although strongly Catholic demographically) are significantly more secular in terms of national identity? Why does Orthodoxy play a significant role in Greek national identity, whereas other nations turn instead towards language, history, or culture?

The specific question here is about *national identity*. There are questions to be answered about the role of the church in moral decisions, or about rates of attendance, or about belief in God, or even about the role of religion in the policy process. The goal of this study, however, is to address one small aspect of the larger puzzle. Groups have a wide variety of tools that can be used for building an identity: language, physical characteristics, skin color, history, culture, food, music, literature, sports, and of course, religion. However, as secularization has taken hold in Europe, the role of religion in this process of identity formation has (or should have) decreased. France, formerly the "eldest daughter of the Church," is now ardently secular and relies on many other factors for national identity. England, the home of Henry VIII and the subsequent fire of Anglican nationalism, is now host to a pluralistic approach to religion and nationality. Others, however, have not made the same progress. Poland, Greece, and Ireland still base their national identity primarily, or at least strongly, on religion. Why?

Why have certain groups avoided the general trend towards secular nationalism in Europe? Why have certain peoples rallied around religion as their unique identifier, while the rest of Europe has turned away from the Church? Why do over 90 percent of Irish and Greek citizens still consider themselves Catholic or Orthodox whereas the rest of Europe has seen these numbers dive well below 50 percent? And why is Polish-ness equated with Catholicism, while French-ness is not?

Clarification of terminology

Religion and nationalism are terms that are used so often and in so many and varied ways that they tend to lose any objective meaning. What exactly do we mean by religion? Are we referring to churches or to theologies? To people or to practices? How do we decide what to call religion and what to call magic or superstition? If we are to understand religious nationalism, we must start by clarifying some of the central terminology. In this case, the heart of the study is nationalism. I seek to explain and describe a specific type of nationalism – a type that is fused with religion. But in order to understand a specific type of nationalism, it must first be clear what is meant by the broader concept itself.

Nationalism has received a great deal of attention in comparative politics. It is still, however, a largely confusing topic for many people. The concepts of nations, states, nation-states, countries, and ethnic groups all blend together to the untrained eye. However, at its simplest, what separates a nation from an ethnic group or other group identity is political ambition – specifically the goal of self-rule or self-determination (Miller 1995). As Ernest Gellner phrases it, "nationalism is the political principle which holds that the political and national unit should be congruent" (Gellner 1983: 1). To risk oversimplification, a movement becomes nationalist in nature when its goal becomes self-determination. When the borders of the social group (nation) are in fact coterminous with the borders of the state, we have the ideal-type nation-state. Gellner furthers his definition by indicating that nations are determined and defined by culture and perception. Essentially, any given nation must have certain shared characteristics. Specifically, they must share a culture, which allows them to relate through understood symbols, ideas, and notions. In addition, any two members of a given nation have to recognize each other as such (Gellner 1983: 83). In other words, two Frenchmen must recognize each other as Frenchmen in order to be national brethren. Therefore, nations are largely self-defined and self-recognized.

Gellner's concept of culture is an important part of the definition of nationalism. There must always be some unifying factor in any given national identity – whether it be history, language, religion, or otherwise. Many scholars of nationalism have pointed to a wide variety of such constitutive factors (Hastings 1997; Kedourie 1960; Kohn 1944; Smith 1989). It seems straightforward, but without a unifying force the nation would be nonexistent. Such is its importance that national movements will often invent a shared culture, literature, or history for the purpose of identity formation. However, it is also important to emphasize the second half of Gellner's equation. The concept of self-recognition is not to be overlooked. Buzan, Waever, and de Wilde point this out in their discussion of the nation:

> Nationhood is not a question of some abstract, analytical category applied to various cases in which it fits more or less nicely. Objective factors such as language or location might be involved in the idea of national identity, but it nevertheless remains a political and personal choice to identify with some community by emphasizing some trait in contrast to other available historical or contemporary ties.
>
> Buzan *et al.* (1998: 120)

There is a choice when it comes to nationalism. The characteristics that are emphasized in any nationalist movement are not set in stone. They may ebb and flow based on the course of history or the choices of individuals; thus there is an option to "create" a national heritage. The goal here is to better understand the circumstances in which people choose to emphasize religion as their primary national identifier despite the presence of other available unifying forces.

Religion

Few concepts in the world are as complex or as disputed as that of religion. Approaching a topic that is, for many people, central to their world view requires careful precision. All too often, scholars of religion talk past one another because they have different ideas of what is meant by religion – traditional, mainstream religious groups versus sects and cults; religious participation versus religious belief or identity; private versus public religion. A discussion of religion in general (and as it is understood in this study more specifically) will help clarify the issue.

The definition of religion itself has varied greatly and has been contested vigorously throughout the years. Some claim that religion is limited to our basic everyday understanding of the term – what the average person would consider "religion." Others expand this concept more widely so that it encompasses anything that qualifies as sacred. Perhaps the most famous definition of religion, at least in the social sciences, comes from Emile Durkheim, who defined religion as "a unified system of beliefs and practices relative to sacred things, that is to say, things set apart and forbidden – beliefs and practices which unite into one single moral community called a Church, all those who adhere to them" (Durkheim 1912 [1995]: 44). Thus, any set of beliefs that focuses on the sacred is a religion. This, of course, opens the debate to what exactly qualifies as sacred. Political scientists and sociologists have classified all manner of subject matter as sacred. One particular line of thought has pointed to the similarities between nationalism and religion, indicating that nationalism has become a sort of modern religion (Anderson 1983; Kedourie 1960). Instead of choosing religious symbols, leaders, and traditions as holy and venerated, national leaders, symbols, and traditions are "worshipped" instead. This, in turn, reduces the need for traditional religions (Kedourie 1960: 55). As such, it seems logical that nation and religion might easily become entwined.

For the purpose of this study, however, the focus will remain on traditional religions as most people understand them. Specifically, this study looks at the link between religion and national identity in Europe. The nature of religion throughout European history has meant that Protestantism, Catholicism, and Orthodoxy account for most of these relationships. Certainly other religions exist in Europe, but none on the national scale.

Although many of the religious relationships are based on national churches, such as the Anglican Church, the national Church of Sweden, the various Orthodox Churches, each of these falls into the broader categories above (mostly Orthodox or Protestant, for reasons to be examined later). Obviously, as we expand beyond Europe, other religions become important in national movements – Islam in Pakistan, Shinto in Japan, Judaism in Israel, etc. – and each of these is recognized as a world religion.

There are many controversies regarding what is meant by religion other than simply definitional ones. For instance, is religion found in ideas, people, or actions? In other words, does a religion exist in its theology or does it exist in its followers? In order for a religion to be strong, must its followers attend church, or do they simply need to state their faith as such? This is a strong and ongoing debate in political science, sociology, and religious studies. As stated previously, attendance figures in Europe have dropped rapidly, and yet polls show that many people still consider themselves religious in spite of their absence from church. In addition, as Heelas and Woodhead point out, "the result [of a decline in religious observance] does not ... appear to have been a rise in secularity" (Heelas and Woodhead 2001: 59). They point out that polls show that indicators of spirituality (i.e., belief in a "higher force" or "soul") have actually risen, while the numbers of those claiming atheism or agnosticism have not risen significantly. Here, religion will be examined by looking specifically at self-identification. Although attendance is a useful tool, cultural and theological differences may distort the numbers – as is the case when comparing the Catholic Church, which puts a heavier emphasis on attendance, with the Orthodox Church, which tends to emphasize other aspects of belief. This will be addressed in the next chapter.

Religious nationalism

If nationalism represents a social movement with goals of self-rule, and religion focuses on the sacred as defined traditionally, then how do the two fit together? The study of nationalism, over the years, has actually devoted some time to addressing the link between these two powerful forces, although it has been rather limited in comparison with the broader field of nationalism studies. The examinations that have taken place have largely looked at the historical relationship between religion and nationalism. Most have either argued that religion helped form nationalism as we know it (i.e., nationalism as a Judeo-Christian concept) or that religion helped shape and define nationalist movements in their earliest stages (i.e., religion as important in the earliest stages of nation formation in Ireland, France, etc.) (Hastings 1997; Kohn 1944).

Max Weber, Clifford Geertz, and Hans Kohn (among many others) recognized that religion can be an important constitutive factor in national identity (Geertz 1963; Kohn 1944). The problem with these studies is that they rarely investigate how or why religion shapes nationalism, and when they do, they look at early nationalist movements and focus briefly, if at all, on modern movements.

The argument that nationalism is, at its heart, a religious outgrowth is a very intriguing one. Peter Berger indicates that religion's importance in group identity stems from the fact that "prior to the rise of nationalism as an idea and to the formation of the secular state as a social institution, religion was often the only thing people had in common bar a language" and that language often led back to religion via the clergy (Bruce 1996a: 107). Adrian Hastings goes so far as to state that "The nation and nationalism are both ... characteristically Christian things ..." (Hastings 1997: 186). Hastings also claims that Israel, as discussed in the Bible, provides the initial model of nationalism (Hastings 1997: 18). Although Hastings likely over-states his point, the importance of religion in early nationalism is clear. However, the role of religion in *modern* nationalism has been under-emphasized. Very few studies have looked at how religion shapes nationalist movements today.

In the conclusion of his book on *Nationalism and Modernism*, Anthony Smith urges that the examination of religion and nationalism go further than it has:

> Given the resurgence of religious nationalisms, it becomes even more important to determine how far earlier forms of ethnic sentiment and later forms of nationalism were similarly imbued with religious beliefs and sentiments. Here we would need to undertake comparative studies of the impact of the belief systems of the various world regions ... to see how far they were able to mobilize people and influence modern, even secular, nationalisms.
>
> Smith (1998: 227)

Certainly Smith is correct. Although political science has been relatively successful in its examination of the early ties between religion and national-ism, the exact relationship between these two powerful forces *today* is remarkably less understood. This can largely be explained by political sci-ence's whole-hearted acceptance of the secularization thesis over the past few decades.

As Smith indicates, the presence of renewed religious fervor and religious nationalism in the Western and non-Western world indicates a need to better understand the relationship between religion and modern national-ism. Issues such as Islamicization and fundamentalism have held the front pages over the past few years, certainly since 11 September 2001 (Berger 1999; Juergensmeyer 1993). As Raimundo Panikkar states, "we are approaching the close of the modern Western dichotomy between religion and politics" (Panikkar 1983: 45). Religion and politics are no longer clearly separable.

Seeking a definition

The link between religion and modern nationalism is not well understood. The first step in understanding the connection is achieving a more precise definition of the concepts involved. As very few people have addressed this issue directly, there are very few clear definitions. Barbara-Ann Rieffer does provide one: "Religious nationalism is the fusion of nationalism and religion such that they are inseparable" (Rieffer 2003: 225). She adds that, in instances of religious nationalism, " ... we see people not only demanding their own nation and sovereignty, but asserting that their nation is religiously based. They want political autonomy *and* recognition of their religion" (emphasis original) (Rieffer 2003: 225).

Although her definition may seem oversimplified, the concept itself is rather straightforward. The difficulties with the issue of religious nationalism do not arise from religious nationalism itself, but rather from the separate concepts of religion and nationalism, which we have already discussed. Rieffer's description points out the characterizations of a manifestation of religious nationalism:

> ... religion is so important to the nationalist movement that it adopts religious language and modes of religious communication, builds on the religious identity of a community, cloaks itself in the religion and relies on the assistance of religious leaders and institutions to promote its cause. Furthermore, when a religious national movement is successful in obtaining some form of political autonomy, often the religious beliefs will be institutionalized in laws or procedures governing the region.
>
> Rieffer (2003: 225)

Thus, religious nationalism is not simply a nationalist movement with a few religious undertones. Nor is it a nationalist movement that may include aspects of religion in the national identity. The concept is stronger than that. Religion must be central to national identity and to conceptions of what it means to belong to the given nation. If religion is not the central feature of national identity, it is at least one of several features. In addition, these other features will nearly always be coterminous with religious identity. In other words, a religious nationalism may focus equally on religion and language, but the individuals engulfed by the religious and linguistic markers are one and the same. For instance, the Greek language may be central to modern Greek identity. However, the Orthodox Church is central as well, and the two concepts are coterminous in that Greek speakers are also assumed to be Orthodox.

This distinction brings us to an important point in our discussion. There are many ways to move forward in an investigation of religious nationalism. Particularly, there are many ways to measure and examine the concepts central to our discussion. As a result, let us take a moment to clarify a few things that are *not* meant by the concept of religious nationalism.

First, and perhaps most important, religious nationalism does not refer to any level of religious adherence or participation. In fact, in many cases in the modern world, religious nationalism drives religious practice as opposed to the other way around. The important point is one that John Coakley brings up: religious identification is more important than religious adherence (Coakley 2002: 218–19). A nation with 90 percent of its population regularly attending mass may or may not have a stronger tie between religion and nationalism than a nation that has only 20 percent of its population practicing regularly. The importance is in the way people identify themselves. A person who has never been to church may still consider herself a Catholic based on the social surroundings she finds herself in. For instance, in Greece, less than 5 percent of the population attends church regularly, and yet 98 percent of the population still consider themselves to be Orthodox. Cyprus has a similar relationship. Religion is still an important part of identity in spite of low attendance figures. In contrast, France has a higher rate of attendance (around 11 percent) while only 29 percent of the population consider themselves Catholic (ISSP 1998). This issue will be addressed and clarified in a later chapter, but it is important to remember that there is more to religion than church attendance.

Second, the term religious nationalism does not necessarily refer to any specific relationship between the church and the state. Again, countries with an established church may not exhibit religious nationalism (Church of England) whereas countries with no established church may. In fact, Jose Casanova argues that a strong church–state relationship may actually facilitate secularization (Casanova 1994). The nature of this relationship is much more complicated than a simple statement of establishment. More must be understood in terms of the church's influence on politics, etc.

National identity

So what is meant by religious nationalism? What exactly will this study look for in each of the individual cases examined? To begin with, this specific examination of nationalism will focus on issues of identity, as discussed previously. Drawing on Walker Connor and Ernest Gellner, the self-awareness of the nation and the collective identity will be examined (Connor 1978; Gellner 1983, 1994). How does the nation see itself? What does the nation associate with? Is it food, language, religion, culture, music, or art? To what extent does religion play a role in the collective identity of the nation? Does being Polish mean being Catholic? Again, the importance here is not in statistics of religious adherence, but in identity. Non-practicing Catholics may still consider Catholicism an important part of their identity in the appropriate situations. Public opinion polls often address issues of identity – how many people consider themselves to be religious, how many consider themselves to be church members, etc. – and will be used for that purpose. However, historic clues will be necessary to fully understand the national self-concept.

Political religion

The second aspect of religious nationalism, although secondary to the first, focuses on the extent to which identification translates into action. Rieffer points out that, in cases of religious nationalism, religion is often "institutionalized in laws or procedures governing the region" (Rieffer 2003: 225). In this sense, the impact of religious identity on political outcomes will be important. To what extent does the church (or religion) influence policy decisions and what role does it play in the governmental process? Here we can see the differences between Spain, where Catholicism is still a strong part of Spanish culture but remains relatively buffered from government, and Ireland, where Catholicism is virtually inseparable from national identity and is consequently reflected in nation-wide bans on divorce and abortion. As mentioned before, few European countries still ban abortion. Yet those that do tend to have a strong tie between religion and national identity – Poland, Ireland, and Malta, for instance. The importance of the church in political matters is a big factor in determining a religious link to nationalism.

Conclusion

This concept of religious nationalism – religious identity and political religion (or public religion) combined into political objectives of self-rule – points us in the right direction. Across the broad range of countries that constitute the modern map of Europe, very few still cling to this model in spite of a long and historic relationship between religion and politics. Something has indeed changed. There is no doubt that religion continues to be important in almost every European state, but in a vastly different way than was the case a few hundred years ago. The push of (and for) secularization has been strong. And yet we still have a puzzle in those countries that have taken a different path: Ireland, Poland, Greece, Cyprus, and Malta. Although social science has recognized that something is different, it has not yet explained why. And that is the goal of this investigation.

2   The current understanding

What do we, as social scientists, know about secularism, religion, and modern nationalism? The answer is "surprisingly little." Some readers will be surprised by this. Others may not be surprised at all. What little debate that does exist has been centered on a small group of sociologists of religion who have examined, with much controversy, the issue of secularization. Although the general debate does not focus on the issue of religious nationalism *per se*, it does address the important concepts surrounding national identity; and a few individuals have made important contributions to our understanding of modern religious nationalism specifically. The goal of this chapter is to wade into the literature and retrieve the useful bits while leaving behind the rest.

As a result, this chapter lays out just a few of the prominent ideas that have brought us this far in our understanding of religious nationalism. Each of the ideas discussed here points in the right direction – either by laying out new ideas about the nature of religious nationalism or by bringing up important questions about our current knowledge. These ideas, however, only reveal a part of the broader picture.

Modernization theory and economic development

As discussed in the previous chapter, the issue of secularization lies at the heart of any debate on religious nationalism. For many years, the concept of modernization was intimately tied to secularization. There was no way to separate the two processes as the latter was defined as an integral part of the former. Despite the reputed death of modernization theory, its basic tenets still play a major role in the overall thought processes of political science. Whether we admit it or not, many social scientists still assume that modernization equals secularization. As a result, we have to understand what is meant by modernization.

Robert Wuthnow succeeds in simplifying the basic idea as follows:

> The central presupposition of modernization theory is that something can be identified that distinguishes "modern" societies from those that are less modern (i.e., "traditional" societies). Among the characteristics

that might signal the presence of greater modernity are higher levels of industrialization, a greater use of advanced technology, overall indicators of higher economic development, more literacy, a more comprehensive educational system, greater urban density, and more extensive administrative capacities on the part of the state.

Wuthnow (1992: 133)

This shift from traditional to modern, according to modernization theory (and other theories since), can portend only doom for religion. At the least, a shift towards modernity weakens religion's standing in society; at most, it completely destroys it.

Most theories about modernity and secularization look at the role of economics in this process. In fact, many studies focus almost exclusively on economic development and its associated patterns of urbanization, education, and rationalization. The basic idea behind secularization and modernization, and one that still holds much attention in the social sciences, is that religion loses its importance as countries develop, or become more modern. Although various factors (urbanization, education, democratization, rationalization) play a role in development, the key aspect is clearly and repeatedly economic development.

Although this theory is quite prominent, I am fairly quick to dismiss it, at least for our purposes here. Clearly, the more secular countries of the world are typically more developed economically. However, the exceptions are strong and difficult to explain away. Table 2.1 shows that the supposed link between development and secularism is weak at best. Ireland appears near the top of the list in both economic status and various religious indicators. Likewise, numerous post-Communist states show low levels of economic development and similarly low levels of religious participation. Granted, these states experienced significant extenuating circumstances, but the fact that they constitute such a large set of outliers points to the problems with the economic argument. In fact, much of the correlation between secularism and modernity can be attributed to the uniqueness of Europe, a region that has experienced both extensive secularization and economic development. Even so, if economic development is sufficient for secularization, then how does one explain Ireland, a country that, although less developed than other European countries, is certainly as advanced as France was in the late 1700s – the period of the French Revolution and the beginning of secularization in French politics? In fact, the purpose of this investigation is to understand why certain economically developed areas still foster religious nationalism.

In spite of these points, it can be argued that the countries in Europe that have, in fact, shown the least movement towards secularism are those that are the least developed economically. Indeed, this seems to be the case. Poland and Greece are certainly less developed economically than France, Germany, or Britain. However, another quick glance at Table 2.1 shows that any correlation between economic development and religiosity in Europe is

Table 2.1 Economics and religiosity in Europe (ISSP 1998)

	GDP per capita (US$)	Percent "religious"	Weekly attendance (%)	Belief in God (%)
Switzerland	31,635.21	39.3	50.5	28.3
Norway	31,601.37	39.8	6.5	18.4
Denmark	28,963.37	28.4	2.1	13.6
Ireland	28,662.22	69.5	63.2	49.8
Austria	27,662.42	62.7	19.1	32.4
Netherlands	27,010.54	54.3	13.8	26.4
France	25,767.16	29.3	11.6	20.1
Sweden	25,617.51	16.7	5.5	12.3
Great Britain	25,427.41	40.8	14.3	22.5
Italy	24,915.27	64.9	29.3	48.0
Spain	20,660.18	56.8	26.5	45.8
Slovenia	18,624.67	38.2	13.1	22.9
Portugal	18,048.04	76.2	29.6	60.0
Czech Republic	15,199.67	25.8	7.5	17.1
Cyprus	15,000.00	81.6	4.0	65.0
Hungary	13,369.73	45.6	15.0	31.1
Slovakia	12,171.80	54.6	29.8	40.8
Poland	9,529.97	84.6	39.3	70.5
Latvia	8,451.23	38.1	5.1	22.9
Bulgaria	6,639.25	51.4		27.9

GDP, gross domestic product.

shaky. In addition, it should be pointed out that, in the grand scheme of things, political scientists would be hard pressed to justify calling even the least developed European states underdeveloped, particularly in comparison with Africa, Latin America, and most Asian countries. It is simply illogical to argue that the factors that are supposedly so important in the shift to modernity (rationalization, economic development, urbanization, etc.) are not present in Greece, Poland, Ireland, or Portugal. These countries are developed. The human values study recognized this fact when it stated that Poland, along with Ireland, was a:

> hyper-Catholic society manifesting relatively traditional cultural values across a wide range of areas. Not only in religion, but also in politics, gender roles, sexual norms and family values, their values are *far more traditional than those generally found in* [other] *industrial societies.* (emphasis added)
>
> Inglehart *et al.* (1997: 30–1)

These countries, in spite of their strong religious ties, are in fact modern and developed. It is only when they are compared with the most advanced European states (which also happen to be the most advanced states in the world) that they even begin to appear underdeveloped.

These states are also very advanced when examined in historical perspective. As stated previously, if one looks at the conditions that began the secularization process in France (notably the French Revolution), there is little doubt that Poland, Ireland, and Greece have reached the same stage of development. There is little doubt that Greece today is at least as urbanized, industrialized, and economically advanced as eighteenth-century France or Britain.

Finally, it should be pointed out that political scientists might be on the right track, although the causal process is likely improperly specified. It is not the case that economic development leads directly to secularization. Rather, economic development means that a state is less vulnerable in the international system, which in turn means they are less susceptible to threats from their neighbors. When this occurs, there is a decreased tendency to emphasize religion in national identity. This idea will be discussed much further in the next chapter, but it is worth introducing here in order to clarify the justification for dismissing, at least partially, the traditional modernization thesis.

Steve Bruce and cultural defense

Many theories of secularization, particularly in sociology, have pushed well beyond the issue of economic development. Of these scholars, Steve Bruce's work is perhaps the most prominent. Bruce is a leading proponent of the secularization thesis, arguing that, although the tide of secularization may ebb and flow in the short term, the long-term trend is undeniable. It is important to note what Bruce means by secularization in order for us to better understand his point. He claims that:

> the basic elements of what we conveniently refer to as "modernization" fundamentally altered the place and nature of religious beliefs, practices, and organizations so as to reduce their relevance to the lives of nation-states, social groups, and individuals, in roughly that order.
>
> Bruce (1996a: 1)

In this process of secularization, Bruce emphasizes a shift towards individuality, which in turn had a negative effect on the large institutional churches of Europe. This "fragmentation of religious culture" eventually leads to a "widespread, taken-for-granted, and unexamined indifference to religion" (Bruce 1996a: 4). This change can be seen in three ways: decline in participation, decline in the influence of religious institutions, and decline in the impact of religious beliefs (Bruce 1996a: 26).

This study, however, is more interested in where secularization fails or is restrained. Bruce, in spite of his strong defense of the secularization thesis, does point out specific circumstances in which he believes religion retains its importance in society. He does so by looking at nonreligious roles for religion. This seemingly oxymoronic statement is best clarified in Bruce's own words: "modernity undermines religion except when it finds some major social role to play other than mediating the natural and supernatural worlds" (Bruce 1996a: 96). In other words, if religion steps outside its traditional roles and takes on tasks or identities that are useful on a broader social scale, then it is possible for religion to maintain itself into modernity. For Bruce, this can be accomplished primarily in one of two ways: cultural defense or cultural transition.

By cultural transition, Bruce refers to the social role religion can play during a geographic or class shift. In such cases, religion acquires "an enhanced importance because of the assistance it can give in helping people to cope with the shift from one world to another" (Bruce 1996a: 96). The first key example is migration. The stress that is endured when moving from one culture to another can lead individuals to fall back on their religion for identity and stability. This trend has been evident in immigrants (both interstate and intrastate) for some time – Africans moving into urban centers, immigrants to America, etc. However, Bruce also points out that social mobility can be important in cultural transition. Here, he addresses the idea of urbanization in a wider context and looks at these changes and their importance in Latin America. While cultural transition is interesting, it says little about the continued importance of religion at the level of the nation-state, instead focusing on individual identity.

Cultural defense, however, plays a much more vital role in group identity. According to Bruce, it occurs when religion takes on the role of "guarantor of group identity" (Bruce 2001: 259). This process can also take on a variety of different forms. The first is when "there are two (or more) communities in conflict and they are of different religions … ." The result is that "the religious identity of each can acquire a new significance and call forth a new loyalty as religious identity becomes a way of asserting ethnic pride and laying claim to what Max Weber called 'ethnic honor'" (Bruce 1996a: 96). He gives the examples of Northern Ireland and the former Yugoslavia to back his argument. The second form that cultural defense can take is "when there is a people with a common religion dominated by an external force (either of a different religion or of none at all), then religious institutions acquire an additional purpose as defenders of the culture and identity of the people" (Bruce 1996a: 96). Although he offers no examples, we can certainly picture Ireland, Poland, or Pakistan before their respective independence dates in this position.

This line of thought appears in other arguments as well. Stein Rokkan also points to the influence of foreign domination in the formation of religious nationalism, although he did not use that term specifically. "The Catholic Church played a major role in the development of peripheral nationalism in some of the territories of Counterreformation Europe" – specifically Poland (Rokkan *et al.* 1970: 128). René Rémond echoes the same sentiment: "For a people who have been conquered, oppressed, subjected to foreign domination, especially if their faith is different from that of their oppressor, religion ensures the preservation of their personality and encourages awareness of their identity" (Rémond 1999: 155). And David Martin, in his seminal work *A General Theory of Secularization*, notes that "A dominated society or a society sandwiched between other societies which throw its identity into high relief turns to its religion" (Martin 1978: 55).

Clearly these theories are strong and explain a great deal of our puzzle. There are still other scholars who have put forth quite similar thoughts on the subject, including John Coakley, whom I will discuss shortly (Coakley 2002: 115, Rieffer 2003: 225–6). However, there are also some very important shortcomings. First, as Bruce is looking at secularization from a sociological perspective, the issue of nationalism is not addressed specifically. Bruce is more concerned with where secularization falls short in general – not specifically why national identities become religious. In other words, Bruce examines why religion has declined in general (attendance, belief patterns, etc.), not in terms of political identities. By looking at this issue not from the perspective of sociological secularization (i.e., the decline of religion, however defined), but rather from a specifically political perspective (focusing solely on the aspect of national identity), we can understand better how identity is affected regardless of changes in attendance and/or practice.

In other, non-political science terms, this thesis is concerned with how people see themselves in a political environment more than with how often people go to church, how often they pray, or whether they believe in a heaven or hell. It is my argument that the effectiveness of the church in politics is controlled more by people's identity than vice versa. To clarify even further, it is possible to imagine a nation that sees a sociological shift away from religion (declining practice and belief) without an accompanying shift in terms of national identity. It is also possible to imagine a nation of largely religious people who do not affiliate religion with their national definition. To summarize, Bruce is looking at a broad social shift away from religion. From a political science perspective, the issue becomes more interesting when examined from a specific angle – looking at political identity and how it is formed.

In addition, Bruce inadequately addresses the issue of what happens after a situation of external domination or inter-religious conflict ceases. Why is it that religious identity has remained so strong in places such as Ireland, Pakistan, and the former Yugoslavia even after situations of "external domination" have ended? These three examples have all made a shift from external domination to inter-religious conflict. What he fails to address, though, is why these groups have adopted a religious basis for identity, rather than a linguistic, cultural, or ethnic one. If secularization is so strong, then why would conflict slow the process? All this indicates that Bruce makes strong arguments, but each must be clarified and aligned more closely with an approach to religion and national identity specifically.

Finally, it is worth noting that the exceptions that Bruce identifies (cultural defense and transition) are not uncommon in world politics. Situations in which groups are involved in conflict with religious "others" or are subjected to external domination are abundant, and the results are clear – throughout Europe in Yugoslavia, Poland, Armenia, Greece, Ireland; in the Middle and Near East in Pakistan, India, Israel, the Palestinian Authority, Lebanon, Iran; in Africa in the Sudan and Nigeria. The list goes on and on. For a supposedly powerful and self-apparent trend, the outliers seem glaring. The significance of these "anomalies" is enough to question the overall assumption that secularization is universal and unstoppable.

John Coakley and "denominational interfaces"

In an edited book written in tribute to Walker Connor, nationalism scholar John Coakley lays out a similar theory regarding the development of religious nationalism. Unlike Bruce, Coakley is addressing the specific issue of nationalism, and he is doing so from a decidedly political perspective. In his chapter, he addresses a variety of subjects dealing with religion and nationalism, but spends a relatively short time discussing modern religious nationalism itself. As a result, an initial discussion of his ideas will be followed by a deeper clarification, explication, and examination.

Because he looks specifically at the issue of religious nationalism, Coakley provides perhaps the best argument in the current debate. He begins by drawing a line between what he calls "ethnic" and "universalistic" religions. An ethnic religion has a message that pertains to a specific group of people, as opposed to a universalistic religion "whose message, it is claimed, is valid for all humankind and which is open to engaging in proselytist or missionary activity … " (Coakley 2002: 215). The examples are fairly simple: Judaism as an ethnic religion, pertaining specifically to the Jewish people; as opposed to Christianity or Islam, both of which proclaim a message for all humanity. Although this distinction may seem minor, the implications for nationalism are strong. There are somewhat obvious implications for the ethnic religion, as can be seen in Judaism's role in Israeli nationalism or, as Coakley points out, Shinto's role in Japanese nationalism. It would be wrong, however, to assume that an ethnic religion necessarily means a subsequent religiously based national identity.

Universalistic religions imply a much more complex relationship between nationalism and religious identity. As Coakley points out, "Unlike nationalism, the great religions are universalistic and transethnic" (Coakley 2002: 213). This means that these two powerful ideals, religion and nationalism, can have counterproductive goals. As Coakley explains, "to the extent that they embrace missionary ambitions and realize their objectives of conversion over a wide geographical area, universalistic religions undermine their own capacity to contribute to processes of nation formation" (Coakley 2002: 215). This is an important point, and one that we shall return to later, yet

Coakley only mentions it briefly. The main idea, though, is that, for France and Italy, Catholicism does little to foster a unique national identity because it does little to differentiate them from one another.

There are, however, important exceptions to this trend. Coakley correctly points out that many universalistic religions play roles in developing clearly non-universalistic national identities. According to Coakley, there are "three ways in which [universalistic religions] may depart from their universalistic logic: by falling victim to doctrinal secession, to organizational fragmentation, or to frontier conflict" (Coakley 2002: 215–16). Each of these is important and thus worth elaborating to some extent. The first exception, "doctrinal secession" refers to "withdrawal from the parent religion because of a conflict over fundamental religious beliefs" (Coakley 2002: 216). The Protestant Reformation is the perfect example. The second typological exception is "organizational secession," which often, but not always, succeeds doctrinal secession. The formation of autocephalous, or independent, Orthodox Churches in Greece, Serbia, and Romania in the nineteenth century is a good example (Coakley 2002: 216). In both these changes, a religious divide is created, which may prove useful in the formation of national identity.

It is Coakley's third category, however, that is most interesting for this study, particularly because it appears to subsume the previous two. Coakley argues that "interdenominational interfaces," or what this study refers to as religious frontiers, are key to understanding this deviation from universalism. "It frequently happens that major political borders fail to coincide with lines of religious division, leaving large minorities on the 'wrong' side of a border ... " (Coakley 2002: 216). Doctrinal or organizational secession may lead to the presence of "interdenominational interfaces," but it is also important to note that many other causes may occur as well – from shifting borders to changing social conditions. It is necessary to note that these divides do not always form religiously nationalist identities, but, as Coakley indicates:

> the consequences could ... be supportive of ethnonationalism: for Polish Catholics in Protestant Germany and Orthodox Russia down to 1918, for Irish Catholics in the United Kingdom before 1922 and to some extent for Belgian Catholics in the Protestant Netherlands in 1815–30, the Catholic Church offered a reassuring bulwark against a hostile culture.
> Coakley (2002: 217)

These "interfaces", however created, are crucial for the formation of a religious national identity.

While Coakley is certainly on to something, he only briefly addresses the importance of these "interdenominational interfaces." In fact, his whole discussion of this causal process takes place in less than three pages, and the resulting implications need further testing to be understood more clearly. In addition, Coakley only looks at borders when they ineffectively reflect the religious divisions of an area. What happens after borders are "corrected" (i.e., after Irish or Pakistani independence)? It is clear that corrected borders do not necessarily mean an end to religious nationalism. What process occurs as these lines are adjusted? It is also worth noting that Coakley's theory explains part of the equation. However, there are many examples of religious divides without a resultant religious nationalism. For instance, Coakley's theory explains Ireland, but what of England? There is something missing from the equation. The missing element is the presence of a threat, which will be discussed in the next chapter.

As we look at Bruce and Coakley, the parallels are clear, but so are the subtle differences in approach and emphasis. What is particularly troubling about both is their brevity of address. Neither author sets out to explain the existence of religious nationalism *per se*. Both address the issue as a side note or exception to some other topic of interest. As a result, both theories provide wonderful insight for a study of religious nationalism today, but both need more examination and testing.

Other theories of note

Steve Bruce and John Coakley are not the only two scholars to have looked at the issue of religious nationalism, either directly or indirectly. Numerous other theories have been proposed. Although Coakley and Bruce provide the most accurate portrayal of religious nationalism, a few others make notable contributions as well and are worth examining in brief.

Demerath and sacralization

Nicolas Demerath discusses the issue of secularization and the rival concept of sacralization. Although his theories do not address the maintenance of religious identity as examined here, they do provide some very interesting insight. Demerath is a supporter of the secularization thesis, arguing that there is a constant process of secularization going on in any given society. In addition, however, there is also an ongoing process of sacralization, or "the process by which the secular becomes sacred or other new forms of the sacred appear" (Demerath 2001: 214). Essentially, Demerath argues that religion and culture are very similar and that cultures continually shift what they consider to be sacred. Something that has been sacred in the past may lose its standing as such. At the same time, something else takes its place in the sacred realm. This argument dovetails well with arguments claiming that nationalism has become a civil, secular religion of sorts.

Demerath's argument becomes interesting for our purposes when he turns to the various paths to secularization. There are two fundamental distinctions in the various types of secularization. The first is the line between secularization that "emerges from within the social context of the cultural system at issue versus secularization that is imported or imposed from outside," or internal versus external secularization (Demerath 2001: 219). The second distinction lies in the divide between directed versus nondirected secularization, or "secularization that stems downward from authorities in control versus secularization that seeps upward from within the cultural system itself." These two divisions result in four ideal types of secularization: emergent (internal, nondirected), coercive (internal, directed), imperialist (external, directed), and diffused (external, nondirected).

Demerath draws some very interesting conclusions. In terms of religious nationalism, however, it seems that only one of his "fundamental distinctions" is important: directed versus nondirected. Nondirected secularization is nearly always more successful than directed secularization. Several examples come to mind: the French Revolution and the Enlightenment as examples of nondirected secularization versus Poland, Turkey, and Ireland as examples of directed. To take the argument one step further, sacralization can be divided into each of these four categories as well, and it can easily be argued that, again, the issue of direction is key. The Spanish Inquisition, the Iranian Revolution–likely failures; versus the sacralization that occurred in Poland, Greece, Turkey, etc. This line of thought fits well with Bruce's argument regarding cultural defense and the resulting resistance to foreign or oppressive power.

Rational choice

Some scholars in the field of secularization take a very different approach to continued religious importance. The idea of rational choice is one that has been central to many debates in political science in recent years, and the study of religion is no different. In this particular case, rational choice scholars, including Rodney Stark, have argued that certain countries manage to maintain a stronger tie to religion because of a freer market (Stark and Bainbridge 1985, 1987). Bruce summarizes the logic as follows: "If we suppose ... that the demand, desire, or need for religion is more or less stable, then the manifest variations in the pace and intensity of religious activity, commitment, and interest must be explained by variation in supply" (Bruce 1999: 44–5).

The United States provides the perfect example. In the case of religion, like so many other things, America is an exceptional case. Rational choice argues that the free market of ideas and choices, meaning the variety of different religions to choose from, leads to a greater vitality because more needs are met by the wide choice of providers (Bruce 2001: 260). In addition, it is easier for new religious movements to form in such an environment. To put it differently, Grace Davie says the following: rational choice theory "offers a supply-side approach to religion, suggesting that a demand for religious activity will increase if the supply is both sufficiently diverse and sufficiently attractive to entice the religious consumer" (Davie 2001a: 275). Thus, more diversity equals stronger religion.

The problems with this approach seem fairly straightforward. The issues with the rational choice approach to religion have nothing to do with rational choice itself. Rather, the observable implications of this theory simply do not occur. One would expect, according to this theory, that a country such as the United States would have a more religious society than most, and many scholars would agree that it does. However, one would also expect that nations with a single strong religion/church would be noticeably more secular, and yet we are faced with the examples of Ireland, Poland, Greece, Iran, and Pakistan. All have a strong focus on a single religion, and yet all are arguably the least secular of their regional neighbors. In addition, other countries with considerable religious diversity, such as the United Kingdom, with increasing Muslim, Jewish, and Catholic populations, are considerably more secular. The evidence does not support the argument. To be fair to Stark, he is looking at religious participation rather than nationalism, but the same issues are relevant.

Casanova and caesaropapism

Jose Casanova also seeks to understand the nature of secularization in his examination of private and public religions. In doing so, he points the finger of blame at "caesaropapism", or the strong linkage between state and church. Caesaropapist states often feature a governmental position that serves as both state and church leader, i.e., the King of England as the Head of the Church of England. According to Casanova, caesaropapism has traditionally been the rule in European politics and, as a result, "It was the caesaropapist embrace of throne and altar under absolutism that perhaps more than anything else determined the decline of church religion in Europe" (Casanova 1994: 29).

Casanova admits that this theory is not a novel one. It is, in fact, one that has been put forth by many scholars, including Marx and Tocqueville. He adds that this point should have been evident "had [Europeans] looked at the striking differences within Europe itself between, on one hand, Catholic Ireland and Catholic Poland, which never had a caesaropapist state church, and, on the other, Catholic France and Catholic Spain" (Casanova 1994: 29). He points to the fact that nonestablished churches have fared better against the trends of secularism than have established churches. "In very simple terms it could be said that the more religions resist the process of modern differentiation ... the more they will tend in the long run to suffer religious decline ... " (Casanova 1994: 214). Here, Casanova gives the example of Poland, where the church was able to resist Communism because it was operating from an independent and decentralized position. This theory ties neatly into Demerath's arguments regarding secularization (and sacralization) from above versus secularization from below, and other scholars have also argued along similar lines, including Ray Taras who has pointed out that the unique nature of church–state relations in Poland has lent itself to a unique modern tie between Catholicism and the Polish people (Taras 2003: 139).

Casanova's theory is both interesting and useful. It is entirely likely that this understanding of religion in Europe is accurate. In fact, it can be argued that the strong linkages between church and state in France led to the push for secularism during and after the French Revolution. However, there are also problems with this theory. There are clear examples of strong "caesaropapist" states today that have not secularized as extensively as we might expect. Greece is a prime example. The ties between the Greek state and the Greek Orthodox Church are strong, particularly by European standards, and yet there has been little decline in the religious nature of Greek society (96 percent still claim to be religious – much higher than in other European states). Portugal provides a similar example. As an overall historic trend, caesaropapism explains a great deal of the secularization phenomenon. However, it does not explain why certain nations have remained religious in spite of strong linkages between church and state.

In addition, an understanding of the church–state relationship does little to help us untangle the mysteries of religious nationalism in stateless groups (ethnonational movements) (Gurr 1993). How can the church–state relationship affect the secularism of a society when there is no state for the church to relate to? Casanova might argue that religion can survive in these nationalist movements purely because there is no "caesaropapist" arrangement between the church and the state. But then how do we explain secular nationalist movements? Clearly, further examination is needed.

Conclusion: making sense of it all

These theories are only a small survey of some of the most relevant approaches to and understandings of religious nationalism in today's world. There are clearly others. There are also many other individuals who have espoused views very similar to those laid out above. I have only touched on those that I consider to be the leading scholars or proponents of their specific ideas.

The sheer variety of theories should tell us something about our understanding, or lack thereof. Some theories argue that religious diversity inhibits secularism (although not necessarily in terms of nationalism) (Stark and Bainbridge 1985, 1987). Others argue the opposite – that groups that are strongly uniform in their religious beliefs are less likely to secularize (Rieffer 2003). Still others claim that strong religious unity is bad for religion, but only when the church becomes tied to the state (Casanova 1994).

What is agreed upon is that religious pressures are a necessary part of our understanding of religion in modern states. Whether those pressures come in the form of subjugation, denominational interfaces, or from the church itself is less clear. What is not clear, and what we must understand in order to understand religious nationalism itself, is the way in which these pressures affect identity. How important are denominational interfaces? Is subjugation a necessary condition for religious nationalism? How important is the church–state relationship? Does it vary from country to country? What role does it play for national groups that do not yet have a state? The next chapter seeks to answer some of these questions by laying out a new theory – one that draws on some of the current ideas (most notably those of Bruce and Coakley) and proposes a new way of understanding modern religious nationalism.

3 A new perspective

If current theories fail to fully explain religious nationalism today, then where do we stand? This chapter argues for a "new" theory, not in the sense of a revolutionary break from the past, but in the sense of small shifts in thinking – a tweaking of the ideas put forth by Coakley, Bruce, and others. The aim here is not to argue that the world is black or white, secular or religious, but to illuminate the shades of gray in between the two, the areas that reflect the real world that we live in every day. With any luck, the result will be a better understanding of modern religious nationalism and its roots. The ideas examined in the previous chapter are insightful. I simply seek to elucidate them further and look at the processes that make them function.

The nature of identity and the importance of "other"

The nature of identity is both complex and important, particularly in any understanding of nationalism. As discussed previously, nationalism is, at its core, an issue of collective identity. In order to understand nationalism, one must first have a grasp of identity and how it is formed.

As such, it is useful to turn to psychological and sociological literature on the subject. This literature indicates that the process of nation building is, by its very nature, a process of differentiation. Nationalism demonstrates well the idea that, in order to know who we are, we must first know who we are not. For example, if the world were composed solely of women, then gender would not likely be a key part of one's identity. What good would gender do as a form of identity? On the other hand, if only half the people in the world had noses, then we would likely consider nose-ness as part of who we are. As of now, if you went around describing yourself as nosed, people would most certainly look at you in a very strange manner.

In the case of nationalism, the same idea is relevant. The nation must first understand what it is *not* before it can realize what it *is*. As a result, nationalist ideas and identities are structured around the unique qualities a particular nation possesses, not the attributes it shares with its neighbors. Max Weber understood this point: "The significance of the 'nation' is usually anchored in the superiority, or at least the irreplaceability, of the cultural values that are to be preserved and developed only *through the cultivation of the peculiarity of the group*" (emphasis mine) (Weber 1994: 25). Walker Connor indicates the same notion: "This essence [of a nation] is a psychological bond that joins a people and *differentiates it*, in the subconscious conviction of its members, *from all other people* in a most vital way" (emphasis mine) (Connor 1978: 379). Benedict Anderson, in his seminal work on imagined communities, argues similarly:

> The nation is imagined as limited because even the largest of them encompassing perhaps a billion living human beings, has finite, if elastic boundaries, beyond which lie other nations. No nation imagines itself coterminous with mankind. The most messianic nationalists do not dream of a day when all the members of the human race will join their nation in the way that it was possible, in certain epochs, for, say, Christians to dream of a wholly Christian planet.
>
> Anderson (1991: 6)

Nation building necessarily focuses on those characteristics that set the nation apart and give it a sense of individuality. A nation must understand what makes it unique.

This concept is especially important for national leaders. Mobilization is crucial for leaders of any group of people, particularly a large-scale national movement. They raise armies, collect taxes (to pay for the army), and create and enforce laws. It is very difficult to mobilize the masses to fight a war against enemies that are seemingly like "us." If an elite wishes to rally support against another group (or simply to rally support via hostility towards another group), an enemy must be conceived of as different. Thus, the importance of uniqueness is clear.

Social identity theory elaborates on the importance of "the other." Simmel's rule indicates that, "the internal cohesion of a group is contingent on the strength of external pressure" (Eriksen 2001: 63). An important corollary of this idea, as explained by Eriksen, indicates that "what *kind* of group emerges depends on where the perceived pressure comes from" (Eriksen 2001: 63). In other words, religious groups form in response to religious pressures; linguistic groups emerge in response to pressures from other linguistic groups; ethnic groups from ethnic pressures. Robert White indicates a similar line of reasoning, stating that "group members develop a social (group) identity in comparison with members of some other group" (White 2001: 133). This is in sharp contrast to Huntington's *Clash of Civilizations*, which argues that groups conflict due to inherent cultural differences (Huntington 1996). Erikson and White, on the other hand, are arguing that differences between groups are emphasized because of conflicts. In other words, Huntington's causal arrow is pointing in the wrong direction. This notion is quite important in understanding the role of religious identity in modern nationalism, and one that has been largely overlooked in the literature on the subject of religious nationalism.

Religion and "uniqueness"

This notion that nationalism is founded upon differences between peoples, though seemingly simplistic, plays an important part in the examination of religious nationalism in the modern world. Many religions (particularly Catholicism, Protestantism, Orthodoxy, and Islam) are, as Coakley points out, universalistic (Coakley 2002). The appeal of Catholicism, for instance, is transnational. The Catholic Church seeks to be a universal church with appeal to all people. One is welcomed into the Church whether you are French, Italian, English, Argentinean, Chinese, or Nigerian. As a result, the Catholic faith prominent in many Western European states is naturally universal. In other words, Catholicism is not unique to French culture, or Italian culture, or any other culture for that matter. In the end, the Catholic nature of France does little to build a nation clearly differentiated from its Catholic neighbors in Spain, Italy, and Belgium. As a result, these nations are forced to turn to other notions for nationalist appeal – whether that be language, history, culture, or religious subdivisions.

In spite of this fact, religion does play a part in national identity in certain modern states and, when it does, the consequences are particularly relevant. Specifically, religion becomes an important factor in nationalist sentiment and nation formation when it is able to play some sort of differentiating role for the nation. This concept draws on Bruce and his notion of religion serving non-religious functions. However, it is more precise and, in many ways, simpler than Bruce allows for (Bruce 1996b). Rather than exploring the intricacies of what is meant by "cultural defense," this study simply argues that religion becomes important for nationalism when and where it is useful in identity formation. This, in turn, occurs at religious frontiers, which brings us back to Coakley (Coakley 2002).

If religion is only useful for nationalism when it helps in identity formation and differentiation, then we must understand when that occurs. Starting from Bruce's ideas regarding cultural defense and Coakley's points in relation to denominational interfaces, we are brought to the concept of religious frontiers (Bruce 1996b; Coakley 2002; Stump 2000). Religious frontiers are seemingly as simple as they sound – geographic borders where two regions or peoples, each prominently influenced by a specific and unique religion, come together. Examples are numerous – the Protestant/Catholic border of Ireland/England; the Orthodox/Islamic border of Greece/Ottoman Empire and Turkey; the Catholic/Protestant and Communist borders of Poland/neighbors; the Islamic/Hindu border of Pakistan/India; and the Jewish/Islamic border of Israel/neighbors. It is in these situations that religion becomes very useful as a means of national differentiation because religion provides the easiest way to differentiate one group from another. Although language or history may also provide distinction, neither is as obvious or as readily useful as religion, particularly for the average person.

Defining frontiers

In order to ensure as much clarity as possible, it is important to elaborate on this concept. *Webster's Dictionary* defines a frontier in many ways. The most straightforward and common usage is "a border between two countries" (Merriam-Webster). Americans tend to associate a frontier with ideas of the rugged West, of expansion, and of manifest destiny. This idea is quite useful for this discussion. But to be precise, it is better to dwell on another of Webster's definitions: a frontier as "a line of division between different or opposed things" (Merriam-Webster). Taylor and Flint define a frontier as "the area between two social systems or entities" (Taylor and Flint 2000: 162). This, of course, takes us back to Coakley's ideas of denominational interfaces, but as stated before, we must go beyond simple examples of group subjugation. We are specifically interested in the frontiers between two religious groups.

The choice of the term "frontier" is intentional for several reasons. First and foremost, it reflects the reality of the situation I am trying to convey. The situations that will be examined in the forthcoming chapters will demonstrate "a line of division between different or opposed things" – specifically religions (Merriam-Webster). Second, and equally important, is the fact that I want to avoid any confusion that the use of the term "border" may cause. The frontiers in this study may or may not be political or national borders as we think of them. For instance, if one were to draw ethnic frontiers on the map of the United States, they would not parallel the national borders. In other words, the frontier between Hispanic culture and American culture would not occur at the Texas/Mexican border, but rather well into the state of Texas itself. A similar ethnic/linguistic border can be drawn between Quebec and the rest of Canada and the United States.

Imagining a map of this nature (displaying religious and cultural rather than political lines of division) would reveal a complex situation in which religious borders exist in a variety of manifestations. The simplest example occurs when two groups of differing religious identities share a common geographical border, as in the case of India and Pakistan. Although the religious border has only been a state border since Pakistani independence, the religious border itself existed long before the partition, separating the Muslim-dominant regions from the Hindu-dominant regions. Another example occurs at the divide between the Republic of Ireland and Northern Ireland. Two separate groups of differing religious identities (Catholic and Protestant) come together at this point. Again, the current political border is the result of a much longer term religious frontier that has been in place since the Ulster Plantation. Clearly these frontiers are not as clear cut as we would like to make them out. There is a blending of cultures at these borders, with a mix of Catholic and Protestant in the counties of Northern Ireland; but on a larger scale, the religious frontier is visible and indisputable.

Some variants of religious frontiers become much more complicated than those discussed above, as there is not a common border. One example occurs when two groups are separated by a body of water (i.e., Spain and the Muslims of North Africa, Ireland and England, etc.). Both these instances are simplified somewhat by the fact that a religious frontier did exist historically. For example, the Plantation in Ireland brought the religious border across the Irish Sea and on to Irish soil. Similarly, the Moorish occupation of Southern Spain did the same in Iberia. Thus, these groups were sharing a direct religious frontier at some point in history. We are, however, faced with a dilemma here. These cases do not fit our specific conceptualization of religious borders. Although Catholic Spain may have shared a historic religious frontier with the Islamic Moors, they no longer do. At some point, that frontier shifted across water. How important is this shift in the broader creation of religious nationalism? This issue will be addressed further in the next section on threat, but a brief clarification is worthwhile.

Religious frontiers can still be important for religious nationalism, even when they deviate from the ideal case; however, when they do, their importance is decreased. Framed differently, the nature of religious frontiers can be imagined as a continuum. A small group surrounded by a larger and very threatening religious group would consider the importance of their religious frontier to be great. However, if two groups of approximate size and strength share a religious frontier, the importance of the frontier will be different for each of these groups than it was for either in the first example. Finally, a large and powerful state that shares a religious frontier with a very small, minor religious group will view that frontier in an entirely different (and less threatening) manner.

It is possible to stretch the concept a bit more, all the while being careful not to break it. A state may not exist directly on a religious frontier, but rather exist in very close proximity to it. It is very possible – likely even – that the frontier will be important to that state's identity. Let us look at this from a non-religious viewpoint. During World War II, although Britain did not share a direct border with Germany, the actions of Germany still played an important role in shaping British identity and actions. However, it would be wrong to say that British identity and actions were affected more than Polish or Belgian identities. Thus, the further from the border, the weaker its impact.

For the purpose of this study, and being careful not to stretch this concept beyond its usefulness, a stricter definition of religious frontiers will be used. Throughout history, it is likely that direct, strict religious frontiers were the only ones that truly mattered, and this thesis will build on that assumption. In the subsequent case studies, only religious frontiers that are obvious and clear (i.e., two groups in direct geographical contact) will be considered.

However, as we move forward, particularly into the twentieth and twenty-first centuries, it is worth conceptualizing religious frontiers less as a hard "yes or no" category, and more as a category in which a group or state can have partial membership.

Finally, it is always important to look at a puzzle from as many angles as possible. Therefore, it is important to examine some cases in which there has seemingly never been a religious border. In Europe, this task is difficult, as religious conflict and religious borders have been an important part of European history. However, some substate groups might provide some insight. A brief example for purposes of concept clarification may prove useful. The Basques of Spain and France do not share a religious frontier with any other groups, nor do they exist near any religious frontiers. Although there are clear threats to the Basque identity, the absence of religious borders means that nationalism is framed in terms of other attributes, such as language and culture. These are the factors that separate them from their neighbors, and thus, they are the factors that matter for identity.

Drawing from the literature on social identity, we understand that you must know who you are *not* before you can know who you are. In this case, a Catholic nation surrounded by Catholic neighbors may be able to use Catholicism as a solidifying factor in its nation-building process, but it will likely be less useful than if a Catholic nation is surrounded by Protestant or Islamic neighbors. A Catholic country in a Catholic region will more likely rely on history, culture, language, music, food, etc. because they do more to separate the state from its neighbors than does a religion that spans international borders. This concept of religious frontiers is therefore central to any understanding of religious nationalism in Europe and likely worldwide.

A "threatened" existence

Yet religious frontiers do not fully explain the existence of religious nationalism. After all, is it not possible, even likely, to imagine a nation existing at a religious frontier without religion playing the central role in that nation's identity? In fact, it is fairly simple to think of examples: England, Germany, Quebec, the United States, many nations in Eastern Europe, etc. There is, in fact, another factor (in addition to religious frontiers) that is equally important in the formation of modern religious nationalism. In the literature on social identity, there is one concept that continues to arise and which scholars repeatedly and consistently mention: threat (Anderson 1991; Coakley 2002; Connor 1978; Eriksen 2001; White 2001).

In addition to the presence of a religious frontier, a threat from that frontier must exist in order for national identity to become solidified around religion. For example, a Christian and an Islamic state existing side by side geographically (at a religious frontier) may exist peacefully with one another and, as a result, the importance of religion as a national identifier may remain limited. Instead, the threats that exist to each nation's identity will define them. Perhaps the Islamic state is threatened by a neighbor that is also Islamic, but speaks a different language. It is likely that linguistic definitions of the nation will be in a position of prominence. However, once the Islamic state is threatened by the Christian state, an identity shift will occur.

Even if the threat is not truly religious in nature (i.e., the conflict is not primarily theological), religion will still play a key role in nationalism because religion provides the easiest, most identifiable, and most useful tool for rallying opposition to the threat. Thus, the dispute may be economic, but the usefulness of religion for mobilization in this case leads to its use by leaders, whether elite or grassroots. As Rene Rémond points out, "The church becomes the Ark of the Covenant of their homeland, the repository of the nation's soul. Events help to make the church and its ministers guardians of the national memory" (Rémond 1999: 115). Although Rémond is speaking specifically of instances in which a group is subjugated, the importance of the church applies when the mere threat of subjugation exists.

Thus, in order for religion to maintain its importance as a nationalist force, the nation must exist at a religious frontier, and that frontier must pose a significant threat to the nation. The result will be mobilization around the distinguishing feature of religion.

National threat

As became clear in the previous section, the importance of frontiers is variable. The factor around which they vary is threat – specifically, a threat to national identity. This concept builds partly out of social psychology and the idea that self-identification is at least somewhat dependent on "otherness" (as discussed in the literature review) (Eriksen 2001; White 2001). Simply put, a religious border alone is not enough to spark a religio-nationalist fire. There has to exist some form of threat to national identity (specifically from the other side of the shared religious border). This is where the ideas of cultural defense and threat as laid out by Bruce, Hastings, and Wallis and Bruce play a role (Bruce 1992: 96; Hastings 1997: 4; Wallis and Bruce 1992: 16–18).

Types of threat

This concept, not unlike that of religious frontiers, comes with several subdivisions. The first, and clearest, is subjugation. This occurs when one religious group is subjugated to the rule of another (i.e., Pakistan under India, Ireland under British rule, Greece under the Ottoman Empire, Poland under the partition, etc.). This concept fits the idea laid out by Coakley in the previous chapter (Coakley 2002). The danger to national identity is imminent when the nation is not in control of its own destiny. Attempts to do away with Irish identity under the rule of the British through the banning of cultural symbols, linguistic ties to heritage, and linkages to Catholicism are clear threats to Irish-ness. The response to the threat is strong, and it takes the form of religion because religion is the most easily identifiable difference between the oppressor (British) and the oppressed (Irish). This same pattern can be seen in Greece under Ottoman rule; in Poland, both during the partition and during Communist rule; and briefly in Pakistan under the Indian flag.

However, there is another form of threat that is also important and which Coakley and Bruce do not address, but which is taken into account in this study. Threat is also present when there is the *possibility* that one group may be subjugated to another. Once again, it is instructive to picture the idea along a continuum, with complete subjugation and national annihilation or assimilation at one end and complete security at the other. By envisioning threat not as a fixed, ideal type, but rather as a fluid variable in which groups can be partial members, we are capable of seeing many more nuances in the building of religious national identity.

Religion and threats

Returning to the importance of religion and frontiers, it is necessary to remember that the nature of the threat determines the nature of the identity. Buzan, Waever, and de Wilde argue that the makeup of the nation defines the threats presented to it (Buzan *et al.* 1998: 124). In other words, a nation composed on linguistic roots will see threats from other linguistic groups. A religious nation will view as threatening any group of another religion. This is not unlike Huntington's claims in *Clash of Civilizations* (Huntington 1996). Although this is clearly a chicken or egg conundrum and, as a result, one certainly reinforces the other, it seems clear that the nature of the threat created the national identity, not vice versa. In other words, it is not the case that religious groups create religious threats, but rather that religious threats create religious groups.

Thus, one can imagine a scenario in which one religious group (or possibly both) fears being conquered by the other. The implications that subjugation might have for their own religious identity and beliefs can lead to mass mobilization around a religious identity, even if that subjugation has not yet occurred. Examples include the clashes between Spain and the Moors; and the fear of Catholicism in England and its resulting suspicions of France, Ireland, and Spain. This distinction is important as it explains a wider variety of cases than Coakley's explanation. Coakley only looks at the role of subjugation, but it is important to note that a group need not be subject to the rule of another in order for religious identity to be strong. This explains the continued religious nationalism in certain nations that have since received independence (Pakistan's threat from India, Greece's threat from Turkey, etc.).

It is important to note that many European countries and substate groups have, at some point, experienced some religious threat. European history has been defined by such threats and conflicts (the Reformation, the Counter-

Reformation, the Inquisition, the Holocaust). However, it is important to look at countries such as Spain and England where a once strong religious threat has diminished substantially. Although the British and the Spanish have both been threatened by religious borders at some point in their history, those threats have diminished. However, the religious frontier still exists. The important change is the shift from a threatened identity to a non-threatened one. Examining these cases will allow us to see how religious nationalism is transformed by changes in outside threats to nationalism and to see whether the predicted changes actually did occur as expected.

Defining threat

Once the importance of a threat is understood, it is essential to clarify the concept's definition. Threat is a term used in international relations much more often than in comparative politics, but it has clear implications for both. A relatively brief glance at security studies in International Relations can help orient us.

Threat can be conceptualized in many different forms – economic, military, cultural, etc. However, the traditional view of security, originating with Hobbes, looks at security as purely material. A threat is, at its most basic, military and material in nature. Military conquest is the primary threat in the international system (Walt 1991; Waltz 1959, 1979). But the security debate has been widening a good deal in recent years. Buzan, Waever, and de Wilde argue that security can be threatened in any number of arenas, or sectors: from the military to the environment to the economy to society to politics (Buzan *et al.* 1998). They go on to argue that security is an inter-subjective process, essentially claiming that security is as much about perceptions as it is about reality (Buzan *et al.* 1998: 30). In other words, perceptions create reality.

There is clearly some truth to this. Two different people may view the same event in a different light, one as threatening and the other as normal. Regardless of the actual intentions of the United States in the Middle East, it is likely that U.S. foreign policy will be viewed as threatening there. Public opinion polls since 11 September clearly demonstrate this effect. In addition, it is clear that threats can come in many forms. The discussion in recent years of cultural domination (particularly by the West) and the threat associated with it by Middle Eastern societies is a pertinent example.

In spite of these points, this study will emphasize more traditional aspects of threats. There are several reasons for this approach. Although economic, environmental, and political threats are important and no doubt have an effect on identity, it is the ultimate threat of annihilation or assimilation that motivates identity formation. Donald Horowitz emphasizes the fact that the fear of extinction is an incredible motivator of ethnic groups. The end of their existence precludes all other threats (Horowitz 1985: 176). This extinction can come through physical extinction or through cultural assimilation.

Buzan, Waever, and de Wilde argue the same: "Societal insecurity exists when communities of whatever kind define a development or potentiality as a threat to their survival as a community" (Buzan et al. 1998: 119). It is likely that a variety of threats affect identity, but existential threats are primary.

This brings us to the second reason for emphasizing existential threats (both annihilation and assimilation): the introduction of subjective threats complicates matters. Looking back at historical examples of threats and their related role in identity formation is difficult enough when one is examining military sectors. Widening the definition too much will open the debate to an enormous amount of subjectivity. For now, this study will tackle more traditional definitions of security and threats.

It is still necessary to explain what is meant by traditional security. For the purposes of this study, emphasis will be placed on military security, or the ability of a neighbor to physically conquer the state, or at least damage it severely through military means. This involves examinations of military threats and military capabilities at a given historic point. In many cases, this will be obvious. When looking at Ireland, it is fairly obvious that Britain posed a threat to Irish identity because there were actual military disputes between the two. In other cases, the examination will be more difficult because it will involve the issue of potential – a state's ability to attack even if it chooses not to.

The nature of the threat will also be incorporated. Some subjectivity is required. Two states may be capable of severely damaging each other militarily (perhaps the U.S. and the U.K. today), and yet their relationship with one another makes such a possibility so remote that it proves essentially non-threatening. In addition, other factors will be considered. Distance, for example, plays a role in determining the severity of a threat. Vasquez points to the importance of proximity by stating that "events closer to home are seen as more threatening than more distant events … ," and Walt similarly says that "states that are nearby pose a greater threat than those that are far away" (Vasquez 2000: 62; Walt 1987: 23). Thus, threats will be examined partly on the basis of military capabilities and the potentiality of subjugation, while the context will always be accounted for. At the same time, it is necessary to account for assimilation threats as well – a more difficult and nuanced process, but one that is still fairly straightforward.

Explaining religious nationalism

This new approach (religious frontiers plus existential threats) aids our understanding in several ways. First, it goes beyond the basic theories of Bruce and Coakley by explaining religious nationalism post partition. In other words, Coakley and Bruce only look at the importance of religion when one group is subject to another. My theory points out that religious nationalism will likely continue after these groups gain independence because: (1) the border still exists, even if it is not a political one *per se*; and

(2) a new threat has not yet emerged to replace the one associated with the religious frontier.

Ireland provides a great example, and will be examined in more depth in Chapter four; however, a brief look is worthwhile. Although Ireland received its independence in 1921, the presence of the religious frontier between Catholic Ireland and Protestant Britain did not go away. It was, in fact, brutally apparent at the border between the newly established Northern Ireland and the Republic. In addition, the Irish had been struggling for centuries against the English. A memory of that sort does not disappear overnight. The lack of national unity between Northern Ireland and the Republic kept Catholic national sentiment central to Irish politics for many years after independence. The Irish were still threatened, and the struggles in the North have only reconfirmed that feeling. Even though they had their independence, religion was still central to national identity.

Second, this study and this theory seek to understand the process by which religious nationalism is maintained. Specifically, what occurs at these religious frontiers that allows for a continued religious identity? Political leaders, grassroots campaigns, and nationalist movements need tools for mass mobilization. At religious frontiers, religion provides the most easily accessible and most powerfully idealistic means of doing so. People identify with religion because it distinguishes them from the "other." As such, elites will use religion as a tool to further political goals.

Third, this theory subsumes the previously accepted notion that economic development leads to a secular national identity. The traditional belief held that secularization was an inevitable by-product of modernization. While this correlation generally holds, the causal mechanism has been misunderstood. It is not the development itself that leads to secularization. Rather, economic development provides, in general, a greater degree of national security – meaning the security of the national identity itself. Thus, an economically developed state is typically less threatened by its neighbors than an underdeveloped and susceptible state. It is a variation in threat (brought about by a shift in economics) that leads to a variation in national identity. This line of thought is useful because it allows us to explain why certain economically advanced states may maintain (or turn to) religious nationalism in times of national insecurity. Thus, should the United States face a serious religious threat, it would likely turn to a religious conception of nation in response – regardless of its status as the world's economic leader. This can be seen in the increase in religious rhetoric following the 11 September attacks. Economic development provides general security, which in turn means that one key independent variable falls out of the equation and results in secular nationalism. But a serious threat could transform even the most advanced state into a religious nation. The upcoming studies of Poland and Britain demonstrate this transition: in Poland in the seventeenth century (economic collapse leads to religious nationalism because of increased threats from Russia and Prussia) and in Britain in the eighteenth and nineteenth centuries (economic development leads to secular nationalism as Britain is less threatened by Catholic Ireland, France, and Spain).

Finally, a study of this sort allows for an in-depth analysis of several theories – both those of Bruce and Coakley, as well as new theories such as the one presented here. Bruce and Coakley each dedicate very little time specifically to the understanding of modern religious nationalism. In-depth case studies and cross-case analyses allow for a much clearer understanding of the causal processes involved in each case, as well as a firmer grasp of the actualities of religious nationalism in Europe today.

The approach

In order to examine the theory laid out above, several historical case studies will be undertaken. I will look at the histories of several European countries, specifically ones that have a clear link between religion and nationalism, and see if the evidence fits the argument. How prominent are religious frontiers and threats in the most obvious examples of religious nationalism in Europe? The historic approach will be useful because it will show the changes in religious nationalism over time – most significantly in response to shifts in religious frontiers or existential threats. For instance, Poland was once considered one of the most religiously tolerant states in Europe, but a shift in Polish security means that it has become one of the most religiously affiliated countries in the region. Without an examination of Poland in the 1600s, we would miss this shift.

Chapter seven will undertake a cross-case approach to testing the theory laid out above (Ragin 2000). This approach will be discussed more thoroughly in subsequent chapters. What is important to note here is that the cross-case approach will allow a much broader test of the theories proposed in this and previous chapters.

A European focus

This book focuses exclusively on the European continent. Area studies such as this are a useful approach to social science that allows for generalization among similar countries, ethnic groups, cultures, etc. Others, however, contend that area studies are based on arbitrary distinctions that have little to do with politics and more to do with our conceptions of the world as tourists and amateur geographers. However, there is justification for such a focus in this case. The phenomenon of secularization is widespread, but its impact in Europe has been unique. Specifically, Europe provides an arena for politics within which religion has seen an unprecedented decline. Europe provides the perfect setting for ideal secularization – modern states that have developed socially, politically, and, most importantly for this study, economically. As a result, secularization has been an indubitable force in European politics. Yet, some states have proven resistant to this trend. A European focus allows us to compare like with like. The level of development, the nature and extent of religion's impact on politics, and the specific religions themselves all allow for a more comparable analysis.

Generalizability is an important issue in political science. An approach that is focused specifically on European states necessarily limits the extent to which the conclusions of this study can be expanded. Although I think it likely that my findings will be pertinent in other parts of the world (i.e., the Islamic world), further studies will be necessary before we can claim as much. What a study of this nature *does* provide is a starting point for that investigation. If we understand religious nationalism in Europe, we have a starting point for our understanding of religious nationalism in Asia, Africa, Latin America, or the Middle East.

Case selection

This study seeks to explain why certain states have retained national ties to religion. As some theories have been proposed (see previous chapters), an examination of religiously nationalist states provides a good opportunity to test the existing arguments as well as the one being proposed here – specifically by examining three of the clearest examples of religious nationalism in Europe in an attempt to find similarities in the historic development of each. Does each case feature some role for religious frontiers? How important have other factors been in the formation of religious identity?

Clearly, the number of national movements in Europe is fairly large, and the importance of religion varies widely. However, Ireland, Poland, and Greece were chosen for this study for the above reasons. Each is economically developed and democratic. The inclusion of an Orthodox country allows the study to be expanded beyond a simple examination of Catholicism and its political impacts. The Irish case will also include a detailed analysis of English and British nationalism, as it is intricately tied to Irish nationalism and allows for the examination of a country that has seen a shift away from a religiously focused national identity.

Choosing three cases of religious nationalism as the main focus of this study will be controversial for some, particularly in light of recent criticisms of selection bias (Geddes 2003). There are certainly issues that arise when choosing cases that do not vary on the dependent variable (in this case, all three case studies exhibit strong religious nationalism). However, all social scientific studies make trade-offs, and I am willing to sacrifice some generalizability in order to gain a fuller understanding of religious nationalism where it does exist. This approach is not novel and, although some will be critical of it, others have pointed out its strengths. As David Collier and James Mahoney point out:

> If little is known about a given outcome, then the close analysis of one or two cases of its occurrence may be more productive than a broader

study focused on positive and negative cases, in which the researcher never becomes sufficiently familiar with the phenomenon under investigation to make good choices about conceptualization and measurement.

Collier and Mahoney (1996: 74)

Collier and Mahoney go on to criticize some of the stronger opponents of selection bias:

> Collier argues that although some innovative issues have been raised, the resulting recommendations at times end up being more similar than one might expect to the perspective of familiar work on the comparative method and small-N analysis. Moreover, Rogowski suggests that some of the most influential studies in comparative politics have managed to produce valuable findings even though they violate norms of case selection proposed by the literature on selection bias.
>
> Collier and Mahoney (1996: 57–8)

Alexander George and Andrew Bennett have also written about the issue of selection bias in case studies, pointing out that "Working with a specified sub-class of a general phenomenon is ... an effective strategy for theory development" (George and Bennett 2005). In addition, they argue that studies that focus on a specific "typology" (i.e., only states that maintain a religious nationalism) may be useful, particularly if process tracing is used to examine the causal processes involved (George and Bennett 2005).

This approach is also bolstered by the fact that the number of observations available in a historic study is far greater than the three "cases", or states, to be examined. By looking at a country over a long period of time, it is possible to see how the dependent variable has fluctuated in response to the various independent variables (Collier *et al.* 2004; King *et al.* 1994). In other words, a study of Poland can be viewed as a simple study of a state that happens to fall into the category of "religious nationalism." However, by examining Poland over the past five centuries, it is possible to look at both a religiously nationalist state (nineteenth- and twentieth-century Poland) as well as a secular nationalist state (Poland during the sixteenth century). A similar transition can be seen in Greece during the rise of the Independence movement and the fall of the Ottoman Empire.

This thesis will undertake an in-depth examination of three of the strongest cases of modern religious nationalism in Europe, partly as a tool of better understanding the phenomenon itself, and partly as a means of testing the various theories that have been laid out. There are other cases that could be included (Yugoslavia, Cyprus, Malta, etc.), and these will be mentioned more briefly throughout the book.

In order to further strengthen the argument in this chapter, a full examination of nationalism across Europe will be carried out in Chapter seven. A variety of approaches were considered for this chapter, including a look at specific counter-cases that provide insight into the development of secular nationalism. Specifically, France was considered because of its status as the preeminent example of secularization in Europe. However, the very uniqueness that makes it interesting (i.e., the French Revolution) also makes it problematic for use as a generalizable test of the theory. The same can be said of other states in Europe. Whereas it is relatively easy to get an accurate picture of religious nationalism through an examination of three cases (there are only five or six in total in all of Europe), it is much more difficult to get an acceptable cross-section of secular nationalisms due to the sheer variety of cases. As a result, a less in-depth but broader approach will be used, and several key states in Europe will be examined in brief. Although depth would be ideal, the nature of the test to be performed means that brief examinations are still very useful. Specifically, in any given case, the absence of either a religious frontier *or* a religious threat should result in secular nationalism. This can be achieved in a much briefer study than is necessary for the first three cases of religious nationalism – cases in which the goal is to truly understand the nuances of religio-nationalist development.

A brief note on measurement

There is a tendency to try to measure in numerical terms all the factors in a given examination. The reasons for doing this are understandable – clear and concise numbers can be easy to examine and interpret. However, they are not always the most accurate way to conduct a study. In a long-term historical study such as this, numerical measurements can be very useful, but only if considered in their proper context.

The issue of religion provides a good example. There has been a tendency to measure secularism or religiosity simply in terms of attendance. Doing so provides a concise measurement of "religion" over an extended period of time. However, this practice has been questioned. Hadaway *et al.* (1996) have looked into the accuracy of self-reported attendance figures, concluding that actual attendance is only approximately half of reported attendance. In this case, attendance is not the factor of primary importance. This study is not concerned with how often people go to church, but whether they consider religion as a key component of identity, particularly at the national level. It is also worth noting that attendance figures do capture some of that essence. Attendance figures are actually indicative of self-identification, but they do not represent the whole picture. I am not concerned by Hadaway's claims that the figures are inflated (at least in the United States), simply because self-reporting is at the heart of this examination. If individuals are over-reporting their attendance, it is likely because of some presumed duty to be attending church. In a truly secular society, it would seem logical that there would be no over-reporting, but the opposite would be the case.

In addition, religious attendance figures can be indicative of phenomena unrelated to religious identity. As Grace Davie points out, the decline in religious attendance in Britain has also been accompanied by a decline in cinema admissions – from nearly 1.5 billion in 1951 to one million in 1991. She makes a very good point – that interest in movies has not actually declined; rather, the advent of television and, later, the VCR and DVD player has resulted in as much interest as ever (look at the revenues), merely altered by changes in technology and society (Davie 2001b: 104–5). This example is a warning to anyone hoping to capture religion by merely looking at church attendance.

The point of the above discussion is to briefly consider the accuracy of attendance measures of religiosity and religious nationalism, particularly in a study that examines national sentiment over the past five centuries. For this investigation, attendance figures will be used, but only in their proper context. Clearly, religious attendance can play a large part in religious identity, but the relationship is not concrete. An understanding of the situation surrounding the statistics must be included in any examination. In addition, the historical nature of this thesis severely limits access to good, continuous data, as desirable as that may be.

Conclusion

I have argued for a new understanding of the conditions leading to the formation of religious nationalism, at least in Europe. This new understanding is not a drastic reconfiguring of the theories that already exist. In fact, it takes most of its logic from existing theories in the field. It does, however, make minor tweaks and adjustments in the hope that our understanding is increased as a result.

The theory begins with Steve Bruce's notion of cultural defense and adds to it John Coakley's arguments about denominational interfaces. In the end, it argues that modern religious nationalism is shaped by (1) a nation's existence at a religious frontier and (2) a clear threat from that frontier. The frontier itself provides the soil. The proximity of another religious group makes religion a useful tool for nation building. However, it is only when the seed of a threat is planted that religion is actually used for that purpose. I do not argue that this combination of variables is necessary for religious nationalism. I do argue that the two factors are jointly sufficient. In other words, there may be other paths to religious nationalism besides the one laid out here. However, if there is a threat across a religious border, then religious nationalism will be the result (Goertz and Levy 2002). The strength of this theory is yet to be examined.

4   Ireland and England

> All that is native to Ireland, all that is social, loyal, moral is essentially Celtic and Catholic.
>
> Father P. E. Moriarty

Ireland provides an ideal case for testing the theory laid out in the previous chapter. Ireland, along with the former Yugoslavia, is the instance of religious nationalism that most non-academics would recognize as such. In addition, most scholars would not hesitate to point to religion as a key component of Irish nationalism. The link between Irish identity and Catholicism has been well documented. The Irish case provides an opportunity to look at the contrasting shifts in English and British identity over time. The nature of each of these identities (British/English and Irish) has been affected by the changes in international and internal threats. As the two nations have reacted to one another, religion has waxed and waned as a key factor in national identity, particularly in Britain.

When turning to the Irish, Catholicism has been a key part of national identity throughout modern history. As Thomas Bartlett indicates:

> Irish history without the Catholic question might seem as improbable as Irish history without the potato … In some respects all Irish history, at least from 1550 onward (if not indeed from the time of St. Patrick), can be regarded as an extended comment on the Catholic question.
>
> Bartlett (1992: 1)

Although the importance of Catholicism in Ireland in 1550 may not be surprising, the fact that it remains so nearly five centuries later makes Ireland unique. By tracing the construction of Irish national identity over the centuries, we can isolate the events and factors that have led to a modern religious nationalism (Ardagh 1995; Bartlett 1992; Colley 1994; Corish 1985; Cronin 1980; Darby 1983; Foster 1990, 2001; McCaffrey 1989; Neville 2003; Tanner 2001).

Religion and the Irish identity

The two key elements of religious nationalism are a religious national identity (how the nation views itself) and political religion (ties between religion
and politics).

Religious identity

The issue of whether or not the Irish people identify themselves as Catholic
is fairly straightforward. Nearly 90 percent of the Irish population belongs to
the Catholic Church. In Northern Ireland, the combined number of
Catholics and Protestants also nears 90 percent. Nearly 65 percent of the
Irish population attends church at least weekly. This number is drastically
higher than in any other Western European state. When polled about their
religious experiences in childhood, less than half of a percent claimed that
they never went to church. In a poll of youth between the ages of 15 and 24,
Ireland was the only state in Western Europe where a higher percentage of
respondents claimed to go to church weekly (69.5 percent) than claimed to
be religious (65 percent). In other words, Irish youth are attending church in
spite of the fact that they are not religious. In contrast, 42 percent of the
youth in France claimed to be religious, although less than 9 percent claimed
to go to church weekly (ISSP 1998).

Religiosity in Ireland exceeds that in other European states. However, the
more important question relates to how the Irish see themselves as a nation.
To use Gellner's criterion, is Catholicism necessary in order for two Irishmen
or women to recognize one another as Irish (Gellner 1983)? Again the
answer is "yes." As Michael Carey points out, "Faith and fatherland does ...
accurately describe Irish nationalism, that is, to be Irish is to be Catholic"
(Carey 1983: 105). Numerous scholars recognize this version of national
identity (Bartlett 1992; McCaffrey 1989; Safran 2003; Tanner 2001). From
the sixteenth century on, Catholicism has been central to the Irish understanding and construction of nationhood.

Political religion

The second half of the equation is also fairly straightforward. There is little
doubt about the importance of the Catholic religion in Irish politics. After
independence, the Church played (and continues to play) a large role in
shaping policy. The 1937 Constitution in Ireland stated that "the State
recognizes the special position of the Holy Catholic Apostolic and Roman
Church as the guardian of the Faith professed by the great majority of the
citizens" (Guelke 2003). Perhaps even more interesting than the overt linkage
between church and state is the fact that the subsequent acknowledgement of
other religions proved to be the controversial point (Guelke 2003: 117).
While some secularization has occurred (as is evident from the removal of

certain religious language from constitutional documents), conservative religious attitudes are still predominant.

> In the 1980s a sizeable part of the Republic made it clear that it wished to remain a Catholic country. Referenda that were intended to liberalize the Republic's moral legislation and thus make it more acceptable to the North backfired. The people voted to remain the only European country that does not permit divorce. Abortion was always illegal but the 1983 referendum made it unconstitutional as well as illegal. In 1992 the judiciary stepped in to close the loophole that had for years allowed a solution to the problem by making it illegal for Irish women to travel to Britain for abortions.
>
> Bruce (1996a: 101)

Lawrence McCaffrey makes a similar point:

> Since over 95 percent of the population is Catholic and mostly devout, and since Catholicism has represented culture and nationality, boundaries between religion and politics are more ambiguous and fragile in Ireland than in more pluralistic societies. Catholic homogeneity encourages the Irish to insist that problems concerning the family, marriage, procreation, and education have moral as well as socioeconomic implications.
>
> McCaffrey (1989: 17)

As Padraig O'Malley phrased it: "secularization in begrudging increments" (O'Malley 1997: xvi).

Although there has been a shift in the role of Catholicism in recent years, it has been slight. The percentage of the Irish population that claims to be Roman Catholic has not declined in any noticeable way since independence. In 1926, the figure stood at 92.6 percent. It rose to as much as 95 percent in the 1960s, and has now dropped, but only to 91.6 percent (McGarry and O'Leary 1995: 183). Attendance figures also continue to be among the highest in Europe, abortion remains illegal, and although divorce and birth control have been legalized, the controls surrounding them are strict. What makes this particularly remarkable is the fact that this continued reliance on religion has taken place in an era of unprecedented economic growth. The Irish economy is one of the strongest in the European Union. In spite of its status as the "Celtic Tiger," religion's demise has yet to occur. Thus, Ireland provides a perfect place to begin our investigation of religious nationalism in modernity.

Pre-Reformation politics

In order to understand why Irish identity has linked itself so strongly to Catholicism, it is necessary to step back to an era before the initial attachment. For Ireland, that takes us to the twelfth century. Although Catholicism has played a key role in Irish history since St. Patrick's return to the island in 432, it was not until many years later that it became inseparable from an understanding of Irishness.

It is impossible to overstate the importance of English involvement in the creation of a national identity in Ireland. Beginning with the Norman invasion of the twelfth century, the English have been involved in Irish politics. As a result, Irish identity has been formed in response to English-ness more so than any other factor. Again, the importance of the "other" in identity formation has been well documented. Up to the Norman invasion, the Irish had successfully absorbed all the conquering civilizations that had come to the island, thus lessening the impact of the "other" in national identity. The Norman invasion marked a breaking point in this trend. The resulting "Old English," as they would become known, went on to play a crucial role in Irish identity formation.

Strongbow and the Norman invasion

The significance of the Norman invasion cannot truly be understood unless one realizes that it was the starting point of a long history of animosity between the English and the Irish. In 1166, a feud emerged between several Irish leaders. At this point in history, Ireland was still quite disjointed politically, and one of the rival leaders, Dermot MacMurrough, went to the English king, Henry II, for aid. The English had various reasons for getting involved in Irish politics at this point. Specifically, a number of trade routes had been established between Dublin and English cities. In addition, Pope Hadrian IV, the one and only English Pope, had bestowed Ireland upon Henry as part of his papal right under the Donation of Constantine. At this point, though, Henry accepted MacMurrough but was unwilling to become involved directly in Irish politics. Instead, MacMurrough went about recruiting English knights to fight on his behalf. The most notable of these was Strongbow.

Richard FitzGilbert de Clare, better known as Strongbow, landed in southeastern Ireland in 1168. He quickly moved north and conquered Waterford and Dublin. The Normans were expected to serve their purpose for MacMurrough and then return to England. More Normans followed Strongbow instead, and the Norman invasion became central to Irish history. The introduction of the French-speaking Normans to the island would forever change Irish politics. Henry, afraid that Strongbow might be gaining too much power, went to Ireland himself in 1171. Henry took control of Dublin and awarded Strongbow a fiefdom for his efforts. The Norman invasion was completed when, in 1177, Henry bestowed the title "Lord of Ireland" upon his son, John.

Adrian Hastings points to this period as the true beginning of Irish nationalism. What had previously been a loose assortment of clans now took on a more united front. "For Wales, Ireland, and Scotland alike, the impact of English invaders, spearheaded by Normans, decisively altered national consciousness from the late eleventh to the fourteenth century" (Hastings 1997: 71). Specifically, Hastings points to the fact that " … the worse the Irish were treated the more like nationalists they naturally became," a trend that would continue for centuries (Hastings 1997: 80). Again, the importance of a threat is evident. But Ireland was unique in the British Isles. Although the Norman invaders now controlled a large part of the island, their control was never complete. The Irish were never fully conquered, nor were they capable of completely absorbing the Normans in the way they had the Vikings and other invaders before (Hastings 1997: 80).

Over the next several hundred years, the Normans slowly became more and more "hibernianized." The settlers began to adopt Irish customs, speak the local language, and intermarry with the natives. The lines between Irish and Norman became blurred to the point that most scholars describe them as "Anglo-Irish." The Normans did not, however, consider themselves Irish. Hastings describes the Old English as "English to the Irish but Irish to the English" (Hastings 1997: 81). Significantly, these "Old English" maintained their loyalty to the English throne. Many native Irish also continued to perceive the settlers as "foreigners" who should be removed from the island. True assimilation was never achieved.

The extent to which the Old English had become like the native Irish became clear in the fourteenth century. In the midst of a long war with France, the English crown sought to solidify its hold on Ireland. The fraternization between the Old English and the native Irish was viewed as problematic for the throne, and a series of rules was established governing the behavior of English lords in Ireland through the Statutes of Kilkenny in 1366. "The Gaelic revival, decreed the statutes, was to be countered by the cultivation of the English language, English surnames, and of archery, the prohibition of hurling and other Irish sports" (Hastings 1997: 46). Horses could no longer be ridden bareback as the native Irish had traditionally done; nor could the Old English trade with the Irish. In reality, the statutes did little to affect behavior in Ireland because the crown was focused on the war in France and made little effort to enforce them. However, it did emphasize the "otherness" that existed between the Irish and the English. It is also important because it demonstrates the focus on language and culture, as opposed to religion, in Irish identity.

Pre-Reformation "nationalism"

This discussion of pre-Reformation politics in Ireland is important for a variety of reasons. First, it is important to notice that Anglo-Irish antipathy began prior to the English Reformation of the sixteenth century. As Hastings points out, "The grounding of late medieval English nationalism lay in economics, geo-political facts, the maintenance of power both at sea and over England's first empire – its Gaelic neighbors. All this precedes the sixteenth century" (Hastings 1997: 55). English nationalism was already forming in the fifteenth century and Irish identity was certainly present, although its status as "nationalism" might be debated. Significantly, both countries were Catholic (the Anglican Church did not exist) and, as a result, religion served only a minor purpose in national identity. Instead, Irish identity focused on cultural and linguistic elements.

There was no religious frontier in the British Isles in the fifteenth century. As a result, English identity was formed in opposition to the French threat and focused instead on linguistic ties. Ireland, or the loss of control in Ireland, did represent a threat to the English throne; however, that threat could not be characterized as religious because there was no religious difference to begin with. Similarly, the threat from France was not religious in any way because the French were also Catholic. The difference was found in language. The Statutes of Kilkenny demonstrate this emphasis on the English language. English lords in Ireland were required to speak English and were only allowed to adopt English surnames. Hastings argues that it is at this point that " ... language is recognized as crucial for the survival of English identity and as a usable tool for policies of state" (Hastings 1997: 46). Language was similarly useful in creating a national identity separate from the Irish, as Ireland "was united by a shared language despite inevitable differences of local dialect ... " (Hastings 1997: 67). Again, there was a threat to both the English and the Irish nations, but the absence of a religious frontier meant that national identity was based on other distinguishing characteristics, namely language and culture.

The changes of the sixteenth century represent a crucial point in both Irish and English nationalism. It is necessary to understand that, upon entering the period of the English Reformation, English and Irish identities were shaped, first and foremost, around language. Cultural factors also influenced national identity, but nowhere did religion play a part beyond a broad association with Catholicism. As the fifteenth century passed, the threat to England from Ireland grew. Most notably, there was widespread support for the losing side in the War of the Roses, which the victorious king understandably did not appreciate. This threat led to stronger nationalism, but not in a religious guise. As Hastings concludes, "At its heart the growth of late medieval nationalism within a society where everyone was a Catholic could owe little to religion until that religion itself came under renewed scrutiny ... " (Hastings 1997: 53). The sixteenth century provided just that scrutiny.

The English Reformation

Henry VIII and the Anglican Church

The spark that ignited the Irish/English division into a seemingly permanent religious bonfire came in the person of Henry VIII. Henry came to the throne in 1509 and was granted papal dispensation to marry his brother's widow, Catherine of Aragon, an act that was frowned upon as unholy. Catherine was unable to produce a male heir for Henry, and he sought another papal dispensation to annul the marriage. This time, however, the Pope was not as amenable. There are many potential explanations for the Pope's stance, but the fact that the Holy Roman Emperor also happened to be Catherine's nephew likely had some impact.

The papal reluctance did not deter Henry, who simply sought a route around Rome. Through the advice of various leading religious scholars in England, Henry used several old laws to punish clergy who continued to profess allegiance to Rome over the English monarchy. As a result, "in 1531 the whole body of the English clergy was found guilty of [treason]. They were fined 118,840 pounds and were obliged to recognize the king as 'protector and supreme head of the church and clergy of England'" (Moynahan 2002: 401). Henry's relationship with another woman likely pressed the issue and, in 1533, Henry married Anne Boleyn in secret. The Pope responded by excommunicating Henry, who subsequently

> realized that papal authority in England had to be overthrown. The king knew antipapal sympathies in England were running high ... So the king calculated that he would face little popular opposition so long as he renounced papal authority in England and avoided troublesome doctrinal questions.
>
> Shelley (1995: 266)

The long-term effects of his decision were important for Irish and English history.

Although Henry's marital situation was the most obvious cause of his separation from Rome, there were others as well. Most notably, Henry was in the midst of costly wars with both France and Spain, and the wealth controlled by the Catholic Church in England was vast. The financial incentives to claim supremacy were strong (Moynahan 2002: 400). What is important is that none of the reasons for Henry's split were religious in nature. As Moynahan points out, there was little religious substance to the English Reformation – rather, "its theology was foggy, and no single strain dominated its brutal flux of beheadings, burnings, confiscations, and revolts" (Moynahan 2002: 398). Henry's split with the Catholic Church was political first and foremost. In fact, Henry was a fervent Catholic, who wrote critiques of Luther's ideas and who heard mass several times a day. "Henry's argument was with the pope, but in terms of doctrine he was deeply conservative and orthodox" (Moynahan 2002: 404). As one contemporary observer from Germany noted, "King Henry's sole concern was the income of the Church ... He stripped the gold and silver from the tombs of the saints ... and robbed the Church of its estates. That was the Gospel that Henry wanted" (Chadwick 1990).

Consequences

Henry's decisions had massive ramifications for European politics generally and for Irish and English politics specifically. What was previously a political dispute between the Irish and the English now became a religious divide as well. Although the nature of the conflict itself had not shifted, the terms upon which it was framed had changed dramatically. The throne was still concerned with Ireland for geopolitical reasons, and Ireland was still interested in ridding itself of foreign oppression. However, there was now a clear difference between the two populations. "It was not until Henry VIII's schism with the Church of Rome in the sixteenth century, his renunciation of papal authority, and his installation of the Church of England as the one official church of the land, that the Catholic–Anglican cleavage emerged" (Squires 2003: 82). Sean Cronin makes a similar point: "Although religion played a major role from the start, it did not become a matter of national 'ideology' until the Reformation" (Cronin 1980: 4). Henry's schism with the Roman Church provided the British Isles with a religious frontier.

Henry's split with Rome may have created the religious frontier, but the threat had existed for some time. The Irish were a thorn in the side of the monarchy for centuries. This was certainly true during Henry's reign. In 1534, Gerald Óg Fitzgerald and his son, Silken Thomas, led an uprising against the throne, to which Henry responded by declaring himself "King of Ireland" and claiming all the land in Ireland as his own. English law now applied to Irish and English alike. The years immediately following Henry's split with Rome were to produce a historic shift in both Irish and English identity. The convergence of a new religious frontier between Protestant England and Catholic Ireland with an increasing threat to both Irish and English sovereignty led to religious nationalism on both sides of the Irish Sea.

Post-Reformation politics and the Elizabethan wars

"Bloody Mary"

After the English Reformation, it only took a few decades for the conflict between the Irish and the English to shift from politics to religion. Henry died seven years after he declared himself King of Ireland in 1541. His death led to a series of successions in which his son, Edward VI, ruled for a brief six years before the Catholic Queen Mary, daughter of the divorced Catharine of Aragon, came to power and restored Catholicism to the kingdom. "Bloody Mary," as she came to be known, was married to Philip of Spain – an alliance that many Englishmen frowned upon. Mary reinstituted Catholicism by force, executing numerous Protestant leaders and solidifying a negative image of Catholicism among many English. "Devoutly Catholic, Mary tried to lead England back to the ways of Rome. In four short years, she outdid her father in intolerance. She sent nearly 300 Protestants ... to the burning stake" (Shelley 1995: 269).

Perhaps the most notable execution during Mary's reign was that of Thomas Cranmer, a Cambridge theologian and Protestant sympathizer whom Henry had appointed as Archbishop of Canterbury. His burning at Oxford unified a Protestant population. As Moynahan points out, "Martyrdom proved the ruination of Roman Catholicism in England, a horror that all Protestants could nurture in common" (Moynahan 2002: 408). The execution of Cranmer united "[t]hose with worldly reasons for resisting the return to the old religion, beneficiaries from the seizure of Church land and property, secular officeholders, nationalists who resented the Spanish alliance," who "now had martyrs to give their self-interest an air of idealism" (Moynahan 2002: 410). John Foxe gathered a variety of the grizzly stories and published them in his *Book of Martyrs*, which "incited the English people to a longstanding horror of Catholicism" (Shelley 1995: 269). Shelley argues that "Aside from the Bible, [Foxe's] book probably did more to shape the mind of Englishmen than any other single volume" (Shelley 1995: 294).

Mary's reign solidified a fear and hatred of Catholicism in England, and the threat to the English nation now had a face and name. The natural reaction to this fear was a shift towards a national identity linked with Protestantism. After all, the Protestant religion now differentiated the English from their enemies in Spain and France, as well as Ireland.

Elizabethan England

At Mary's death in 1558, Elizabeth I, Henry's daughter by Anne Boleyn, restored England to a Protestant realm. Elizabeth sought a solution that would mitigate the tension between Catholics and Protestants and, although she reigned as a Protestant, her theological stances were quite moderate. This, however, did not mean that her transition back to Anglicanism was peaceful. Although Mary's reign earned her the title "Bloody," Elizabeth's conversion program was equally brutal. In the end, the damage had been done, and Elizabeth's attempt to find a middle ground did little to nullify animosity between Protestants and Catholics. Her reward was excommunication from the Catholic Church in 1570.

Although the wars of succession began as a political issue, focusing on Mary's right to the throne, they ended as a solid battle between Catholicism and Protestantism. Other than in the case of Mary, there was no theology involved, but the result was a strong Protestant identity in England. Hastings argues that English nationalism was already becoming strongly Protestant by the sixteenth century. "There is ... a fairly widespread willingness even among modernists to admit that late Elizabethan England was already becoming a genuinely national society, with tinges of nationalism strongly fed on Protestantism" (Hastings 1997: 35).

Of course, the threat to English Protestants came from sources other than "Bloody" Mary. Mary's husband, Philip II of Spain, had strong animosities towards Elizabeth. After Mary's death, Philip decided to conquer England under the guise of rescuing it from the Protestant heretics. In 1588, the Spanish Armada sailed from Portugal for the British Isles. The plan involved bringing troops from the Netherlands across the English Channel to march on London after the Armada had taken control of the sea channels. Ultimately, the Armada was famously defeated and its remnants returned to Spain, but a later Spanish landing at Kinsale in Ireland brought the threat home once again.

The English Reformation under Henry VIII created a religious frontier in the British Isles. The subsequent events of Mary's reign, the Spanish plots, and ongoing tension with France added a significant threat to that frontier. Most notably, the Spanish landing at Kinsale showed that England's Irish neighbors were a direct threat to its survival. Winston Churchill wrote that the relations between Ireland and England "were established during centuries when the independence of a hostile Ireland menaced the life of England" (Churchill 1929). Irish politics now took on a new significance for the English. Although the actual disputes between the Irish and English were not directly religious (sovereignty, economics, etc.), religion provided the easiest form of differentiation between the groups. Adrian Hastings does a wonderful job in making this distinction:

> There was nothing inherently nationalist about Protestantism. The linkage was largely fortuitous. The excommunication of Elizabeth by Pope Pius V in 1570, the massacre of St Bartholomew two years later, the Armada, Foxe's Book of Martyrs and Gunpowder Plot combined to heat up English nationalism from the middle of Elizabeth's reign while reshaping it as a thoroughly militant and Protestant force determined to take on the Spanish threat not only in the straights of Dover but in the Netherlands, Ireland and the New World. When the danger from Spain receded, that from France replaced it and the liberation struggle – as English people saw it – against foreign political and religious tyranny went on.
>
> Hastings (1997: 55)

A new form of English nationalism based on Protestantism was forming.

The Irish response

This new English nationalism had profound effects in Ireland. In 1598, an uprising led by Hugh O'Neill, the Earl of Tyrone, defeated an English force in Ireland. When the Earl of Essex blundered the response, he was beheaded, and another prominent Englishman, Lord Mountjoy, took command of the English forces. His march across Ireland was brutal, and the situation came to a head in 1601 when Spanish troops landed in Kinsale to offer support to O'Neill's Irish rebels. Although Mountjoy defeated the Spanish troops, it was clear to the English monarchy that something had to be done about Ireland. England was now a Protestant state; the wars it had been fighting with France and Spain took on a religious dimension, and a Catholic Ireland on England's doorstep simply would not do. "The war with Spain, the threat of a Spanish invasion of England and the manifest collapse of any sort of English state control of most of Ireland had produced a new determination on the part of government to subdue the island definitively" (Hastings 1997: 81).

The subsequent English response took the form of a "white man's burden" for the seventeenth century. The common assumption was that the Irish would have to be civilized by the English; and that included conversion to Protestantism. "Queen Elizabeth herself spoke of the need 'to bring that rude and barbarous nation to civility', and another English observer wrote of how 'the Irish live like beasts ... are more uncivil, more uncleanly, more barbarous in their customs and demeanors than in any part of the world that is known'" (Neville 2003: 93). Edmund Spenser spoke out boldly against the Irish in his *A View of the Present State of Ireland*. He concludes that force must be used against the Irish for their own benefit (Spenser 1596).

> Great force must be the instrument but famine must be the means for till Ireland be famished it cannot be subdued ... There can be no conformitie of government whereis no conformitie of religion ... There can be no sounde agreement betwene twoe equall contraries viz: the English and Irish.
>
> Gottfried (1949: 148)

These attitudes led directly to the plantations of the seventeenth century, which had an indubitable impact on Irish identity.

Perhaps the efforts of the English in the sixteenth and seventeenth centuries would have been successful had it not been for the Old English. Whereas the Old English had, up to this point, remained loyal to the English crown, the events surrounding the English Reformation left them in a nationalist no man's land. Although the Old English thought of themselves as English, they maintained a strong link to the Catholic Church, which gave them a common bond with the native Irish.

> Probably the most crucial factor in the religious history of reformation Ireland was that, by and large, the Old English stuck to Catholicism and became in due course both a recipient and a producer of Counter-Reformation clergy. Their loyalty to the English Crown did not carry them into the English church of Elizabeth and therefore made them increasingly unreliable subjects in the eyes of her government and of the new English Protestant nationalism ...
>
> Hastings (1997: 81)

This also contributed to the logic of the Plantation. "Though in the past the crown had always largely relied upon the presence of the Old English to see its policies through, their religion now made them inherently unreliable" (Hastings 1997: 81). The English needed faithful subjects in Ireland, and the religion of the Old English aligned them with the papists of the world, including the hated Spanish and French.

The Old English stance on Catholicism contributed to a shift in Irish nationalism in other ways as well. " ... [T]he fact that the Old English had finally sided against England helped to demonstrate that the speaking of English was no longer in principle a threat to the [Irish] nation" (Hastings 1997: 89). As the Irish language was subsequently forced out of use, national identity could cling to the new unifying force of Catholicism. Here, as in England, a religious frontier had been created. The shift in the Old English population meant that Catholicism was a more useful tool for nation building than was language. Catholicism allowed the Irish and the Old English to come together, whereas the former unifying power of language was diminished. Although religion played a role in the politics of the Anglo-Irish conflict, the issues of sovereignty, economics, and basic freedoms were truly at the heart of the matter. Religion simply provided the most convenient tool for group mobilization.

The failure of the English to convert at least the Old English in Ireland was critical to the outcome of Irish nation building.

> Ireland's failed Reformation injected a religious element into a still older conflict between the English settlers who had colonized Ireland in the Middle Ages and the Gaelic natives. Resistance to authority became clothed in the white of martyrdom, and rebellion took on the colours of a crusade.
>
> Tanner (2001: 11)

The shift from a political disagreement to a religious conflict had reached fruition.

The series of events in post-Reformation England and Ireland were critical to the solidification of a religious nationalism in both states. The actions of "Bloody Mary," the war with the Spanish Armada, the Spanish landing at Kinsale, and the refusal of the Old English to reform all solidified the presence of a religious frontier in the British Isles and a related political and cultural threat across that frontier. As Moynahan points out, the end result of these events was England's transformation into:

> ...the greatest Protestant power. ...Early attempts to kill off Protestantism, by execution and by invasion, produced ingrained hostility and persecution of Catholics. To this day no Catholic can be regent, Lord Chancellor, Keeper of the Great Seal, or king or queen of England.
>
> Moynahan (2002: 398)

The Catholic tie to Irish identity is intact to this day.

Plantation

In September 1607, Hugh O'Neill and Rory O'Donnell fled Ireland for Rome. Their departure was significant because of their titles: O'Neill was the Earl of Tyrone and O'Donnell the Earl of Tyrconnell – both significant landholders in Ireland. This legendary "Flight of the Earls" had enormous repercussions for Irish politics, and many Irish still hold the Earls in contempt for their actions. The flight resulted in a vacuum of power in Ireland. Specifically, when O'Neill and O'Donnell fled, all their landholdings became available for redistribution by the English monarchy. The solution proposed by James I in 1610 was the Ulster Plantation.

The plantation laid the groundwork for the introduction of nearly 24,000 new settlers over the next twenty years. In order to gain access to the newly available land, the settlers had to agree to support English customs, including Protestantism (Neville 2003). In addition, the native Irish were subjugated to an extent previously unseen. The Irish had access to less than 10 percent of the land, and the land that was available to them was the least productive. The best tracts of land went to English and Scottish settlers. Two decades later, the religious frontier between the Irish and the English had been made abundantly clear. The animosity between the English and the Irish had been solidified through the legalized discrimination of the Ulster Plantation. More significantly, it had been formalized along religious lines. At this point in national development, both the English and the Irish identities were focused on their respective religious cultures.

Adrian Hastings argues that "large-scale settlement in a foreign land is bound to go one of three ways in terms of nationhood" (Hastings 1997: 92). He identifies these as (1) assimilation *into* the existing population, (2) elimination *of* the existing population, or (3) the failure of both assimilation and elimination. The third " ...is what actually happened in Ireland ... This is only likely to happen if there is some great factor, real or perceived, racial or religious, preventing assimilation" (Hastings 1997: 93). In Ireland, the opposing sides of the conflict had become so entrenched in their respective religious identities that neither was willing or able to be assimilated. Thus, with two distinct populations attempting to share a single land, the divisions between them became increasingly polarized. The Protestant English used their power to impose restrictions and limitations on the Catholic Irish, which further emphasized the religious cleavage. Steve Bruce summarizes the impact of the plantation:

> The people who came from Scotland were Calvinist Presbyterians. The natives were Catholics ... The Reformation was anti-Catholic and the Counter Reformation was anti-Protestant. The settler and native support of competing religions was an important reason for the two populations remaining distinct, and it was used by both sides in theodicies of success and failure. The settlers were able to explain and justify their

privileges by seeing these as the natural result of having the true religion. Catholics were poor because they had not been saved and were kept in bondage by their priests. Religion also provided consolation for the subordinate population and the Catholic Church acted as the main repository of Irish identity.

Bruce (1996a: 101)

It is important to note that the true issue behind the conflict was not religion, but rather economic and political discrimination. This is not to say that religion was unimportant. Certainly by the early seventeenth century, religion had entered into the equation in a substantial way. By now, the Protestants regarded Catholic actions and beliefs with disdain and vice versa. But a great deal of this disdain can be traced to historic animosities on the political and economic fronts. However, as in most religious conflicts, a shift occurred along the way so that these other contentions were veiled in religious garb. "Throughout the conflict, although political and economic factors were always at stake, the principle cause of contention has been *held up* as religion" (emphasis added) (Squires 2003: 86).

The combination of Elizabethan attitudes of superiority towards the Irish and the subsequent plantation strengthened nationalist sentiment in both countries. In England, the ongoing threat from the papist "others" drove national identity to the Anglican Church, which was the most useful tool for establishing English uniqueness and superiority. The Irish settlement is where "the new English Protestant nationalism appears at its purest, here too that the Reformation decisively alters the relationship between the English and the Irish and by doing so provides us with a classical scenario for the relationship between religion and nationalism" (Hastings 1997: 74). In Ireland, the formalized repression of the Ulster Plantation led to a strengthened Irish identity. It so happened that the repressor had built its unique national identity around Protestantism. Catholicism provided the most reasonable and useful tool for mass mobilization in opposition to English injustice. Although other factors could have been emphasized, religion provided the simplest and most virtuous route, particularly as Irish language and culture had been more successfully attacked and weakened by the English. This "snowball effect" continued to build in the latter half of the 1600s. The events leading up to and culminating in Cromwell's intervention in Irish politics further cemented the religious nationalism of both states.

Cromwell

The English Civil War and the Catholic uprising of 1641

In the mid-seventeenth century, politics in England took a series of major turns. Most notable was the English Civil War between the monarchical forces of King Charles I and the Parliamentarian forces of Oliver Cromwell.

Significantly, the reasons behind the Civil War not only focused on issues of Parliamentarianism and constitutional government, but also on religion. Puritanism had become a growing force in English politics, and the Puritan forces in Parliament did not look favorably upon the supposed Catholic sympathies of the new English king, Charles I, who came to the throne in 1625. Charles had married Henrietta Maria, a French Roman Catholic princess, and the marriage was seen in a very negative light by the English Parliament, an issue that was to have major implications over subsequent years.

The English Revolution can be directly traced to a religious issue as well. In 1637, Charles attempted to impose the Anglican religion upon Presbyterian Scotland, and the result was a Scottish rebellion. In order to financially support his war against the Scots, Charles was forced to call Parliament to order. The Parliament demanded reform in return for their aid and, by 1642, the political conflict had erupted into a military one. But before this could occur, events in Ireland once again took center stage.

Disenfranchised and relegated to a subservient position by the Ulster Plantation, the Irish simply needed an excuse to rebel. The Plantation had brought a large number of Presbyterian Scots to the island, resulting in an increasingly complex dynamic. The Presbyterians were fierce in their identity, and they were also persecuted for their faith, a fact that led to a strengthened Scottish nationalism. The Irish responded in turn by building even more strongly on their Catholicism for unity and inspiration. The Old English were upset as well; however, their displeasure had more to do with the fact that the large number of planters threatened their political position in Ireland. All these factors – when combined with Charles' supposed Catholic sympathies, Parliamentary troubles, and anti-Presbyterian actions of 1637 – led to a belief that an Irish rebellion would be supported by the monarchy. In 1641, the Irish did rise up. Charles, however, had his own problems to address.

The uprising of 1641 was the source of a great deal of English folklore regarding the Irish. Stories of Catholic atrocities against Protestant settlers circulated widely. Many of the stories were drastic exaggerations, but there is no doubt that some atrocities were committed. Conservative estimates put the number of Protestants killed at 4,000, nearly 20 percent of the Protestant population at that time (Foster 1990). The facts of the events are less important than the impact. The October 1641 date became entrenched in the Protestant mentality, and a new fear of Catholicism rose to the surface. "With the Jesuits active, and reports of the massacre of Protestant settlers, religious panic and fear of Catholic reconquest added to the existing crises of church government, parliamentary rights, and taxation" (Moynahan 2002: 468).

Cromwell in Ireland

Although the Irish found a strong leader in the Counter-Reformation-inspired Owen Roe O'Neill, the rise of Oliver Cromwell in the English Civil War was the ultimate determinant of the Irish fate. Cromwell's

Parliamentary forces achieved their goals in England when, in 1649, Charles was beheaded and a Commonwealth was established. Having achieved success in England, Cromwell turned to Ireland. Cromwell was a strong Puritan, a fact that was apparent in the Civil War. As Shelley points out, "In their [Cromwell's forces'] eyes, the war was a Puritan crusade against the enemies of righteousness. The just end sanctified force as a means" (Shelley 1995: 298). Thus, Cromwell's march on Ireland had a religious fervor to it that subsequently made him one of the most hated men in Irish history.

In 1649, Cromwell landed in Ireland with a force of 20,000 troops that quickly swept through the Irish countryside. Cromwell's mission was religious: the Catholics had demonstrated their barbarity in 1641 and had only worsened things by supporting the monarchy in the Civil War. As Neville points out:

> The nuances of Irish politics meant little to [Cromwell], and he cared not one jot that ... [the] Anglo-Irish lords had been loyal to the English Crown. In Cromwell's eyes Papists were Papists, and his task was to impose Protestantism on the whole of Ireland and restore order. He also, like all Protestants, remembered the massacres of 1641 and regarded himself as the agent of a wrathful god.
>
> Neville (2003: 105)

The most prominent episode in Cromwell's march was the infamous siege of Drogheda. After landing, the English troops marched on the town, a key defensive point for the north. Although the Irish expected the siege to be prolonged, Cromwell proceeded to bombard the walls of the city until they were breached. Once inside, the orders were given to grant no quarter to the Irish defenders. In the end, over 3,500 citizens of Drogheda were killed, including many who were burned alive in the Church of St. Mary and the royal Governor who was reportedly bludgeoned to death with his own wooden leg. Cromwell later wrote of the siege at Drogheda: I

> forbade [my men] to spare any that were in arms in the town: and, I think, that night they put to the sword about 2000 men ... I am persuaded that this is a righteous judgment of God upon these barbarous wretches. ... It is good that God alone have all the glory ...
>
> Cronin (1980)

The conflict had become a religious war.

After his conquest, Cromwell instituted a series of brutal reforms that pushed the Irish into a further place of repression. The decision to force the native Irish to the western region of Connaught, which was significantly less hospitable than the eastern portion of the island, is perhaps the most notable. "To Hell or Connaught" became a key part of Irish history, and the "curse of Cromwell" is still an Irish tradition.

The Irish uprising of 1641 and Cromwell's reaction to it clearly demonstrated the importance of the religious frontier once again. By the late seventeenth century, the Anglo-Irish conflict had taken on definitive religious overtones. Both the Irish and the English identities were being formed in response to one another. The events of 1640–50 only solidified stereotypes on each side. "The Rising of 1641 against the Planters provided a Protestant massacre, and the Cromwellian conquest in the 1650s a Catholic one" (Darby 1983: 15). The threat was clear to each side, and it was religious. Catholicism represented a danger to English freedom and sovereignty, and the English people rallied in support of their Protestant uniqueness.

The Glorious Revolution

The religious nationalism of both the Irish and the English was once again demonstrated and reinforced during the Glorious Revolution of 1688–89. In 1660, Charles II was restored to the throne of England. English suspicion of Catholic leanings had not died when his father was beheaded. Their mistrust was reinforced when Charles' brother, James II, took the throne. James' actions, including the support of alliances with Catholic states in Europe and toleration of Catholics at home, proved very unpopular in Protestant England. Although the Irish welcomed James' reforms, Parliament felt otherwise, and they invited William of Orange to take the throne.

When William of Orange landed on English soil, James was forced to seek support from Catholic France, further damaging his support at home. He eventually fled to Ireland, where his presence brought back renewed fears of another 1641. The situation culminated in the Siege of Derry, where the citizens of the city refused to allow troops loyal to James to enter the city. The subsequent siege lasted more than six months, and the Protestants in Derry did not see relief until an English ship succeeded in breaking through the blockade with support. William of Orange pursued James to Ireland in 1690 and succeeded in defeating him at the Battle of the Boyne.

The result of the Irish obstinacy was yet another round of punitive laws aimed at suppressing Irish culture and Catholicism. Throughout the 1690s, a series of Catholic Penal laws were enforced. John Darby explains:

> Having established an exclusively Protestant legislature in 1692, a comprehensive series of coercive acts against Catholics were implemented during the 1690s and after: they were excluded from the armed forces, the judiciary and the legal profession as well as from Parliament; they were forbidden to carry arms or to own a horse worth more than £5; all their bishops and regular clergy were banished in 1697, although secular clergy could remain under license; Catholics were forbidden to hold long leases on land or to buy land from a Protestant, and were forced to divide their property equally among their children in their wills, unless the eldest conformed to the Anglican faith … Their main effects were to

entrench the divide between Catholics and Protestants, to strengthen Irish Catholicism by adding a political component to it, and to drive underground some aspects of the Catholic Gaelic culture, notably education and public worship.

Darby (1997: 23)

This formalized repression only emphasized the religious divide and the threat to Irish identity, and points to the importance of religion in the national identity of both the English and the Irish. Adrian Hastings points out:

The fact that the threat to national identity in the seventeenth century was so clearly a Protestant one, and that Protestantism went necessarily with the dominance of England, inevitably identified Catholicism with Irish resistance to loss of national identity.

Hastings (1997: 89)

Again, the conflict was not primarily religious, but a threatening religious frontier meant that the Irish and English both turned to religion for national mobilization. This linkage between religion and nationalism would finally start to shift in the nineteenth century, but the results would only be enduring for Britain.

Eighteenth- and nineteenth-century Ireland

The United Irishmen and a Protestant Irish nationalism?

The eighteenth and nineteenth centuries revealed some interesting shifts in national identity in the British Isles. The dawn of the 1700s in Ireland and England revealed a strong tie between religion and nationalism in both states. The Catholic Penal laws aimed to break the Catholic Church in Ireland once and for all. In 1720, the British Parliament gained the right to legislate for Ireland, and the result was renewed Irish nationalism, but this time it took an unexpected turn, largely because it was inspired by the American and French Revolutions.

The American Revolution in 1776 inspired Irish leader Henry Grattan to demand legislative independence from Westminster, which he eventually achieved. However, this independence was not very reassuring for the Irish. Grattan was a Protestant, which meant that many Irish Catholics simply viewed legislative independence as another opportunity for the Protestants to exploit the Catholic population. As for the Protestants who were allowed to serve in the legislature, there was skepticism about the likelihood of continued deference once the British recovered from their war in America.

The French Revolution in 1789 reinforced the nationalist sentiment among many of the Protestant Anglo-Irish, who sought political freedoms from British rule. In response to the events in France, a group was formed under the title "United Irishmen." Unlike Grattan's movement previously, which was focused on the Protestant population, the United Irishmen had a goal of Irish nationalism built upon a union between Catholics and Protestants. The religious divisions in Ireland were too sharp by this time, and the United Irishmen were never successful in their attempts. They were, however, important for other reasons. One of the leaders of the movement, Wolfe Tone, fled to revolutionary France and, in 1796, returned to Ireland aboard a naval fleet carrying 15,000 French troops. The French had declared war on the British in 1793, and Ireland provided an opportune point for invasion, as it had for the Spanish previously. Unfortunately for the Irish, the winds turned and the French were forced to retreat. The British retaliated with a brutal campaign against the United Irishmen.

The French returned in 1798. A British attack on the United Irishmen in Wexford led to a large-scale uprising, this time with support from both the Catholic citizens and the Protestant United Irishmen. The French, again seeking to maximize their opportunities, returned to Ireland. They arrived too late, however, and were quickly defeated by British troops.

The importance of the Wexford uprising and the French response is clear. As had been the case in earlier English history, Ireland proved to be a threat, both directly and indirectly, to the English nation. The use of Ireland as a staging post by the French simply reinforced the need to control the Irish people. Once again, this was attempted via a series of legislative acts that further repressed the Irish. In 1800, the Act of Union was passed, abolishing the Irish Parliament. All Irish Members of Parliament would serve their terms in Westminster. Although Catholics were still banned from serving as MPs, they did have access to some positions, although their rights were severely restricted. After the Act of Union in 1800, "Those Catholics who did take on any public office did so under the condition that they swear that they would 'never exercise any Privelege to which I am or may become entitled to disturb or weaken the Protestant religion or Protestant Government in the United Kingdom'" (Squires 2003: 83).

Marcus Tanner explains the impact of the 1798 uprising and the end of the United Irishmen:

> … Irishness became ever more strongly identified with Catholicism, while Protestants, both Anglican and Presbyterian, retreated into a British identity. For them, the Act of Union of 1800, which joined the British and Irish parliaments, took on an almost sacred significance.
>
> Tanner (2001: 13)

Although Catholics did eventually win emancipation in 1829, their rights remained limited until the events of the twentieth century and Irish independence. What could have potentially led to a shift away from a Catholic-centered understanding of Irish identity fell victim to the same factors that had historically built Irishness around the one characteristic that most clearly differentiated them from the English: religion. P. J. Corish makes an interesting argument: "In the eighteenth century Irish patriotism had been very much a Protestant preserve. After the crucial decade of the 1790s it was well on its way to becoming a Catholic one" (Corish 1985: 150).

Eighteenth-century English nationalism

Whereas the events of the eighteenth and nineteenth centuries in Ireland failed to shift national sentiment away from the Catholic Church, the rising power of the British did have an effect on the other side of the Irish Sea. In order to understand the significance of these changes, it is important to recognize the depth of the national link to Protestantism prior to the 1800s.

In her book, *Britons: Forging the Nation, 1707–1837*, Linda Colley lays out a very persuasive argument that British identity was shaped around war with "a powerful and persistently threatening France." According to Colley, France was "the haunting embodiment of the Catholic Other that Britons had been taught to fear since the Reformation in the sixteenth century … " (Colley 1994: 368). Certainly in the eighteenth century, English national identity was still intricately tied to the French "other" and their own Protestant uniqueness. Hastings uses a similar logic: "The nationalism that England would export abroad … and pass on as core to an enlarged British nationalism in the eighteenth [century] was certainly very Protestant … in its self-understanding and sense of righteous mission" (Hastings 1997: 36). Claydon and McBride support this logic by arguing that eighteenth-century British identity consisted of two key elements: the "sense of Englishness … founded on a profound horror of a papist 'other'" and the model of an "elect nation" – the inheritors of "God's true faith" (Claydon and McBride 1998: 10).

Eighteenth-century British national identity was clearly centered on the Anglican Church and its position as an "elect nation." However, there is a discernable shift in the notion of British nationalism beginning in the nineteenth century. As British power waxed to its fullest, the threat from both Catholic France and Catholic Ireland subsided. Clearly the threat did not vanish, but the ability of the Irish or the French to threaten the very existence of the English nation was reduced. The British Empire now stretched around the globe and was recognized as the world power. Despite the fact that the religious frontier between Ireland and England still existed, the threat coming from that frontier was fading. As a result, the notion of what made the British unique and superior also shifted. There are a number of arenas in which this shift can be seen.

One school of thought argues that France was still threatening (although less so), but the nature of the French threat had changed. Hugh McLeod claims that the very secularism of the French Revolution was critical to the British change. The opposition to France now took the form of an emphasis on British Christianity in contrast to the overt secularism of France (McLeod 1999: 46). The colonial expansion of the British Empire also exposed the British to the "heathen masses" around the world. There was certainly a revival of religious values in Britain in the nineteenth century, as evidenced by the "white man's burden" to civilize the world. In a similar vein, McLeod also emphasizes the importance of British prosperity. The growth of the British economy provided another means for the British to set themselves apart as "elect." As McLeod indicates, " ... the proof of their own superiority lay in the nation's prosperity" (McLeod 1999: 48). A state that was the world's economic and military leader had little to fear in terms of national annihilation or assimilation. Britain was, instead, the annihilator and assimilator.

These changes in British national identity, seemingly subtle though they are, signify an important change in the politics of the nineteenth century. Prior to the emergence of the British Empire as the dominant world power, the religious frontier created by Henry VIII's schism with Rome provided a major point of insecurity for the English nation. The combination of that religious frontier with a significant threat from Ireland, Spain, and France provided the ideal breeding ground for religious nationalism. As British power and prosperity grew in the eighteenth and nineteenth centuries, the threat diminished, and British nationalism shifted its focus to other fronts. Although the initial shift meant an identity tied to a general Christianity as opposed to Protestantism, the ultimate result would be a nationalism severed from the Anglican tradition. British power would be perceived differently across the Irish Sea. An increase in British power translated into more insecurity for the Irish, and that meant a continued emphasis on Catholicism as differentiator.

Independence

Home Rule campaign (1880s–1910s)

As British power waxed and the Irish threat waned, a shift in British attitudes could be detected in the mid-1800s. Still disdainful of the Irish, the "superior" British adopted the nineteenth-century attitude of pity as opposed to hostility. This can be seen in the increased political leniency by the British at the time. The goal of Catholic emancipation was achieved in 1829 under the leadership of Daniel O'Connell, who argued that a Catholic country should have a Catholic Parliament. In 1869, Gladstone repealed the fifth article of the Act of Union, disestablishing the Church of Ireland. Although this was largely symbolic (attendance was dismal), it was still significant. In addition, the combined effects of the potato famine and changes to voting laws "meant that by 1853 88.7 per cent of the Irish electorate was registered for voting" (Neville 2003: 154).

In the 1870s, a new movement emerged that advocated legislative independence through peaceful and constitutional means. The Home Rule Party was established by Isaac Butt, but Charles Parnell quickly emerged as the movement's definitive leader. Although Parnell was a land-owner and a Protestant, he understood the importance of the Catholic Church in Ireland and wisely earned its support. Although Parnell was successful in achieving some concessions in the Land Act of 1881, a series of events led to the temporary demise of the Home Rule movement. Legally, Home Rule proved to be too progressive for many in the Westminster Parliament, and the Home Rule Bill of 1886 failed to pass. A significant reason for its failure can be traced back to the unwillingness of Ulster Protestants to live in an independent Ireland. Just as significant was Parnell's fall from grace. An affair led the Catholic Church to denounce Parnell, and his Irish followers followed suit. Although his mission had failed, Parnell had a deep impact on politics in late nineteenth-century Ireland and Britain. As Neville indicates, he made Home Rule the leading Parliamentary issue of the day (Neville 2003: 162).

World War I and the Easter Rising of 1916

The failure of constitutional approaches to Home Rule led to a general feeling of betrayal in Ireland and a consequential return to violent means. Although the Irish Catholic threat to the British had diminished, the threat to Ulster Protestants had increased. As the possibility of Home Rule entered the political debate, the fear of life under Catholic Ireland became central to Ulster Protestant identity. Thus, another shift occurred. The Irish identity was still threatened by British control; however, the Protestant nationalism previously central to a larger British nationalism now became central to a more focused Ulster nationalism. The Ulster Protestants had already played a central role in the fall of Home Rule, and in 1913 the Ulster Volunteer Force (UVF) was formed. The purpose of the UVF was to use "all means which may be found necessary to defeat Home Rule" (Neville 2003: 162). Numbering over 90,000, the UVF was certainly a menacing presence. On the Catholic side of the conflict, the Irish Volunteers had begun to arm themselves as well, preparing for what seemed like an inevitable civil war. But things fell apart in Europe before they had a chance to in Ireland.

The outbreak of World War I distracted the British from the issue of Ireland and, while it did distract some in Ireland as well, there were some who aimed to take advantage of the circumstances. On Easter Monday 1916, the Irish Republican Brotherhood, led by Padraig Pearse, rose in revolt. A German ship had been sent to supply the rebels, but it was captured before it reached its destination. The uprising went ahead, despite the improbability of success. The rebels, though small in number, put up quite a fight, and the British response was strong. In the end, over 500 people were killed – 300 of them civilians.

The uprising itself was not as important as the subsequent events. Initially, most Irish citizens were incensed by the rebels, going so far as to throw tomatoes at the captured rebels in the streets. But the British response to the revolt was harsh. Fifteen rebels were executed, including some who were already severely wounded. The result was Catholic outrage and a renewed national sentiment in opposition to British rule. A group of national leaders emerged after the crisis, including Michael Collins and Eamon de Valera, who had somehow avoided execution for his role in the events of 1916. In 1918, Collins' party, Sinn Féin, won a landslide victory and proceeded to establish an assembly in Ireland, the Dáil Éireann – an act that was illegal under British law. Shortly thereafter, the first clashes of the War of Independence changed Irish politics.

In 1919, Michael Collins unleashed the newly formed Irish Republican Army (IRA) in an attempt to provoke the British troops in Ireland. The war between the IRA and the British "Black and Tans" dragged on for two years, and by 1921 most Irish citizens were eager for peace. In 1920, the Government of Ireland Act was passed, dividing Ireland into the North and South and providing each with an independent parliament. The following year, the Anglo-Irish Treaty was enacted, which created the Irish Free State. The treaty was a compromise in that the North was left under British control. In addition, the new Irish state would be forced to swear allegiance to the crown, although no such allegiance to the British government was required.

Post-independence Ireland

A threatened North

Irish independence marks an important shift in the Irish story. In many ways, it would seem that independence from British rule would mark the end of the British threat, and thus an important factor in the formation of religious nationalism would wither away. The logical result would then be a shift away from religious nationalism in Ireland. Had there been a united Ireland in 1921, this might have been a possibility. However, the fact that all of Ireland was not "free" meant that a sense of subjugation remained. In particular, an independent South proved to be significantly threatening to the Protestant population of Ulster. The nationalist sentiment in the North had already solidified around Protestantism, and the increased threat of a unified Ireland merely fanned the flames. The increase in religious rhetoric also meant a continued threat to the new Catholic minority. Although the larger picture seemed to show a conflict moving towards a solution, the presence of a threatening religious frontier was as real as ever in Ulster.

The Catholic population of Ireland was not pleased by partition and, in 1922 a civil war erupted between those who supported the Anglo-Irish Treaty and those who were opposed to the division of the island. Both before and after the Treaty was enacted, the IRA made a policy of using violence against the new state, and their tactics opened the door for the passage of the Special Powers Act in 1922, which provided the Northern government with extensive powers over Catholics in the region. Certainly the Northern Unionists (meaning union with Great Britain) had reason to be afraid. The

1937 Constitution in the Republic began by recognizing the "Most Holy Trinity" and paid tribute to the Catholic Church as "the guardian of the Faith professed by the great majority of the citizens." (Note the clear tie between Catholicism and government in the Republic.) In addition, the treatment of Protestants in the South did little to ease Northern fears. "A fact often cited by Ulster Protestants in explaining their hostility towards the concept of a united Ireland has been the fate of the Protestant minority in the South after the partition of Ireland in the 1920s" (Guelke 2003: 116). The number of Protestants in the Republic has steadily diminished to the point that they now make up less than 3 percent of the population (C.I.A. 2004). Today these fears have been lessened as the influence of the Catholic Church has weakened.

A modern religious nationalism

The result of the Anglo-Irish Treaty in Ireland has been the emergence of several distinct national sentiments, each of which needs to be addressed. To begin with, the Irish national identity has, in recent years, begun to show some signs of secularization. John Ardagh, in his description of the modern Irish people, points out that:

> the Church's influence, once so massive, has been declining steadily in the past thirty years, as society grows more secular. Many practicing Catholics no longer follow its moral laws in their private lives. They may still believe in God ... but they have grown critical of the Church as an institution.
>
> Ardagh (1995: 158)

Ardagh's point is important. Particularly in recent years, there has been some backlash against the Catholic Church and its emphasis on sexual and social mores. However, there has not been a massive shift away from the Catholic identity. Catholicism continues to be an important part of Irishness despite the fact that church attendance has declined. The importance of religion in religious nationalism is not so much theological as it is socio-logical and political. Religion provides unity to a wide population. As such, many people may still consider Catholicism a key part of their identity while paying little or no attention to Church doctrine. This is central to our understanding of religion in today's Northern Ireland.

Although the Catholic Church has weakened in the Republic, Ireland still represents one of the most religious states in Europe. Abortion remains illegal, and divorce and birth control are strictly regulated. There has been some flexibility in recent years on issues of abortion and birth control, but the Church clearly still has a prominent position in national political debate and policy. Should Ireland continue to prosper economically and strengthen its own position in the world arena, the importance of religion for national identity will also likely continue to wane – not because they are wealthy or developed *per se*, but because that development provides security and diminishes the threat of national assimilation or annihilation.

However, this transition has not yet occurred in Northern Ireland. Perhaps even more than in the South, religion plays a key non-theological role in the identity of Protestants and Catholics of the North. "An advantage of the terms Protestant and Catholic is that they convey much more effectively than any political label the sense of people's involuntary membership in a group" (Guelke 2003: 102). Steve Bruce provides an example of how this identity plays out:

> The distinguishing feature of ethnic religion is that it remains a powerful emblem, even for those members of the ethnos who do not personally share the faith. Thus one has the working-class Ulster Protestant who, though now not terribly pious, was raised in Sunday School, listens to the familiar prayers and Bible readings at the start and end of his Orange Lodge meeting, encourages his children to go to church, and is proud of his wife who is church-going and "good living."
>
> Bruce (1996a: 105)

The continued threat to the Unionists of the North means that religion will continue to play a role in national identity there.

In Britain, the story is different. No longer threatened by the Irish issue, British nationalism has turned to other sources for identity. Religion no longer provides the central focus of British nationalism. "Although the Church of England ... is the established church in the United Kingdom, its hegemonic role is now almost extinct" (Squires 2003: 92). Britain's leading role in the world over the past 150 years has focused national attention on colonial holdings abroad and on crises nearer to home, such as the World Wars. This is not to say that religion is no longer a factor in British identity. In recent years, the influx of Islamic immigrants has led to a new sense of Britain as a Christian nation in certain sectors of society. Josephine Squires explains the importance of the Islamic community today: "Considerable social and political tension exists between Islamic groups and non-Muslims in Britain ... 'Muslim' has become a word of abuse and Islamophobia appears to be the aversion of the day" (Squires 2003: 89). At this point, the threat from Islam is minor. But should the Islamic population continue to grow, or should Britain fall victim to further Islamic terrorism, it is likely that the importance of religion in British nationalism will increase once again in spite of its economic development.

The strange story of the Gaelic language

Space must be set aside here for the purpose of addressing the Gaelic language. Any discussion of Irish nationalism has to address the issue of language, if only because of the unique circumstances surrounding its near demise. The fact that the near total loss of the Gaelic language did not diminish the Irish cause is noteworthy. Adrian Hastings points out that the Irish example of nationalism without language is surprising, given the importance of language in other nationalisms.

> It seems strange that Irish nationhood suffered so little from the abandonment of its strongest redoubt, the language, and it was only possible because Gaelic had in a very real way been replaced by an alternative principle, that of Catholicism. The fact that the threat to national identity in the seventeenth century was so clearly a Protestant one, and that Protestantism went necessarily with the dominance of England, inevitably identified Catholicism with Irish resistance to loss of national identity.
>
> Hastings (1997: 89)

Larkin insinuates that the loss of the Gaelic language may have actually encouraged the entrenchment of Irish nationalism in Catholicism.

> Because the Catholic church became the most important institutional element in sustaining the ongoing Irish identity after the collapse of the aristocratic Gaelic order, it was inevitable that Irish and Catholic over time would become virtually interchangeable terms.
>
> Larkin (1989: 103)

The loss of the Gaelic language, often a crippling blow for other nationalisms, only pushed Irish nationalism more towards the one distinguishing characteristic that remained: the Catholic Church.

Let us return for a moment to the working theory. This book makes the argument that a religious frontier is important in the formation of religious nationalism because it isolates religion as a key differentiator between two hostile or threatened groups. As such, it makes sense that the loss of the Gaelic language would encourage religious nationalism. Had the Gaelic language survived more extensively, it is likely that it would have remained a key ingredient in Irish national identity. It is unlikely, however, that it would have replaced Catholicism as the defining characteristic. The historic animosities between the English and the Irish along religious lines made it virtually inevitable that Irish identity would be shaped in opposition to English and British Protestantism. In addition, the role of the Old English in the sixteenth century determined that language was not the crucial difference between the oppressive English and the subjugated Irish. It was Catholicism instead.

Conclusions

This book argues that religious nationalism forms under certain geopolitical conditions. Specifically, the combination of a religious frontier and a national threat leads to a link between national identity and religion. In many ways, the story of Irish and English nationalism provides the perfect illustration of this argument. Throughout history, Irish nationalism has been shaped in contrast and in resistance to an English "other." English identity, on the other hand, was strongly impacted by an Irish threat up to the nineteenth century. However, what began as a strongly Protestant image of nationhood shifted towards more secular conceptions as the threat from Catholic Ireland and France diminished.

An emphasis on the "other"

There are two important points to make here. The first is to re-emphasize the fact that identity is based on "otherness." In other words, our self-conception is built around what sets us apart – what we are not is as important as what we are. In terms of national identity, nationalism is structured around the characteristics that set one nation apart from others. In addition, identities are shaped by the pressures placed upon them. In the British Isles, Ireland proved to be a continual thorn in the side of the English monarchy and Parliament. In particular, the repeated use of Ireland as a staging post by the Spanish, French, and Germans for invasions into the English homeland proved to be highly threatening. On the other hand, the English and British mistreatment of the Irish beginning in the twelfth century proved to be the strongest pressure on Irish nationalism. The result was that both sides built their identities in response to one another.

The presence of a threat only meant that the Irish and English nations were mutually constituted. The focus of that construction could have been language, culture, history, or any number of other factors. The fact of the matter is that religion provided the easiest, clearest, and most accessible tool for national mobilization. The English Reformation determined that the nationalist movement in Ireland would be primarily religious, as opposed to cultural or linguistic. Michael Carey explains how the English pushed the issue into the religious realm:

> Unwittingly, the English colonizers provided a very clear point for Irish cultural identity, the identification with Roman Catholicism by the native population. The English Ascendancy, with its own church, then proceeded to define political loyalty as religious loyalty too, and aggravated this split with specific policies to promote the English Church and denigrate and suppress the Irish Church.
>
> Carey (1983)

The presence of a religious frontier meant that political and economic grievances could be easily wrapped in religious garb. The result, as history has shown, was a political conflict along religious lines. Unfortunately, religious conflicts and identities, by their very nature, lend themselves to intractability.

One reason for the strength of opposition to religious interpretations of the Northern Ireland problem/conflict is that they tend to the conclusion that nothing can or should be done to promote a political settlement on the grounds that the differences at the heart of the conflict are not amenable to compromise.

Guelke (2003: 105)

However, religious divisions *were* a key factor in the ongoing formation of national identity in both Ireland and England. As Hastings indicates:

If there had been no nationalist spirit in Ireland, maybe its people, Catholics included, could have been as satisfied with a British identity as were the Scots or the Welsh in the heyday of the British Empire. But such an "if" requires the absurdity of forgetting the whole history of Ireland prior to 1829, and how the role of religion in all of that ... had been decisive. It shaped the lines which have still not gone away and much as church leaders may wish to affirm that the conflicts of today are not about religion and are not between religious people, the fact remains that without the impact of religion they would be totally incomprehensible.

Hastings (1997: 90–1)

The important point is this: had there been no religious frontier in Ireland, English and Irish identity may still have been formed in contrast to one another; however, they would not have been formed along religious lines. Had there been a religious frontier but no Irish threat to England, English identity would have been formed in contrast to another threat and, as a result, would likely have focused on a different constitutive factor – language, culture, history, etc. But the course of history dictated that, for both the Irish and the English nations, the religious division created by the English Reformation was a crucial and conspicuous threat to both nations, and each responded by rallying around religion as a key differentiator in nation building.

An emphasis on politics

An important corollary of this theory is the fact that, although religion is central to national identity in Irish history, the factors that led to the linkage were political, not theological. As discussed in the literature review, some argue that religious groups create religious threats (Buzan *et al.* 1998): a Catholic nation (Ireland) will be threatened by a non-Catholic nation (England). While there is certainly truth to this argument, it proceeds to put the cart before the horse. The Irish case shows that, in fact, religious threats produce religious groups. To clarify, the Irish nation and the English nation were already threatened by one another before the introduction of a religious element. Once religion entered in, the identities formed around it. Thus, it is not the case that Ireland and England were threatening because they were of different religions, although this was eventually true. Rather, Ireland and England focused on religion because they were threatened, and Catholicism and Protestantism were the easiest ways to rally the nation in response to that threat.

This can be seen in Irish politics today, most notably in the North. Religion has been so central to identity for so long that it has become indistinguishable from political identities. However, at the core of things, religious identities in Ireland are largely political and very seldom theological. The clash between Catholicism and Protestantism is certainly doctrinal for some; but for most, religion is simply a matter of identity. As Jonathan Tonge points out:

> Labelling [sic] by religious denomination remains the most convenient method of identifying the division between the communities. The terms Catholic and Protestant are preferred to nationalist and Unionist or republican or loyalist as they embrace the vast majority of the people and are less problematic than other labels.
>
> Tonge (1998: 81)

For many, religion's role as a social category is, at the core, more important than its theological role. "What matters is not an individual's religiosity but the individual's incorporation in an ethnic group defined by a particular religion" (Bruce 1996a: 102). Josephine Squires makes the same point:

> Social segregation of Catholics and Protestants still exists, entrenched though it may be, but this is due to the reliance on historical memory as a guide for present and future actions. Although religion played a large role earlier in the England–Ireland conflict. ... it has now become a scapegoat, an easy label, while the true reasons for the current conflict, which are more difficult to explain or justify, are, to a large extent, neglected.
>
> Squires (2003: 82)

It would be wrong to dismiss the importance of religion's role in Irish politics simply because it is a social container. Religion is remarkably important in Ireland, as can be seen by the very high levels of religiosity. Wright points out that a number of Irish Protestants view the Northern Irish conflict in "religio-political" terms, or a "battle between two religious systems carried on in the field of politics" (Wright 1973). And, as Guelke indicates, religion and national identity have become coterminous. " ... [T]he number of Protestant nationalists [in Northern Ireland] is virtually insignificant. In fact, not a single respondent out of a survey of over two thousand identified himself or herself as both a Protestant and a supporter of either of the two nationalist parties ... " The same is also true of Catholic Unionists (Guelke

2003: 104). Religion is indubitably important. However, it must be understood that the religious division is a result of political conflict.

This chapter has argued that the introduction of a religious frontier into the Anglo-Irish conflict meant that religious nationalism in each country would be formed around their unique religious identity instead of another potential constitutive factor such as language or culture. This process was certainly furthered by the near elimination of the Irish language. However, religion was the most efficient tool for subsuming the various groups in Ireland under a single national identity. To this day

> Protestants and Catholics are divided by religion by definition, but they are also divided by differences in economic and political power, by historical experience, and, most intensely, by national political identity … Religion is the key ethnic marker, facilitating the residential, marital and educational segregation which helps reproduce the two ethnic/national communities. Because religion is the key marker its importance is exaggerated.
>
> McGarry and O'Leary (1995: 211–12)

In England, religion served the same purpose until the mid-nineteenth century, when British power grew to the point that the Irish threat was no longer critical for national identity. As such, the religious frontier did not vanish, but its importance for British identity was diminished. This combination of a religious frontier and a national threat is not isolated to the Irish and British cases. As will be seen in subsequent chapters, this pattern is evident in a number of European settings.

5 Poland

The Polish state is a Catholic state ... This is so not just because the great majority of its population is Catholic, not even because the size of the majority is so overwhelming. It is fully Catholic because our state is a national one, and our nation is a Catholic one.

Roman Dmowski (1926) *The Church, the Nation, and the State*

The real reason for the existence of Poland is to realize on earth the kingdom of heaven, to merge politics and religion, to found the future Church of humanity and to show the whole world that sovereignty does not reside in a king or in a people but only in the nation.

Count Zygmunt Krasinski, 1847 (Taras 2003: 138)

Poland provides another good example, in some ways purer than Ireland, of a state that has maintained a tie between nationalism and religion (Corona 2000; Curtis 1994; Davies 1982; Dziewanowski 1977). Poland is, and has seemingly always been, Catholic. Throughout the history of the Polish state, one finds quotes and claims similar to Roman Dmowski's above. In whatever way it is examined, Poland stands out as Catholic. The wider European secularism has been avoided here. Jose Casanova indicates that "The typical positive correlation of education, industrialization, urbanization, and proletarianization with secularization either did not obtain in Poland or was significantly attenuated" (Casanova 1994: 93). Thus, Polish nationalism provides another case in which religion has maintained an undeniable presence. Casanova goes on to point out the similarities between the Irish and Polish cases:

Catholic Poland, like Catholic Ireland, is an example of a Catholic country, which, in the absence of the typical fusion of absolutism and caesaropapism, deviates significantly from what David Martin has termed "the French-Latin pattern of secularization."

Casanova (1994: 92)

Like Ireland, Polish nationalism was formed in opposition to specific forces throughout its history. Whereas the British provided this counter-image for the Irish, the Russians and the Germans have done so for the Polish. Although my discussion of Russian and German nationalisms will be significantly briefer than my discussion of British nationalism, it will still be useful to see how the Russian case, in particular, has fluctuated between religious and secular conceptions of the nation based on their varying political and economic situations. As was true in Ireland, the presence of a religious frontier is clear in the Polish case. Ever since Poland became a Christian state in 966, it has been at the "frontier" of Latin Christianity, and that has left a heavy imprint on national consciousness. However, unlike Ireland, the threat from Poland's neighbors has varied dramatically. Whereas a religious frontier and an existential threat were introduced to Ireland nearly simultaneously, in Poland there was great variation. Although Poland has been at a religious frontier since it accepted Christianity in the tenth century, the Polish identity did not become truly threatened until several centuries later. "Periods of independence and prosperity alternated with phases of foreign domination and disaster" (Curtis 1994: 3). Religious nationalism fluctuated in unison with these shifts in threat. This allows an examination of the proposed relationship between frontiers and religious nationalism from a new angle.

Although many scholars have examined the actions of the church during the Communist years, it is really essential to look earlier in time. The conventional wisdom is that the Catholic Church was very clever in its handling of the Communist situation, a fact that allowed it to remain central to Polish identity. However, by the time Communism took hold after World War II, there was very little that could have been done to *prevent* the church from taking a central role. Rather, I agree with Stewart Steven that " ... it could not have been otherwise, because for so many long years only the Catholic Church kept the bright flame of freedom alight" (Steven 1982: 156). Catholicism had been solidified as a part of national consciousness hundreds of years before, and the presence of a religious frontier and a hostile other (specifically Orthodox and Communist Russia) meant that Catholicism would have been central to Polish resistance whether the Church wanted it so or not.

Religion and the Polish identity

Religious identity

As with Ireland, there is little doubt regarding the religious identity of the Polish people. Statistics of Polish religiosity are even more robust than in Ireland. Ninety-three percent of Poles are members of the Catholic Church, according to a 1998 study (ISSP 1998). According to a 1992 study, a meager 2 percent of the population claimed some religion other than Catholicism (Weclawowicz 1996: 110). In addition, 85 percent claim to be religious, compared with a European average of less than 50 percent; and over 70 percent of Poles attend church at least once a month. The European average is just over 30 percent (ISSP 1998).

However, the link between religion and national identity extends far beyond simple statistics of religiosity. Returning to Gellner's concept of mutual recognition, it is clear that Catholicism is central to the Polish understanding of Polishness and has been for ages. Norman Davies points to " ... the unbroken presence of the Roman Catholic Church [in Poland], whose establishment reached back to the very beginnings of recorded history, and whose supremacy was only briefly threatened" (Davies 1982: 160–1). Religious symbols are a key part of Polish identity. Specifically, the Black Madonna of Czestochowa is "believed to have rescued Poland miraculously from invasions by the Tatars and the Swedes, and some Solidarity leaders wore replicas of the icon" (Curtis 1994: 98). She was declared the Queen of Poland in the Second Republic after World War I, and Lech Wałesa wore her image on his lapel throughout his Solidarity days. As the subsequent history shows, " ... the Church in Poland has become synonymous with the Polish nation. The two are seen by the people as indivisible, he who harms one harms the other" (Steven 1982: 162).

Political religion

In terms of political religion, the link between the Catholic Church and Polish politics is apparent. As was the case in Ireland, Polish politics reflect the privileged position of the Catholic Church. The 1997 Polish constitution:

> ... incorporated references to both the Christian heritage of the Polish nation and to all Polish citizens, as well as to God as the source of "truth, justice, goodness, and beauty" and to universal values that were the source of these ideas for non-believers.
>
> Taras (2003: 150)

In addition, the Concordat, reached with the Vatican, "began with the assertion that 'The Catholic Religion is practiced by the majority of the Polish population'" (Taras 2003: 150). Abortion remains illegal except in a few special circumstances. A World Values study has pointed to the conservative nature of politics in Poland:

> Almost all of the socialist or ex-socialist societies are characterized by (1) survival values, and (2) a strong emphasis on state authority, rather than traditional authority. Poland is a striking exception, distinguished from the other socialist societies by her strong traditional-religious values.
>
> Inglehart *et al.* (1997: 27)

Bogdan Szajkowski points to the importance of the Catholic Church in contemporary Polish politics:

... the Church's unique role in Contemporary Polish politics intertwined moral and political authority with national, historical and cultural traditions and with the current demands and expectations of national survival. As long as there exists a sovereign Poland the Church can and will promote the nation's interests.

Szajkowski (1983: 226)

There is a clear link between Catholic values, the Church, and modern Polish politics. The Polish identity, " ... called by one scholar a 'civil religion,' combined religious and political symbols in Poles' conception of their national history and destiny" (Curtis 1994: 92).

Although there has been some backlash against the Church's involvement in politics in recent years, there is little doubt that it maintains a special position in Poland. This is certainly true when compared with other European states, particularly post-Communist countries. After the fall of communism, there has been a clear effort to link the Polish state to the Catholic heritage that had helped preserve the nation's identity. Polish nationalism is religious nationalism.

Early Poland

Catholicism and the Polish state

An understanding of Polish nationalism, like Irish nationalism, requires an examination of early Polish history. Although many scholars focus on church–state relations in the Communist era, a clear appreciation of the religious links to Polish nationalism is not possible without first stepping back to the origins of the Polish state.

Although there is evidence that the Polish people began organizing prior to the tenth century, tradition puts the origin of the Polish state at 966 AD. The Polish people had migrated westward along with various other Slavic peoples and, in 966, Prince Mieszko married a Bohemian princess and accepted Christianity on behalf of the Polish people. Although Mieszko's decision did not actually establish a Polish state, it did earn a level of autonomy previously unknown to the "Polanie" or "people of the plain." The circumstances of Mieszko's choice are significant. The Slavic expansion had brought the Polish people into contact with the Holy Roman Empire, which had earned a reputation for invading its neighbors under the guise of spreading Christianity. Mieszko thus opted to accept the religion voluntarily in order to preempt any Germanic invasions. "The Poles thus accepted membership in the Christian community initially as a stratagem to counter the missionary as well as colonizing zeal of their Germanic neighbors" (Dziewanowski 1977: 2).

This series of events is important for a number of reasons. This interaction began a long history of Polish involvement with the Germanic peoples. From the beginning, the Poles shaped their identity in reaction to Germany, and they would continue to do so, off and on, through the twentieth century. As a result, Germany, along with Russia, provided the most significant "other" in Polish history and, although both states were Catholic in the tenth century, subsequent religious divisions would mean than Catholicism would provide the most significant factor in the differentiation of the Polish nation. The second reason why Mieszko's decision is important for Polish history is the obvious fact that it introduced Catholicism into the equation. When Prince Mieszko adopted Christianity for the Polish people, he did so by accepting baptism directly from the Vatican in order to avoid the involvement of the Holy Roman Empire. By doing so, he "inaugurated the intimate connection between the Polish national identity and Roman Catholicism that became a prominent theme in the history of the Poles" (Curtis 1994: 4).

The decision to accept Roman Catholicism became significant twenty-three years later when, in 989, Poland's neighbors in Kiev opted for the Byzantine version of Christianity.

> Consequently, from the dawn of its existence, Poland faced the dilemma of siding with one or the other of the two opposing centers of civilization, Rome and Byzantium. By accepting Latin Christianity through dynastic connection with Bohemia, Poland chose Rome and thus allied itself with the West.
>
> Dziewanowski (1977: 2)

This Slavic split would color relations between the Poles and their eastern neighbors for centuries to come. As in Ireland, the subsequent feuds between the Russians and the Poles would be largely political in nature, but the cleavage created by the religious frontier would mean that the national identities of each would take on decidedly religious overtones.

> From its beginning, Poland drew its primary inspiration from Western Europe and developed a closer affinity with the French and Italians ... than with nearer Slavic neighbors of Eastern Orthodox and Byzantine heritage. This westward orientation, which in some ways has made Poland the easternmost outpost of Latinate and Catholic tradition, helps to explain the Poles' tenacious sense of belonging to the "West" and her deeply rooted antagonism toward Russia as the representative of an essentially alien way of life.
>
> Curtis (1994: 7)

The German threat

Although the division between the Polish Catholics and their Orthodox neighbors would be important later in Polish history, in the tenth century, the primary threat to the Polish nation came from the Germanic peoples to the west. Significantly, Germany was still a wholly Catholic state as the Reformation had not yet occurred. As a result, the Catholic identity did little to differentiate the Poles from the Germans. In fact, the Catholic religion was only accepted in an attempt to prevent German aggression.

Polish leaders continued to use the Catholic Church as a buffer against the expansionist Holy Roman Empire. Mieszko's son, Bolesław I, was successful in a series of conflicts against the Empire, and he was rewarded with more territory for the Polish state. In addition, Bolesław was recognized in 1025 as the first King of Poland by the Vatican for his support of the papacy against the Holy Roman Emperor, Henry VI. Again, the links between Rome and the Polish people were strengthened. As Dziewanowski indicates, " ... Poland could strive to be independent of the Empire by supporting its strongest antagonist, the papacy ... " (Dziewanowski 1977: 3).

In the first hundred years of the Piast Dynasty, as the era became known, Poland had significantly expanded its territorial claims and had become a power in central Europe. Otto III, the Holy Roman Emperor, had recognized Poland as a state in 1000, and the Polish people had quickly taken to the Catholic faith. However, the only religious frontier that existed in the eleventh century was between the Catholics of Poland and Bohemia (modern-day Czech Republic) and their Orthodox neighbors to the east. This frontier, however, did not represent an existential threat to the Polish people. Rather, the one sure threat came from the west and the Catholic Holy Roman Empire (Germany). The Polish response was an emphasis on the Catholic Church, but not in a religiously nationalist way. The use of the Catholic faith was more utilitarian and elitist, not relying on a broad nationalist sentiment as we understand nationalism today. However, this utilitarian adoption of Catholicism would have major ramifications for religious nationalism a few hundred years later.

Beginning in the eleventh century, a series of new threats did begin to put the Polish nation in a more tenuous position. A series of poor leaders came to the throne after Bolesław I and resulted in a severely weakened state. Land and power had been divided repeatedly under the Piast dynasty, leaving Poland susceptible to foreign menace. The trouble began in 1226, when Duke Conrad of Mazovia invited the Teutonic Knights to help him conquer neighboring pagan tribes in the Baltics. The Knights, formally known as the Order of St. Mary of the Germans, had participated in the Crusades to retake Jerusalem from Islam. After they returned, they served as a mercenary group of sorts. In exchange for their services in Poland, they were promised control over some of the lands they helped conquer. The Knights were unsatisfied with this arrangement and proceeded to set up an autonomous region along the coast of the Baltic Sea, thus expanding Germanic influence deeper into Polish territory and cutting the Poles off from crucial maritime access.

The Teutonic Knights would continue to torment the Poles for many years, but another threat to the Polish nation arose in 1241 when the Tatars, or Mongols, arrived on Poland's doorstep. The Tatars were Islamic, and when they "cut a swath of destruction through the country" in 1241, a whole new religious frontier was introduced into the Polish equation (Curtis 1994: 6). Although they left Poland a year later, they continued to launch raids into Polish territory for another half century. Between the Holy Roman Empire, the Teutonic Knights, the Tatars, and the Bohemians, Poland's status as a state was in serious jeopardy. As Curtis points out, by the end of the thirteenth century, over two-thirds of Poland was under foreign control.

Therefore, by the end of the Piast dynasty, Poland had shrunk rapidly from a regional power to a state on the brink of extinction. Significantly, the religious frontiers were as strong as ever, but the threat from them was still not prominent. Although the Poles were on the verge of subjugation, the main threat still came from the Germanic peoples to the west, which were notably still Catholic. Religion was a strong part of Polish society, as it was in all of Europe at the time, but this period of weakness did see a strengthening of Polish Catholic identity.

> By the thirteenth century, Poland had produced numerous missionaries and saints and was soon to become a bulwark against the Tatars and, later on, against the Turks. This was the origin of the still-popular notion of Poland's historical mission to defend Western Christian culture against the hostile forces threatening it from the East.
>
> Dziewanowski (1977: 4)

In the years that followed the Piast dynasty, a number of interesting shifts occurred that saw Polish identity swing away from Catholicism and then return to it with renewed vigor as the German and Russian threats peaked once again.

Jagiellon Poland

As the strength of Piast Poland waned, it was forced to look outward for aid. Although there was something of a Polish Renaissance in the late fourteenth century, the Piast dynasty came to an end in 1370 when Kazimierz III died without an heir. After a brief reign by the Hungarian king, the Polish crown passed to a ten-year-old princess named Jadwiga. The Polish monarchy was in a state of confusion, and the geopolitical situation of the Polish state was still precarious.

> Driven from the lower and middle Oder, barred from access to the Baltic Sea, and deprived even of the use of the mouth of its chief river, Poland by the fourteenth century was engaged in a life-and-death struggle with the Germanic princes encircling the nation on three sides ... The only potential ally against the Teutonic Knights was Lithuania.
>
> Dziewanowski (1977: 8)

The Lithuanians controlled a large swathe of land to Poland's east, and the two states shared several enemies in common – most notable among them were the Teutonic Knights. A marriage was thus arranged between Jadwiga, the Polish princess, and the Lithuanian leader, Duke Jagiello, who adopted the title Władysław II and the throne of Poland. In 1385, under the Union of Krewo, Poland and Lithuania were joined into a single commonwealth, and Władysław's subjects in Lithuania were converted to Christianity. The union between the states increased Poland's boundaries dramatically and created an alliance with Lithuania that was to last for 400 years.

The linkage between the Polish and Lithuanian nations marked a major shift in Poland's threat level. Previously vulnerable to the Germanic groups surrounding them, the new Polish–Lithuanian state took on the Teutonic Knights and, in 1410, was successful in handing them a significant defeat. The defeat of the Order was a major turning point in the affairs of the Polish people. As Dziewanowski indicates, the victory over the Teutonic Knights "put an end to the expansionist plans of the Order and the Luxemburgs; it broke the predominance of the German element in the Baltic area; and it transformed the Polish–Lithuanian confederation into a great power" (Dziewanowski 1977: 10–11).

The Polish successes did not stop with the Teutonic Knights. "The Polish–Lithuanian union considerably altered the balance of power in Central and Eastern Europe … " (Dziewanowski 1977: 10). Significantly, this new power meant that Poland became a central player in European politics. Specifically, " … both nations gradually became drawn into the affairs of the Black Sea region, where the rising might of the Turkish Empire was already casting its shadow over Byzantium and the southern Slavs" (Dziewanowski 1977: 10). The concern over the Muslim invaders was not isolated to the Polish people. Rather, the Islamic question had become central to European politics, as the Turkish invaders had begun to press into the heart of Europe. In 1440, a mere thirty years after the monumental defeat of the Teutonic Knights, Poland sought to rid Constantinople specifically, and Europe in general, of the Muslim influence. They did this by forming an alliance with the Hungarian state, thus building a bridge across the Catholic–Orthodox divide. This is significant because it illustrates the power of religious pressures. The threat from the Islamic invaders was such that it pushed various Christian groups together in a common bond of religion, in spite of denominational differences. Had the conflict been between the Hungarians and the Poles, the emphasis would have certainly been on a more specific Orthodox and Catholic identity. Again, the conflicts shape the identities, not vice versa.

The Polish–Hungarian Union was to prove a failure. The Battle of Varna in 1444 and the later Battle of Mohács in 1526 saw the Poles and Hungarians defeated at the hands of the Turks, and the Union between the two states soon dissolved, along with hopes of any reconciliation between the Eastern and Western branches of Christianity. Again, it is

interesting to consider what may have happened here if the Islamic threat
had continued to be central to Polish and Hungarian identity. It is likely that
a prolonged existential threat would have meant a more unified Christian
identity as opposed to the more specific Orthodox and Catholic identities
that formed throughout much of Eastern Europe.

Russia rising

There was another significant change around this time (sixteenth century).
Up to this point, the primary threats to Polish identity had been from the
Germanic peoples to the west and from the Islamic peoples to the south and
east. The Russians had not been a significant factor in Polish identity
because they had not yet been threatening in any major way. But the union
between Poland and Lithuanian and the subsequent defeat of the Teutonic
Knights now meant that the German threat was greatly diminished. The
Islamic threat had played an important part in Polish identity previously,
and would certainly do so again in the future but, for the moment, the Polish
state was strong enough to eliminate any serious Islamic threats to the Polish
nation. The Russians, however, were finally beginning to emerge as the
regional and world power they were to become.

The Muscovites (or Russians) began to solidify the Eastern Slavic peoples
into a single powerful state in the fourteenth and fifteenth centuries.
Although Poland had previously been fairly homogeneous, its union with
Lithuania had introduced a wide variety of minority groups. " ... [M]ost
Lithuanians were Catholic, like the Poles, but large Ukrainian and
Belorussian groups (Slavs, like the Poles) were incorporated into this mini-
empire and belonged predominantly to the Eastern Orthodox faith"
(Taras 2003: 138). Although they had been an unremarkable threat up to
this point, the Russians " ... hoped to free their Orthodox brethren from
the Latin yoke and unite with them in one state" (Dziewanowski 1977:
13). This, of course, included the Orthodox minorities in Poland–
Lithuania.

The divide between the Orthodox and Catholic populations thus became a
factor in the identities of various groups in Central and Eastern Europe.
"'This Slavonic domestic feud,' as the great Russian poet Alexander Pushkin
wrote in 1830, was destined to plague the relations of the two neighboring
states up to our day" (Dziewanowski 1977: 13–14). A new dimension was
added to the Polish fight for the Catholic faith:

> In the mid-fifteenth century, Poland's role in Europe was widely seen in
> terms of an *antemurale christianitatis* – the easternmost bulwark of
> Roman Catholicism. It was regarded as a nation lying on the fault line
> of Western and Eastern civilizations, under constant threat of becoming
> absorbed by the non-Catholic East.
>
> Taras (2003: 139)

But at the time, the Polish state continued to grow in power and influence. The Russian menace loomed, and it did so in the form of a foreign religion, but the threat was not significant. If anything, the Poles were the threatening power. As Kennedy and Simon point out, " ... Poland came to be a regional power in East Central Europe, dominating regions that were not ethnically Polish, and even attempting to 'Catholicize' Orthodox believers in the East in the sixteenth and seventeenth centuries" (Kennedy and Simon 1983: 130). This Polish "Golden Age" is an important point in our analysis of Polish nationalism.

Before continuing, it is worth reiterating a few points. First, it is necessary to realize that Poland has existed at a religious frontier since its inception as a state. When it was founded, Poland was sharing borders with pagan states, Orthodox states and, later, Islamic groups. Although Catholicism quickly became a key feature of Polish society, it did not become intricately tied into Polish nationalism, at least not more so than in other nations at the time. This is because the primary threat to the Polish nation came from the Germanic Holy Roman Empire, which was itself a Catholic state. The second point to emphasize is that the nature of national threats did change after the defeat of the Teutonic Knights. Specifically, a threat arose from Islamic invaders to the south and from a rising Orthodox Russia to the east. However, these threats increased at a point in time that also revealed a new and strengthened Poland. The union with Lithuania led to increased security for the Poles, so that the rise in Orthodox Russia was not a significant threat. The "Golden Age" of Polish politics reveals a great deal about the importance of threat in national identity.

Golden Age

The sixteenth century in Poland marked what became known as the "Golden Age" of Polish history. Although Poland–Lithuania had been badly beaten at the Battle of Mohács in 1526, a peace agreement was reached shortly thereafter. This "Eternal Peace," reached in 1533, meant that the Islamic threat to Poland was still present, but not severe. In addition, the defeat of the Teutonic Knights had brought the Poles to the center of politics in Central Europe. During this era of peace, Poland prospered at a variety of levels. As Curtis points out, the kingdom became the breadbasket of Europe, profiting from vast agricultural exports. The Poles excelled culturally during these hundred years as well. The Renaissance in Italy inspired the arts, several universities were founded, and one of history's most famous Poles, Nicolaus Copernicus, forever changed the way we view astronomy.

These successes in the political and cultural realms led to an obvious pride in the Polish nation – specifically among the elites. As Dziewanowski indicates:

> The mood of the ruling class during Poland's "Golden Age" was affected not only by the long series of military victories and political

successes, but also by the nation's substantial material and cultural progress. In the light of these achievements one can understand the pride and, indeed, the arrogance of a Polish nobility convinced that Poland was the freest, most advanced nation of the world.

Dziewanowski (1977: 15–16)

Understandably, the perceived threat to the Polish state was minimized. This did not mean that the religious frontier had changed. It was, in fact, as prominent as ever. Orthodox Russia continued to grow in strength, and the Islamic Tatars continued to launch raids into Polish territory. However, the cultural, economic, and political power of the Polish–Lithuanian commonwealth meant that these frontiers were not threatening. The result was a Polish nationalism that did not emphasize the Catholic link.

The most prominent and interesting manifestation of this security was found in the level of religious tolerance in medieval Poland. At the time, the rest of Europe was embroiled in conflicts over the newly formed Protestant sects. Poland was tolerant towards these reform-minded groups.

Political freedom was paralleled by religious and ethnic tolerance without equal in a Europe where religious nonconformists were burned at the stake. While fierce denominational disputes and bloody religious wars raged in the rest of Europe during the Reformation, Poland was a "haven for the heretics."

Dziewanowski (1977)

Even more remarkable, given Poland's more recent history, is the fact that Poland during the "Golden Age" was tolerant toward Jews as well, illustrated by the fact that Poland had the world's largest population of Jews at the time. The level of religious acceptance meant that "[l]ife was simply more tolerable for Jews in Poland than elsewhere" (Weintraub 1971: 13). All these factors led Haskins and Lord to declare, in 1920, that "In the sixteenth and seventeenth centuries this republic [Poland] was the freest state in Europe, that state in which the greatest degree of constitutional, civic, and intellectual liberty prevailed" (Haskins and Lord 1920). All this "liberty" was possible because of Poland's strength relative to its neighbors. Had Poland been susceptible to Russian interference, there would have certainly been a much stronger emphasis on Catholic nationalism, and that would have meant a corresponding decline in liberties for non-Catholics.

Because of these facts, Ray Taras points out that the link between Catholicism and Polish identity was already weak in the sixteenth century. "The adage that being Polish meant being Catholic, then, was already an oversimplification of the ethnic and religious makeup of Poland in Medieval times. Even equating an ethnic Pole with a Catholic was imprecise" (Taras 2003: 138). Taras goes on to point out that "Even further condemning the myth that to be Polish was to be Catholic was the presence of about 80 percent of the world's Jews in the country at this time" (Taras 2003: 138). Although Taras is certainly correct about this "Golden Age," events to occur in the following centuries would mean that a previously peaceful and prosperous nation became severely threatened, and the result was a clear shift to a religious notion of nationhood focused on the Catholic Church, as predicted.

This weakness started to emerge in the late sixteenth century. In 1572, the Jagiellon dynasty came to an end when Sigismund II Augustus died without a male heir. Subsequently, the Polish nobles instituted a system of elective monarchy. The result, to be examined later, was a severe weakening of political power in Poland. As Polish power waned and Russian power waxed, there was an obvious shift in the religious sentiment of the Polish people. Likewise, the attitudes of the Russians became tied to Orthodoxy.

> ... Poland's geographical position dictated its mission: to be the rampart of the Latin west against schismatic Russia. As for Russia itself, Byzantium's heir since the fall of Constantinople and invested with the dignity of the third Rome, its destiny was also expressed in religious terms. It was holy Russia, guardian of orthodoxy and charged with responsibility for all those people who shared its faith.
>
> Rémond (1999: 110)

This nationalist shift was already visible in the far eastern territories of Poland, where Catholicism was not the predominant religion of the people. There, the familiar pattern of religious frontier and threat meant that minority groups were among the first to shift towards a religiously based national conception.

> ... [I]n the eastern territories of the kingdom a Polish or Polonized aristocracy dominated a peasantry whose great majority was neither Polish nor Catholic. This bred resentment that later grew into separate Lithuanian, Belorussian, and Ukrainian nationalist movements.
>
> Curtis (1994: 114)

The threat did not reach the entirety of the Polish population until "The Deluge" over fifty years later.

The Deluge

The period from 1648 through 1667 has great significance for any understanding of Polish nationalism. The tendency of scholars is to skim over this period and jump straight into the partitions of the eighteenth century. However, in order to understand how Poland went from a powerful and tolerant state to a subjected religious nation, we must understand this interim period.

When Sigismund II Augustus died in 1572, the fact that there was no male heir to the throne was seen as an opportunity for the growing numbers of Polish nobles. The nobles had always played a large part in the governing of Polish lands, but the end of the Jagiellon dynasty signaled the dawn of a new era of elite power. In an attempt to avoid another strong ruling dynasty, the nobles began to opt for foreign leaders who would not threaten their unique situation. As Curtis points out, "this policy produced monarchs who were either totally ineffective or in constant debilitating conflict with the nobility" (Curtis 1994: 15). The result was a gradual weakening of centralized power, which was particularly demonstrated through a stronger and stronger veto power given to the nobles. "The liberum veto gave opportunity to vested factional or local interests – and to foreign agents as well – to paralyze the entire machinery of state" (Dziewanowski 1977: 21). This eventually led to a state that was virtually helpless in its own self-defense – a factor that became increasingly important in the years to follow. In addition, the election of foreign rulers meant that the interests of Poland were often subjugated to those of the ruler's own country, again bringing Poland into conflicts that could have been avoided.

The period known as "The Deluge" officially began in 1648 and marked the beginning of Polish decline and, significantly, the rise of Catholic nationalism. The crisis began with an uprising of Ukrainians in eastern Poland–Lithuania. When the Poles were unable to put down the uprising, the Ukrainians were successful in lobbying for Russian intervention. "Because of the limited resources of the treasury, the standing army [in Poland] was hardly sufficient for the defense of vast, open frontiers" (Dziewanowski 1977: 19). Within seven years, Russia controlled much of the eastern half of the commonwealth. The Swedish King Charles X took advantage of Poland's struggles and invaded from the north. Meanwhile, the Ottoman Turks continued to menace the Polish–Lithuanian state, although the Polish involvement with Russia and Sweden now meant that the Islamic groups to the south were much more threatening. The Swedish forces quickly conquered a great deal of the Polish state and, although the Polish forces did rally to push back the invaders, the damage had been done. The weakness of the commonwealth became abundantly apparent to the self-serving nobles who proceeded to shift their allegiances to the various powerful neighboring monarchs.

The defeat of the Ottoman Turks at the siege of Vienna in 1683 under the leadership of Jan Sobieski marked the last military victory of the Polish–Lithuanian commonwealth. The series of military conflicts within the state and against its neighbors had left Poland severely weakened. "The economic and social consequences of the Cossack and Swedish wars may be compared only with the effects of the Hundred Years War on France or the Thirty Years War on Germany" (Dziewanowski 1977: 19). By 1700, Poland had become a virtual puppet of Russia under Peter the Great, who " ... repeatedly interfered in the domestic affairs of the commonwealth, stationing

Russian troops on its territory, systematically bribing deputies of the Diet, and encouraging the anarchic proclivities of the nobility" (Dziewanowski 1977: 23). Curtis similarly points to the destructive power of the Deluge: "When Jan II Kazimierz abdicated in 1668, the population of the commonwealth had been nearly halved by war and disease. War had destroyed the economic base of the cities and raised a religious fervor that ended Poland's policy of religious tolerance" (Curtis 1994: 16).

Curtis makes an interesting point. The partition is often pointed to as a key influence in Polish nationalism. While I agree, the impact of the period leading up to partition is equally important in understanding the religious aspects of Polish nation building. What we see in seventeenth-century Poland is a religiously tolerant and powerful state reduced to a weak, Catholic-centered state in a very brief period of time. The correlation between religious tolerance and state/national power is not coincidental. As Polish power waned economically, politically, and culturally, the threat to the Polish nation became increasingly real and immediate. It so happened that the primary threats came from Russia, an Orthodox state, and the Ottoman Empire, an Islamic state. The result was a Polish focus on Catholicism as a central and key factor in national differentiation and resistance. In Poland, the religious frontier was always there; the threat changed. Thus religious tolerance became strong religious nationalism in the "Deluge."

> Religious tolerance had been observed fairly scrupulously until the beginning of the seventeenth century. The situation changed, however, during the Cossack and Swedish wars ... By the middle of the seventeenth century many Poles came to believe that there could be no true national unity without religious orthodoxy, and that members of schismatic and heretic (i.e., non-Catholic) groups were not trustworthy citizens. Incidents of discrimination against religious dissenters grew increasingly frequent, and nonconformists were more and more denied the political equality enjoyed during previous times.
>
> Dziewanowski (1977)

The consequences of the Deluge in the larger picture of Polish nationalism have been vastly underemphasized. The seventeenth century represented the beginning of a rapid political decline in Poland. The importance is two-fold. First, the Deluge shows that subjugation is not central to the formation of religious nationalism. The rapid economic and political erosion of the Polish nation led to a strong religious infusion in national identity prior to the actual subjugation of the Polish people in the late eighteenth century. Second, this example shows the importance of a threat once again. The religious frontier was not enough to create a religiously based nation. However, economic and political decline provided reason to rally around Catholicism.

The eighteenth century would firmly cement Polish nationalism in Roman Catholicism. As Hans Kohn points out:

> The Poles ... disintegrated at a time when all other nations gathered their strength ... Yet the only nation to disappear in the eighteenth century had been one of the great powers of Europe in size and population, stretching from the Baltic to the Black Sea, an enormous and amorphous land mass in the borderless plains of Eastern Europe. Like Sweden and Turkey, it declined at the end of the seventeenth century under Moscow's pressure westwards to join Europe through the Baltic and Black seas.
>
> Kohn (1944: 518–19)

The Poles had come to see themselves as "under the special protection of Providence" as confirmed through signs and wonders. But as Kohn points out, " ... no signs and wonders helped in the eighteenth century: there was nothing but shame and decay, destroying the nation and inviting greedy neighbors to partition it" (Kohn 1944: 520). The fact that those "greedy neighbors" happened to adhere to different religions would mean that the Catholic faith would be central to Polish-ness for the subsequent three centuries.

The partitions

Eighteenth-century Poland

Throughout the eighteenth century, Poland's circumstances continued to decay. Essentially a puppet state at the turn of the century, Poland was engaged in various wars between Russia and her rivals. "Unlike Spain and Sweden, great powers that were allowed to settle peacefully into secondary status at the periphery of Europe at the end of their time of glory, Poland endured its decline at the strategic crossroads of the continent" (Curtis 1994). Poland was forced to play a part in the emerging struggle for control of the continent. To make matters worse, the continued erosion of monarchical powers left the state impotent. The veto power and the greed of the nobles combined to destroy any attempts to control national defenses.

Throughout the 1700s, the weakness of Poland continued to be exploited by her neighbors. In 1740, Frederick II became the leader of Prussia (Germany). He had a goal of uniting all the Prussian lands into a single state, beginning with Silesia and Pomerania and continuing eastward. This, in turn, posed a problem for the Russian Tsarina, Catherine II. Poland had essentially become a puppet state of the Russian tsars, and it provided a key buffer to Russia's west. The Russians interfered with Polish politics again in 1764 by placing Stanisław August Poniatowski, Catherine's former lover, on the Polish throne.

This combination of events – Prussian expansion and Russian intervention – led to a revival in Polish nationalism. Under the leadership of Stanisław August, drastic reforms were made to the Polish government, including a moratorium on the crippling liberum veto. These reforms meant that the Polish monarchy was actually gathering strength, a prospect that pleased neither the Russians nor the Prussians. The Russians again intervened.

> Catherine, among the most displeased by Poniatowski's independence, encouraged religious dissension in Poland–Lithuania's substantial Eastern orthodox population, which earlier in the eighteenth century had lost the rights enjoyed during the Jagiellon Dynasty. Under heavy Russian pressure, the Sejm restored Orthodox equality in 1767. This action provoked a Catholic uprising by the Confederation of Bar, a league of Polish nobles that fought until 1772 to revoke Catherine's mandate.
>
> Curtis (1994: 18)

Perhaps more than any other event, the Confederation of Bar demonstrates the extent of the linkage between Polish nationalism and Catholicism prior to the partition of Poland. "The purpose of the Confederation of Bar was to defend 'the Holy Roman Faith,' allegedly threatened by the concessions made to the dissenters, and to end Russian interference in Polish affairs" (Dziewanowski 1977: 26). As Hans Kohn indicates, the central focus of the Confederation was religion, and the former class divisions in Polish society were dissolved:

> What first aroused the Poles to action was … a movement of religious fanaticism, directed against Catherine's desire to put the Greek Orthodox citizens of Poland on the same footing as the Catholics. "The faith is in danger" became the rallying cry … In 1768 the Confederation of Bar started an armed insurrection to defend religion to the last. For the first time all classes were united, to oppose equal rights for the non-Catholics.
>
> Kohn (1944: 522)

The threat from Poland's various religious frontiers had become abundantly clear, perhaps more so than at any other time previously. The subsequent reaction was an obvious return to Catholicism as a central factor in Polish nationalism. However, the issues involved were primarily political – Russian control and Polish sovereignty. It was simply the response that was religious.

The division of Poland

The response from Russia and Prussia is equally important. Russia, previously the dominant power in Poland, faced several new challenges. Along with the Prussian goals of expansion, the Ottoman Turks took advantage of Russian preoccupations and declared war in 1768. Russian involvement in the Balkans to the south also brought the threat of an Austrian invasion into Polish territories. Clearly spread too thinly, Catherine met with Frederick of Prussia and Maria Theresa of Austria in 1772 and agreed to partition Poland between the three states. Troops from each of the three partitioning powers quickly moved into Polish territory, and Poland lost nearly one-third of its land.

The first partition did not put an end to the Polish state. As Curtis points out, "the first partition in 1772 did not directly threaten the viability of Poland–Lithuania. Poland retained extensive territory that included the Polish heartland" (Curtis 1994). It did, however, further encourage nationalist sentiment. Further reform was pursued under Stanisław August, resulting in Europe's first written constitution in 1791. The Industrial Revolution also had effects on the Polish economy, which up to this point had been heavily agricultural. Reacting to this Polish rejuvenation, Russia once again invaded Poland "under the pretext of defending Poland's ancient liberties" (Curtis 1994: 20). In 1793, the partitioning powers revoked the constitution and implemented the second partition of Poland, which proved to be much more severe than the first. A Polish rebellion led by Tadeusz Kościuszko in 1794 gave Austria, Prussia, and Russia the excuse they needed to completely dissolve the Polish state. In 1795, the third partition was carried out and the Polish–Lithuanian commonwealth ceased to exist. "In 1796, Russia, Prussia, and Austria made reciprocal pledges never to use the term 'Kingdom of Poland' in its official documents. It was to be 'Finis Poloniae'" (Dziewanowski 1977: 29).

Poland under partition

Partitioned Poland provides the perfect example of a threatened nation. There was no longer any opportunity for the Polish people to deny the dire situation they found themselves in. Poland had descended from the heights of European power to nonexistence. Although a religious frontier had always been present, the threat level had clearly shifted. As Polish power declined, the national reliance on Catholicism rose. The correlation between the two factors is clear.

The partition of Poland only reinforced the Catholic link to nationalism. Now stateless, the Polish people were on the verge of extinction – particularly if the partitioning powers had their way. Russia and Prussia each instituted harsh anti-Polish laws that rallied support for the Catholic Church. "The first impetus for an expanded church role was the social repression Poles experienced during the era of the third partition, from 1795–1918" (Curtis 1994: 92). The Polish language was banned in the Russian and Prussian partitions. (Significantly, Catholic Austria lifted these restrictions after 1867.) In addition, drastic limitations were placed on education, publication, and organization rights in the partitions. As in Ireland, the restrictions on language rights simply pressed the nation further towards religion as the one factor that could unify them across political and economic classes. In particular, the fact that the Polish people were divided between a variety of oppressors meant that Catholicism not only unified the nation in resistance, but it unified it across state borders. Catholicism was the one factor shared in common with other Poles that clearly differentiated them from their occupiers in Prussia and Russia.

The Poles, however, would not go easily. The clarity of the national threat continued to rally nationalist sentiment. The growth of Polish patriotism that had begun in the mid-eighteenth century simply gathered pace as the Polish state was dissolved. "Thenceforth the Poles became a divided and oppressed people struggling, often arms in hand, to preserve their cultural identity as well as to regain unity and political independence" (Dziewanowski 1977: 31). Jean Jacques Rousseau advised the Polish people that "If you cannot prevent your enemies from swallowing you, at least do not allow them to digest you" (Dziewanowski 1977). The Poles would, in fact, fight for their national identity with incredible vigor.

Variations between partitions

The fact that each of the partitioning powers claimed a different religion provides an interesting examination of this study's argument. Whereas Russia was Orthodox and Prussia was largely Protestant, the Austrians were Catholic. Therefore, the different partitions provide an interesting contrast. All three partitions experienced a major threat. However, only two faced a threat from a religious frontier. The Austrian partition still shared the collective Polish experience, but for nearly 150 years the threat was primarily Catholic. Thus, an investigation of the different partition experiences can be quite illuminating.

The Prussian partition

It was in Prussia and Russia that the national struggle proved to be the hardest. Dziewanowski describes life in the Prussian partition as a "grim everyday struggle against germanization" (Dziewanowski 1977: 44). Unlike in the Russian and Austrian partitions, in the Prussian partition, "No common culture could be claimed, and the Germans felt themselves superior in every way to the Poles. They tried to force German culture on the Poles rather than allow them to adapt to it ... " (Corona 2000: 42). The Poles reacted with great hostility to this attempted assimilation. "The sturdy Polish peasantry of Prussia, mobilized by a militant catholic clergy, was thoroughly disaffected, and ... determined to defend its Polish-ness with a will" (Davies 1986: 171). The Church played a key role in this process: "In the part of Poland that was under German rule, the Church opposed the policy of forcible Germanization" (Cviic 1983: 93). This policy provided a central point for Polish solidarity.

The tension between the Germans and the Poles was perhaps most clearly demonstrated by Bismarck's *Kulturkampf* in the 1870s. The *Kulturkampf*, or cultural struggle, specifically targeted the Catholic Church. The Poles in Prussia had begun to organize in resistance to the Prussian occupation, establishing newspapers, banks, and mutual aid societies. The German Chancellor, Otto von Bismarck, grew suspicious of the Poles and set out to destroy the Polish nation. "Polish Catholics responded to the challenge with a redoubling of their religious and national zeal. The furious Bismarck replied to this by launching a vast colonization scheme to gain more land for the Germans. His slogan was 'tear the Poles by the roots'" (Dziewanowski 1977). Bismarck's plan included the resettlement of German citizens into the Polish territory, as well as concerted efforts to ban the Polish language and Polish education. Polish literature could be taught, but it had to be taught through a German translation.

The Polish peasants were furious. "The deeply Catholic Silesian farmers and miners, faced with Prussian governmental politics that would rob them of both their mother tongue and their religion, awoke and began to fight" (Dziewanowski 1977: 47). The result was solidified resistance to a clear effort at assimilation. As Dziewanowski indicates, "by the 1880s, the Poles were sufficiently developed nationally to offer stiff resistance to the colonization drive" (Dziewanowski 1977: 45). As a result, nationalism was centered on the uniqueness of Polish Catholicism because of its ability to transcend other social divisions and unite the Polish people.

> During the nineteenth century, Catholicism, romantic nationalism, and Slavic messianism fused into a new Polish civil religion. At first, this process was restricted to the gentry and the intelligentsia. But in the 1870s, the threat Bismarck's Kulturkampf posed to the linguistic and religious identity of the Polish peasantry pushed this group into the nationalist cause.
>
> Casanova (1994: 92–3)

Just as the religious divide in Ireland had brought together the Old English and the native Irish, the religious divide in the Polish partitions brought the various social and economic classes into a unified national resistance. Catholicism was the easiest tool for national mobilization in resistance to drastic Germanization. A similar pattern emerged in the Russian partition.

The Russian partition

The Russian partition was similar to the Prussian partition. The Russians also attempted to assimilate the Polish population, but the shared Slavic heritage meant that Russian rule had the potential to be more palatable. In fact, the integration of the Poles into the Russian state brought a surge in economic prosperity. Railroads linked major Polish cities with their counterparts in Russia, opening a whole new level of trade. However, in 1864, a Polish group led an uprising, seeking to free not only the Polish people but all peoples oppressed under Russian rule "who, despite differences of faith and language, shall enjoy equal rights in free determination of their fate" (Dziewanowski 1977: 36). This threat was quickly defeated by the Russians, who proceeded to crack down on the "Polish menace." Dziewanowski argues that " ... [t]he defeat of the uprising of 1863–64 was a milestone in Polish history, the dying gasp of the old Romantic Poland. ... Russian was made the official language, and Polish law courts and schools were supplanted by the Russian system ... " (Dziewanowski 1977: 36). Russian troops were garrisoned in Poland in large numbers, an action that truly angered the Polish citizens who could not overlook the history of Russian–Polish relations.

Religion once again provided the key for national mobilization. The Polish language was banned, and the Slavic heritage of Poles did nothing to distinguish them from their Russian oppressors. In addition to differentiating the Poles from the Orthodox Russians, the Catholic Church also provided the one place in society where Polish could be spoken freely. Adrian Hastings points out the difference between the Polish example and the other groups subjugated to Russian rule:

> Russia could conceivably ... [incorporate] its Slav neighbors who shared not only a linguistic but also the same religious tradition. It is noticeable how different it was to try to incorporate Catholic Poles or Armenians from incorporating Ukrainians, most of whom were Orthodox Christians.
>
> Kohn (1944: 119–20)

In addition to unifying the Poles in the Russian partition, the Catholic Church provided unity across partitions.

> The Catholic Church "was one of the links which maintained the sense of nationhood across dividing frontiers. In the part of Poland under Russian rule, religious differences between Orthodox Russians and Roman Catholic Poles helped to shield the national identity against Russification ... " The Church penetrated national life in both cultural and social spheres. Polish religiosity blended with traditional Polish culture and customs.
>
> Chrypinski (1984: 127)

There was also a noticeable shift in thinking after the failure of the uprising of 1864. Polish leaders shifted their focus from armed struggle to an attempt to lift Poland through economic means. The result was political and economic development, but the continued distrust of the Russians meant that Catholicism remained central to Polish identity in spite of economic growth.

The Austrian partition

The Austrian partition provides an interesting contrast to the other two partitions. Most significantly, the fact that Austria was a Catholic state meant that the religious element was eliminated from the equation. If the Poles in Galicia, as the Polish partition became known, were to differentiate themselves from their Austrian oppressors, then the focus would have to be on cultural or linguistic ties rather than Catholicism.

Second, and perhaps related to the first point, is the fact that the Austrians were far less threatening to the Polish people. The Polish language was allowed and the Poles had considerable autonomy in education and legislation. This freedom was encouraged by wars between Prussia, with a Russian alliance, and Austria, with a French alliance. The Austrians needed Polish support in the war, and Galician loyalty "was soon repaid in the form of a series of decrees that established Galicia as an autonomous province within the Dual Monarchy. The administration, the law courts, and the school system were thoroughly polonized" (Dziewanowski 1977: 43). By the late 1800s, Poles were becoming fully integrated into Austrian society, with nearly 20 percent of the seats in the Austrian Parliament from Galicia. The lack of threat from the Austrian authorities was clearly demonstrated in 1864, when the Polish Democratic Society rose in revolution. In a stark contrast to the Russian insurrections, the largely upper class rebellion was put down by the Polish peasantry who viewed the rebels as a bigger threat than the Austrian monarchy.

The Austrian Poles remained loyal to the Austro-Hungarian crown until the events of World War I in the twentieth century, when the Poles felt betrayed by the Treaty of Brest-Litovsk, which essentially agreed to give more Polish territory to the Germans. As Rémond indicates, " ... relations with the occupying power were the least strained in those territories annexed to catholic Austria" (Rémond 1999: 115). This peace was made possible by Austrian Catholicism, which meant that the Catholic Poles were less threatening to Austrian sovereignty. In fact, wars with Russia and Prussia revealed the level of similarity between the Poles and Austrians and resulted in a great deal of Polish autonomy. The fact that the religious frontier was virtually eliminated (as opposed to the other partitions where the frontier was unavoidable) and the fact that Polish identity was allowed to flourish in Galicia (as opposed to the other partitions where identity was repressed) meant that the Poles were relatively content to remain Austrian citizens, a fact that contrasts dramatically with the other two partitions.

Results of the partition

Although "The Deluge" began the shift from a tolerant, powerful nationalism to a threatened, Catholic nationalism, the threat of assimilation became abundantly clear when Poland's neighbors eliminated the Polish state. Polish nationalism became firmly rooted in Catholicism because it " ... played a complex but significant role in preserving Polish nationalism and preventing the full assimilation of the nation into its neighbors' societies" (Kennedy and Simon 1983: 131). The previously divided Polish nation now found a new unity.

> The common Catholicism of many ethnic Poles ultimately proved to be a decisive factor in developing a nationalism that cut across social classes ... The struggles against the Protestant Prussians and Orthodox Russians helped to end the peasants' isolation from the nationalism of the nobles and the intellectuals. In fact, it was religious and cultural suppression that drew workers and peasants to Polish nationalism.
>
> Kennedy and Simon (1983: 131)

Catholicism was chosen by the Polish people because it was the most obvious differentiating factor between the Poles and their neighbors. Had there been no religious frontier, Polish nationalism would have centered on some other factor – language, culture, history, etc. But as it stood:

> The Catholic Church gave the Poles a distinctive character, different from the Germans and Russians. The Prussian Germans were Lutheran and the Russians were Orthodox. Both denominations, at that time, were instruments of absolute power for the Kaiser and Tsar, and hostile towards Catholicism. The administration of the Catholic Church embraced the old Polish territories and so unified the divided Polish kingdom. The old places of pilgrimage were venerated and visited with no regard for the tripartite division and there the pilgrims were as one nation. They prayed together and discussed common problems, encouraging each other to be loyal to God and the nation. The often misinterpreted saying "Polak-katolik" – to be a Pole is to be a Catholic – was at that time well understood.
>
> Gula (1994: 10–11)

The clear contrast between the Austrian partition and the Russian and Prussian partitions only reinforces the importance of religious frontiers and threats in the formation of religious nationalism. When the Polish state was finally reinstated following World War I, the linkage between Poland and the Catholic Church was formalized and clear.

World War I and the Second Republic

In 1914, the Archduke of Austria–Hungary was assassinated in Serbia. The event set in motion a chain of events that immersed the continent of Europe in World War I. The war pitted the various partitioning powers against each other – Austria–Hungary was allied with Germany against Russia and its

allies. As a result, the Poles received concessions from each of the partitioning powers in return for loyalty and allegiance. Through the course of the
war, 450,000 Poles died. In 1917, the Russians withdrew from the war and
the United States entered it. This shift meant that Woodrow Wilson, the
great advocate of self-determination, had a strong say in post-war politics –
a fact that drew Polish support firmly to the Allied side. As the war drew to
a close, Józef Piłsudski, a pre-war socialist leader, was returned to Warsaw
from a German prison. In November 1918, he became president of the
Second Polish Republic, which gained its independence for the first time in
over 120 years.

Although the specific details of interwar Poland are not important, the
general situation is. Poland's new independence represented an obvious
decrease in the threat to the Polish nation. Self-rule meant that, at least to
some extent, the Poles were in control of their own destiny. In addition,
interwar Poland experienced a great deal of economic growth. Arguably, the
result was a decrease in Catholic nationalism as the threat of assimilation
similarly declined. Jose Casanova argues that this trend was clear, and that a
more normal pattern of secular and modern government would have continued to emerge had it not been for the outbreak of World War II.

> With the establishment of a Polish independent state after World War I,
> the unity of the nation against foreign enemies began to dissolve. There
> appeared the standard cleavages between classes, parties, and ideologies
> while the chauvinism of every nationalism in power began to show its
> ugly face in the treatment of the Jewish and Ukrainian minorities. The
> unity between church and nation also began to dissolve, and there
> appeared splits between a conservative hierarchy and the more radical
> lower clergy.
>
> Casanova (1994: 93)

Certainly the relationship between church and nation shifted, but it would be
wrong to argue that the change was fundamental. The Polish nation was not
without threats. There was a border dispute with Czechoslovakia to the
south, and the old menaces in Russia and Germany were still present. Both
states were dissatisfied with the settlement that came from the Treaty of
Versailles, and Germany's dissatisfaction would ultimately play a large part
in the outbreak of World War II. In 1920, Poland and Russia went to war
over disputed territory in Belorussia and Ukraine – a war that seemed to
doom the Polish state once again. The Poles, however, managed to emerge
from the conflict with a compromise settlement. The threat to the Polish
state remained very clear in spite of their newfound freedom. As a result, any
decline in the importance of religion in the Polish nation was muted. Later,
economic problems during the depression contributed to the unease.
Whereas Casanova indicates that the church and nation were separating in
interwar Poland, Stachura states that:

During the Second Republic the Church consolidated its role as the ultimate non-political repository of a nationalism which was sharpened by the difficult problems confronting Poland at home and abroad ... In particular, the Polish state's uneasy relations with its large ethnic minorities – Ukrainians, Germans, Byelorussians and Jews – especially during the disturbed years of the depression, gave rise to a militant brand of nationalism.

Stachura (1999: 139)

In addition, Christopher Cviic points to the hybrid version of religious nationalism:

From 1918 to 1939, during the existence of the First Republic, the Church lost the support of a large part of the intelligentsia, which was put off by the Church's traditionalism, exclusivism, and ... intense anti-Semitic prejudice. But it retained its hold over the masses, particularly the peasantry, who constituted the bulk of the Polish population.

Cviic (1983: 93)

Essentially, the decline in threat was enough to see some shift in national ideology, but not significant (or lengthy) enough to produce a true secularization of the Polish nation. In fact, the power of Catholicism was reflected in the politics of the age.

The Catholic Church had been the mainstay of "Polishness" in the nineteenth century, and effortlessly coalesced with patriotism to emerge as a major social and moral influence after 1918. The Polish–Vatican Concordat of 1925 formalized its leading role and status.

Stachura (1999: 28)

Roman Dmowski, a leading Polish nationalist at the time, formed the Nationalist League, a group that "wanted Roman Catholicism to be the official, or even only, faith in Poland. Thus, supporters ... thought that the best thing for Poland would be if each ethnic group had its own territory within Poland, or better yet, left Poland altogether" (Corona 2000: 58).

Clearly, the link to Catholicism held sway over a significant part of the Polish population. This linkage would only be strengthened by the events of World War II, which perhaps affected Poland more than any other European state. The Poles were specifically targeted by the Soviets and the Germans because of their past:

Not only were Germany (particularly after 1933 under the National Socialists) and the Soviet Union under Stalin the avowed enemies of Poland, intent on reversing the terms of the Treaty of Versailles ... , but a host of domestic economic, political and social matters also threatened her hard-won independence.

Stachura (1999)

As the war drew closer and closer, Catholicism remained central to Polish identity.

> ... the Church, which drew support from all sections of ethnic Polish society, including the peasantry, middle classes, landowners, and, to a somewhat lesser degree, from the industrial proletariat and intelligentsia, not only legitimized herself but also personified mainstream Polish nationalism on the eve of the Second World War.
>
> Stachura (1999: 139)

The link would be critical for the events to follow.

World War II

The era of the First Republic ended quickly. Polish independence, earned in 1918, would barely last twenty years before the Polish ordeal began again. Unhappy with the settlements after World War I, Germany began making plans for its reestablishment as a European power. Although the story of Hitler's rise is unimportant for this study, the impact of his foreign policy is. After a series of political and military moves to annex the Sudetenland and other territories, Germany set her eyes on Poland once again. Hitler insisted that parts of western Poland be returned to Germany – a demand that Poland saw as a simple foretaste of Germany's future plans. Although Poland received some backing from the French and British, the deterrent effect was not enough to prevent a Nazi invasion.

The Soviets, however, did present a major obstacle to the German invasion of Poland. Thus, in a series of secretive meetings in the summer of 1939, the two states negotiated an agreement: the Soviets would produce finished goods for the Germans in exchange for food products. Therefore, the Germans could continue to supply their military with the necessary tools for war while the Soviets profited. What later became clear after the fall of the Soviet Union in the 1990s was the fact that the two countries also agreed to partition the Polish state once again. The Nazi–Soviet Non-Aggression Pact, or the Ribbentrop–Molotov Pact, granted the eastern half of Poland to the Soviets in exchange for a Soviet agreement to remain neutral in the upcoming conflict. Essentially, the pact was a repeat of the partition agreements a century and a half earlier. Both states wanted Polish territory, but neither was willing to fight a devastating war against the other over it. As Steve Bruce points out:

> Hitler wanted nothing less than the eradication of the Poles. For the two years following the Ribbentrop–Molotov pact of 1939, which cynically

divided Poland between Germany and the USSR, Stalin agreed that
Europe could do very well without a sovereign Poland.

Bruce (1996a: 98)

This agreement only reemphasized the villainy of the Soviets in the eyes of
the Polish people. This continually reinforced threat proved to be critical in
the politics of the Communist era.

Having ensured a peaceful Soviet response, the Germans launched their
invasion of Poland in September 1939. The result, of course, was the official
beginning of World War II – France and Britain declared war two days later.
Two weeks later, the Soviets moved into the eastern territories and eliminated the Polish state once again. The emphasis in recent studies of Poland
has been on Soviet treatment of Poles in the post-World War II years, but
it is also important to look at the impact of Soviet and Nazi policies *during*
the war.

The Germans are, of course, infamous for their actions in Poland during
the occupation years. From 1941 through 1944, Poland was the center of the
Holocaust. It is estimated that six million Poles were killed during World
War II, half of them Jewish. The major centers of the genocide were found in
Poland – Auschwitz, Treblinka, etc. The brutality, however, extended far
beyond the Jewish population. As Bruce has previously pointed out, Hitler
had issues with the Catholic Church and the Polish people, and he wanted to
see nothing short of the destruction of the Polish nation. As a result, the
Catholic Church was targeted with particular vitriol. "About a third of all
the clergy were executed by the Germans or died in concentration camps"
(Cviic 1983: 93). The threat to the nation was clear.

The Soviet occupation of eastern Poland was equally brutal. Although the
Germans pushed the Soviets out of Poland in 1941, two years proved to be
more than enough time to wreak extensive havoc on the Polish people.
Although the public eye typically falls on Nazi death camps, approximately
one and a half million Poles were deported to Soviet work camps in the early
years of the war. The massacre of approximately 10,000 Polish officers in the
forest of Katyń and their subsequent discovery in 1943 simply reinforced the
negative Polish view of the Soviets. The Katyń massacre would prove to be a
symbol of Soviet menace throughout the Communist era.

Further evidence of the Soviet threat came as the war was coming to a
close. In 1944, the Red Army pressed the Germans back through Polish territory. The Polish Home Army, a resistance group formed after the German
occupation, sought to free Poland on its own and rose up in revolt against
the German occupying forces. The Polish Home Army had been given the
go-ahead by Allied leaders because the Soviet troops had entered Praga, an
eastern suburb of Warsaw. The reaction of the Soviets, however, was to halt
their advance while the Germans crushed the Polish forces. Although the
fighting lasted for over sixty days, in the end the Soviet troops were able to
take Warsaw with little resistance and without having to acknowledge the

fact that the Poles freed themselves. This subsequently played into Soviet claims over Poland after the end of the war.

Because of Soviet and German involvement in Poland during World War II, any shifts away from Catholic nationalism were undone. Jose Casanova argues that, had the Polish reemergence (as expressed in the Second Republic) continued, it:

> ... might have put an end to Polish exceptionalism. But [it was] cut short by World War II and by the renewed experience of partition, foreign occupation, and unified historical resistance. National solidarity was once again strengthened by the extreme ordeal, and the Polish church found itself once more on the side of the nation ... Any grudge Poles may have had against their church was soon forgotten.
>
> Casanova (1994: 94)

The similarities between the partitions and World War II were striking. Curtis calls the period from 1939 to 1945 "the most severe wartime occupation conditions in modern European history" (Curtis 1994: 36). Not only was the threat to Polish nationalism explicit, but it also reemphasized the fact that Poland could seemingly never trust its neighbors – essentially enforcing a permanent state of threat. The previous experiences of the Polish people had unified them under the banner of Catholicism. When the threat from Orthodox Russia and Protestant Germany arose again, the natural reaction was to fall back on Catholicism as the easiest tool for national differentiation. The fact that the church itself was targeted by both the Soviets and the Germans only fed into this concept of the nation.

> The profound suffering and barbaric devastation endured by Poland during the war only served to strengthen further the role of the Church as the bedrock of nationalist sentiment in a situation where virtually all other institutional and organizational support systems dating from the pre-war period had disappeared.
>
> Stachura (1999: 139)

This return to Catholic identity reinforced the anti-Semitism that was already present in Polish society. Fueled by the mass killings of the Holocaust, as well as by the boundary shifts following the war, Poland became a nearly homogeneous country in terms of religion. "In 1791, before the partitions, it was only 54 percent Roman Catholic; in the Second Republic it was 65 percent Catholic (1931); but in 1946 it was 96.6 percent Catholic" (Kennedy and Simon 1983: 132). The Jewish population in Poland, previously the largest in the world, now dropped to historically low levels. This is important for several reasons. Religious homogeneity certainly leant itself to a stronger conception of religious nationalism. However, it is important to point out that Poland was a religious nation prior to this homogeneity. Religious homogeneity did not cause religious nationalism – it simply reinforced it. The historic presence of Poland at a religious frontier and the threat from the Russians and Germans during the partitions had created religious nationalism long before Poland became a purely Catholic nation in terms of population. The advent of Communism enforced the linkage even further.

Communism

Most scholars of Polish nationalism focus their investigation almost exclusively on the Communist era. I disagree with that approach. Although the Communist era was clearly a formative time for Polish nationalism, I argue that the linkage between religion and nationalism was already in place. Communism strengthened this bond; it did not create it. As such, I will deal with Communist Poland relatively briefly – emphasizing the important aspects, but also demonstrating that the Communist era fits into a much bigger picture of religious frontiers and threats throughout Polish history.

In 1945, the Red Army occupied Poland. Subsequent negotiations between the United States, Britain, and the Soviet Union placed the Polish states in the Soviet sphere of influence. In the elections that followed, a democratic government lead by Stanislaw Mikolajczyk proved very popular but, because of Soviet tampering, the Communist party was placed solidly in control of Polish politics. The promised economic progress was slow in coming (although there was a dramatic shift in urbanization and industrialization), and the Polish resistance began to strengthen again. Once more, the Catholic Church was at the center of this resistance and, as a result, the Stalinist regime stepped up its persecution of the Catholic Church. Believing that the Nazis had begun the process of destroying the Church, the Soviets quickly set about finishing the job. But the secularist results that were achieved in other Eastern European states were not to be achieved in Poland.

> The communists ... perceived neither the nature of Polish Catholicism nor its peculiar relationship to Polish nationalism. Motivated by atheism and monistic ambitions, they opened an offensive against religion and the Catholic Church in the belief that administrative measures would provide a final push toward an ultimate destruction of the "remnants of capitalism." To their great disappointment, these "relics of the past" not only survived but actually became stronger and have come to enjoy greater moral authority than ever before.
>
> Chrypinski (1984: 123)

The open attacks on the Church simply reinforced the linkage between Catholicism and the nation. The religious frontier was no longer a Catholic/ Orthodox frontier – it had shifted to a Catholic/Secular Communist frontier. The result, however, was the same. The continued Soviet threat combined with the atheist, Communist frontier led to a continued reliance on Catholic identity. Again, the emphasis is on *continued*. Communism did not create religious nationalism in Poland.

The continued importance is clear. Compared with pre-Communist Poland, there were increases in the number of churches and parishes, as well as members of the clergy. In addition, statistics regarding religious participation increased regardless of the fact that they were extremely high before Communist rule (Casanova 1994: 93). Tomka tries to explain this phenomenon by pointing to the unifying power of the Catholic Church:

> Religion happened to be the only source of counter-culture in the Communist era which had an effect on every social strata (in contrast to the explicit political opposition which was restricted to the narrow circle of intellectuals in the field of human and social sciences). Since that time there has been no other agency of comparable size undertaking the role of preserving and transmitting national cultures and basic values.
>
> Tomka (1995: 19)

Bruce clarifies Tomka's point, saying that:

> Being a staunch Catholic was one of the ways in which a Pole could assert his or her Polishness against the international Communism that the USSR wished to force on Poles. The attitude of the Church towards the State was always complex. It rarely engaged in outright defiance. To have done so would have brought down state oppression. Instead, it offered measured criticism and allowed itself to become associated in the mind of the people with a nationalism that was independent of the Communist Party.
>
> Bruce (1996a: 99)

Davie elaborates on this idea by emphasizing that the Catholic Church became associated with resistance to (rather than support of) the illegitimate force of Communism. She shows that resistance to secularization became equated with resistance to communism. "[T]he combination strengthened rather than diminished the position of the Church and resulted in unusually high figures of religious practice throughout the Communist period" (Berger 1999: 78–9). The Church was also active in its resistance, officially ruling that all active members of the Communist Party should be excommunicated. In 1949, "implementation of the Vatican decree in Poland became a crime punishable by law" (Cviic 1983: 95).

The importance of the Church is worth emphasizing. However, I again want to separate myself from other scholars who point to the actions of the Church as central to continued religious nationalism. Certainly Church actions were supportive of Polish nationalism, but there are few things the Church could have done to destroy this link. Historical forces meant that

Catholicism was simply the best tool for unifying the Polish people regardless of church actions. "As a result … , Poland is the only country where the advent of communism had very little effect on the individual citizen's practice of organized religion" (Curtis 1994: 89). As Casanova indicates, "All the strategies of forced secularization from above, used relatively successfully first in the Soviet Union and then throughout Eastern Europe, were also variously tried in Poland, albeit with little success" (Casanova 1994: 95).

The interactions of the Church and the state demonstrate the power of the Catholic identity. "Popular conceptions [held] that the socialist state is a foreign implant, the creation of a Soviet-dominated communist party" (Kennedy and Simon 1983). This threat meant that the Church had tremendous power. "The ultimate goal of the regime was clear, and it never ceased proclaiming it: the complete elimination of the church and of religion from Polish life" (Casanova 1994: 95). However, the strength of Catholic nationalism meant that the "Communist authorities were cautious in attacking the privileged position of Catholicism" (Taras 2003: 141). The state was forced to deal with the Church in ways that were unheard of in other Eastern European states. When the state did overstep its bounds, the Church benefited from renewed popular support. As Patrick Michel indicates, " … when the government attacked the Church and sought to compromise it or force it to compromise, it merely helped the Church to gain in influence" (Michel 1991: 196). In fact:

> All attempts to rewrite Polish history and to depict the church as an enemy of the nation and an enemy of the people backfired. The official propaganda machine lost all its credibility, and the church became the cherished trustee of the nation's history, culture, and traditions, and of the collective memories of the Polish people.
>
> Casanova (1994: 95)

The Communist state tried various attempts to weaken the power of the Church, including an emphasis on economic development. But:

> … secularist planning through economic development also failed to bring the expected results. The hopes … that economic development, borrowed from the West materially and ideally, would have the same secularizing effects in Poland it had apparently had in the West were also unrealized.
>
> Casanova (1994: 96)

Whereas Catholicism had been central to the Polish identity dating back to the Deluge of the seventeenth century, Communism was successful in bringing the Church into the political realm. As Stewart Steven wrote in 1982, "The very act of going to Church is a political act. The man or woman who wears a crucifix is making not merely a religious but a political statement as well" (Steven 1982: 162). This linkage would have a profound influence on the Solidarity movement of the 1980s – eventually leading to the fall of Polish Communism.

Solidarity

The balance of power between the Catholic Church and the Polish state was forever altered in 1978 with the election of Karol Wojtyła to the papacy. Wojtyła, who took the name John Paul II, was the first non-Italian pope in nearly 500 years and the first Slavic (and Polish) pope ever. The selection had massive repercussions in Poland. Stewart Steven quotes a Communist journalist's reaction to the news: "I was out of the country attending an international seminar in Prague. And a Czech came up to me, knowing I was Polish and told me the news. My first thought was this means trouble; my second thought was this means very big trouble" (Steven 1982: 153). Big trouble was certainly to come. The pope visited his home country the following year. Over three and a half million Poles came to hear him speak at Czestochowa – the world's largest recorded human gathering.

The pope's visit brought about an enormous rejuvenation of nationalist sentiment. "Surveys of young people in the 1980s showed an increase in professed religious belief over the decade, from 74 percent to 96 percent ... and church attendance was higher in the communist era than it had been before World War II" (Curtis 1994: 97–8). In addition, the Church became a solid symbol of political resistance. This was most clearly demonstrated by the emergence of the Solidarity movement in 1980. Led by Lech Wałesa, workers at the Gdansk shipyard went on strike. Although their demands were political – specifically the right to unionize – their methods were religious.

> During the Gdansk strike, photographs of Pope John Paul II were displayed everywhere. Walesa decorated his lapel with a badge with the picture of the Black Madonna of Czestochowa. Crucifixes were prominent in the conference hall during negotiations. Priests conducted mass in the occupied shipyard.
>
> Kennedy and Simon (1983: 129)

In addition to political demands, the workers also called for Catholic Mass to be broadcast on Polish state radio and television. The Catholicism of the workers united them in the same manner that Catholicism had united the Polish people as a whole.

> Thus, in addition to the protective role offered by the powerful, institutionalized Catholic Church, the very Catholicism of the workers provided a means of identification with each other, an allegiance to the Polish nation, and a clear opposition to the officially atheistic communist party.
>
> Kennedy and Simon (1983)

Soon, more than one in four Poles was a member of the Solidarity movement. As the Solidarity movement gained more and more strength, the Communist party reacted by declaring martial law in 1981. The goal was as much to prevent Soviet intervention as it was to lessen the power of Solidarity.

Although the Solidarity movement was slowed by martial law, the subsequent arrest and murder of Father Jerzy Popiełuszko sparked outrage among the Polish people (Moynahan 2002: 700–1). As Moynahan indicates:

> ... the Communist Party in Poland did not recover. Like the other regimes imposed on Eastern Europe by the victorious Red Army after 1945, it had already been rendered morally moribund by the methods of its arrival, through rigged elections, intimidations, and imprisonments and by their continuation.
>
> Moynahan (2002: 700–1)

In 1989, Solidarity was allowed to take part in the national elections and succeeded in sweeping the Communist party out of power in a landslide victory.

The role played by the Catholic Church, both in its support of Solidarity and in its unifying power across Polish society, is recognized as a central reason for the movement's inauguration and success. Throughout the Communist era, the Catholic Church continued to provide the easiest form of resistance to an illegitimate government. This, however, was nothing new. Such a pattern had been occurring since the partitions of the eighteenth century. More importantly, this pattern was made possible by the presence of a religious frontier and a very clear existential threat to the Polish nation. The Poles had been targeted for elimination or assimilation from the period of the Deluge, through partition, into World War II, and certainly during Communist rule. As Stewart Steven argues:

> Some Western leftists find it hard to understand why the Church had such a powerful influence on Solidarity. The answer is that it could not have been otherwise, because for so many long years only the Catholic Church kept the bright flame of freedom alight.
>
> Steven (1982: 156)

Steven is right. There is little the Church could have done to destroy its linkage to the Polish nation, short of siding with the Soviet oppressors. The presence of a religious frontier meant that the Polish people latched on to Catholicism because it differentiated them in their nationalist struggle – not because the theology or teachings of the Catholic Church dictated such. The Church used this national linkage to further its goals of political power and the strengthening of the Polish faith. It did not, however, create the linkage to begin with. This is demonstrated to some extent by the actions that followed the fall of the Communist party.

Poland today

In much of Eastern Europe and the Soviet Union, the fall of communism led to a resurgence in the importance of religion in society. Although the Church was already a key factor in Polish society, the early years of democratic rule saw the Church's power further consolidated. "After ultimately winning the struggle to protect Polish spiritual life from the effects of communist dogma, the church immediately took a powerful role in determining social policy in the transition period" (Curtis 1994: xliii). Catholicism became intricately tied to government. "In 1989 virtually every significant public organization in Poland saw the church as a partner in its activities and decisions" (Curtis 1994: 95). An attempt was made to eliminate the separation of church and state and, as in Ireland, conservative Catholic beliefs were integrated into public policy. The most obvious example of this is the ban on abortion in nearly all circumstances.

The strength of the Catholic Church was not palatable to the larger Polish population. Religious influence in politics began to be viewed with suspicion, and a fairly large portion of the Polish population wanted to see Catholicism return to more traditional roles. The Church, no longer the focus of resistance, seemingly lost ground. Bruce points out that:

> Although it is too early to be confident of the statistics, it is interesting to note that recent research shows that the success of Solidarity, the collapse of the Soviet Union, and the creation of a genuinely autonomous Polish state has been followed by a marked decline in the popularity of the Catholic Church.
>
> Bruce (1996a: 99)

In fact, Weclawowicz points out that "The activity of the Catholic Church reached nearly 87% acceptance in the late 1980s … Since 1989, however, approval has dropped substantially, to its lowest level of 46% in November 1992, and stabilizing afterwards at 54%" (Weclawowicz 1996: 110). He goes on to indicate that "If the imposed communist system, together with urbanization and industrialization, created the first phase of secularization of Polish society, the last years of transformation to democracy could be treated as a second phase of secularization" (Weclawowicz 1996: 112). As William Safran indicates, "Today, Poland is officially as much committed to religious pluralism as it is to democracy; yet the Roman Catholic leadership remains powerful and continues to attempt to impose Catholic values upon the country that are not always conducive to democracy" (Safran 2003: 7).

This shift in the power of the Church is important for our understanding of Polish nationalism. Although Poland still exists at a religious frontier with Orthodox Russia and Protestant Germany, the threat (for now) has subsided. As was the case in the interwar period, Polish independence has created a sense of security and strength. The Poles are no longer threatened with assimilation. In fact, they have experienced a fairly strong economic recovery (although the initial economy in post-Communist Poland was devastated), and their inclusion in the European Union will likely continue this growth. It is also reasonable to expect that continued development will provide the Polish people with even greater security, thus leading to a further shift away from Catholicism in national sentiment.

It is also important to realize that the experience of the Poles is still fresh in the national memory. Poland still maintains strong residual economic ties to Russia. Less than twenty years have passed since the fall of communism, and change is slow in coming. Poland still remains one of the most religious states in all Europe. Peter Stachura argues that:

> A Church that, in the absence of any other national institution commanding a widespread respect and affection, still remains the most potent symbol of Polish nationhood, is well placed to provide leadership to nationalism feeling in the aftermath of Communism. The encouragement and example given by the Polish Pope, John Paul II, are vital factors in this regard.
>
> Stachura (1999: 140)

With over 85 percent of the Polish population still considering themselves "religious," Poland is still clearly a religious nation (ISSP 1998: li). As the threat from her neighbors subsides, Poland will continue to shift away from a religious conception of the nation – particularly if the Church becomes the source of threat rather than the opposition to it. But the Polish national consciousness will first have to come to grips with the presence of a Russian and German state that have previously represented such a tremendous menace to the Polish people. But until then, "The Catholic–Nationalist symbiosis ... is still the most cherished and vibrant manifestation for Poles of their sense of national pride and identity" (Stachura 1999: 140).

Conclusions

The Polish story confirms the crucial importance of religious frontiers for the formation of religion-based nationalism. It is at such frontiers that religion becomes a useful tool for national differentiation. Poland clearly supports this argument. It also supports the contention that a threat is essential for a religious turn in national identity. Although Poland had existed at a religious frontier since Prince Mieszko accepted Catholicism in 966, religious nationalism cannot truly be seen in Poland until the Deluge of the seventeenth century emphasized the weakness of the Polish position.

Particularly important is the fact that, during the Golden Age of Polish politics, Poland had been a very wealthy state in comparison to its contemporary neighbors. The theory laid out here manages to subsume modernization theories that argue that economic development is central to the process of secularization. While the modernization argument is true, the

actual causal mechanism is missed. Economic development leads to secularization because it increases national security and decreases assimilation
threats. A prosperous state instead becomes the assimilation threat. As a
result, most economically advanced states do not demonstrate strong linkages between religion and nationalism. However, an economically developed state may still be threatened, and thus susceptible to religious
nationalism, as is demonstrated by an increasingly developed Poland and
Ireland. The following quote by the great Polish poet Czesław Miłosz
demonstrates the process by which a powerful state may, in fact, come to
foster a religious nationalism:

> The history of Poland seems extravagant and full of incongruities: a huge
> state which for centuries stood up to the Teutons, Turkey, and Muscovy
> but ... literally fell apart while its once weaker neighbors partitioned
> it and erased it from the map of Europe for some one hundred and
> twenty years; ... habits of religious and political tolerance which gave
> way, as a result of collective misfortunes, to wounded, morbid national-
> ism. This chaos of elements so disparate, yet interrelated by a logic of
> their own, may contain some lessons of universal portent.
>
> Dziewanowski (1977: 1)

An emphasis on the "other"

I would like to address two points about the relationship between religion
and nationalism in Poland. As was the case in Ireland, Polish national
identity was continually shaped by a threatening "other." In Polish history,
that threat has consistently come from the German and Russian empires.
Polish identity has historically been shaped in opposition to these two forces.
Both states had tampered with Polish politics leading up to the partition, at
which point they agreed to dismember the Polish state completely. "The
partition experiences of the eighteenth through the twentieth centuries produced an acute awareness that the very existence of the Polish nation was in
jeopardy" (Kennedy and Simon 1983: 121). Later, the Germans were guilty of
some of history's most infamous actions during World War II, and the
Soviets were guilty of similar crimes under Communist rule. As Adam
Bromke points out, the attitude of the Poles towards the Russians is still
clear today:

> What then is the attitude of the Poles toward Russia and the Russians?
> No doubt, it is primarily characterized by enmity accompanied by a
> large dose of contempt. The reasons for this are natural. They stem from
> the past and present pattern of Polish–Russian relations. Since the
> beginning of the 18th century, when the pendulum swung against them,
> it has been the Poles who have been systematically hurt by the Russians.
>
> Bromke (1987: 210)

Stewart Steven, in his interviews with average Polish citizens, found a similar sentiment:

> "If we Poles are anti-Soviet, it is because the Russians have made us so," says one prominent university professor. "They believe they liberated us and gave us socialism, and so we owe them a debt of gratitude. We believe they killed many of our people and took away from us our independence of thought and action, and so we have nothing to thank them for."
>
> Steven (1982: 150)

Nationalism in Poland has been developed in stark contrast to Germany and Russia. The fact that each of those states resided across a religious frontier simply assured that Polish nationalism would focus on Catholicism to emphasize their uniqueness and their status as a "chosen" people. Had there been no religious frontier, it is likely that Polish nationalism would have focused on their Slavic heritage in contrast to Germany or linguistic and cultural ties in contrast to Russia. However, "Polish Catholicism has been repeatedly at the forefront of Catholic expansion or Catholic defense against other religions in Eastern Europe, to wit, different versions of paganism, Orthodoxy, Islam, Protestantism, and, finally, atheistic Communism" (Casanova 1994: 92). Jose Casanova argues that "Church and nation became identified at a time when the Catholic church was the only institution capable of cutting across the partition of Prussian, Russian, and Austrian Poland" (Casanova 1994: 92). Although Casanova makes a good point, I argue that Polish nationalism was becoming linked to Catholicism in the period leading up to partition, particularly during the "Deluge." The threat was clear before partition was enacted. However, Casanova is certainly correct in pointing to the unifying force of religion in the history of Polish nationalism. It remains important to this day:

> Religion has been both a spiritual and cultural force maintaining national identity in a country historically vulnerable to external domination. As a consequence of the lack of legitimacy of the various authorities during most of Poland's modern history ... the Church has become in popular consciousness the most credible and respected national institution.
>
> Kennedy and Simon (1983)

An emphasis on politics

I also want to address, albeit briefly, the role of religion in politics. In the previous chapter, I argued that religious identities were convenient containers for a variety of political grievances. Although the conflict in Ireland seemed to be a Protestant/Catholic conflict, the religious labels were actually the simplest way to identify a series of political beliefs dealing with self-determination, political equality, etc. This is also the case in Poland. A large percentage of the population still remains active in the Catholic Church, but that identity has been encouraged because it was symbolic of resistance to a variety of conquerors and oppressors. As Kennedy and Simon indicate, "It is common knowledge that a sizeable portion of Poles ignore Church positions on birth control, sexual mores, and even abortion" (Kennedy and Simon 1983: 128). The Church is central to Polish identity, although it may not be central to Polish personal life. Theology is less important than identity.

Gregorz Węcławowicz argues that, in spite of high attendance figures, "The religious rules and principles [of the church] ... have been treated less rigorously." He goes on to point out that "In 1992 more than 82% of respondents rejected the involvement of the Church in political life, and 68% were against shows of religiosity by employees of the state administration" (Weclawowicz 1996: 110). This is not to say that Poles are not Catholic. It simply shows that there is a distinction between national identity and personal religious practice. A Pole need not go to church weekly in order to consider himself or herself a Catholic. "Whether during the partitions, under German occupation in World War II, or in the Communist period, [the Catholic Church] served as a galvanizing force of national resistance and constituted the principal institutional opposition to alien rule" (Taras 2003: 140). As a result, the Polish nation still holds Catholicism dear, in spite of disputes over its proper role in modern society.

This chapter has argued that Polish nationalism has proven to be unique because of its particular conditions: first, its presence at a major crossroads of religion in the middle of the European continent; and second, a persistent and savage threat from its Orthodox, Muslim, and Protestant neighbors. The Polish case also demonstrates the importance of a threat in the equation. Although the Poles had lived at the frontiers of Catholicism, religion was not tied to Polish nationalism until after the Deluge, which saw the previously powerful and tolerant state reduced to a weak and Catholic state. This combination of a religious frontier and an assimilative threat remained constant throughout Polish history – through the partitions of the eighteenth century, into the horrors of World War II, and continuing into the Communist era. In each instance, Catholicism proved to be the easiest, most central factor in the uniqueness of the Polish people. Although the Polish nation has become more hesitant about the Catholic Church since the elimination of the Communist threat, the importance of Catholicism will remain below the surface for easy retrieval should another threat emerge across the religious frontier.

6   Greece

The nation (ethnos) and Orthodoxy ... have become in the Greek conscience virtually synonymous concepts, which together constitute our Helleno-Christian civilization.

President Constantine Karamanlis, 1981 (Stavrou 1995: 39)

The Greek nation ... has and will always have need of religion.

Alexander Papadiamantis

Greece is an interesting puzzle. The Greek nation, like the Irish and Polish nations, is undeniably linked with religion (Boatswain and Nicolson 1995; Brewer 2001; Carey and Carey 1968; Clogg 2002; Curtis 1995; Sarafis and Eve 1990; Toynbee 1981; Vacalopoulos 1976; Woodhouse 1991). But Greece also provides an opportunity to examine the issue of religious nationalism from new angles. Specifically, whereas Ireland and Poland were each Catholic countries, Greece is strongly Orthodox in its faith – a fact that has implications in terms of attendance figures. In addition, the Greek state has taken on an almost theocratic structure, certainly more so than either Ireland or Poland. Language and descent are also important factors in Greek nationalism, whereas Ireland and Poland feature a purer focus on Catholicism. Therefore, the historic trajectory of Greece is of particular interest.

Greece is, however, very similar to the previous cases in other ways. Like Ireland and Poland, Greece has existed at a religious frontier for much of its history. Since the expansion of Islam in the twelfth century, the Greeks have faced a near constant threat from the Muslim world. This frontier became very real in the 1400s, when Constantinople fell to Islamic forces. Even before this, historic animosities between the Eastern and Western branches of Christianity had led to a religious identity in the Balkans. To this day, the Turkish–Greek border represents the presence of a religious frontier that plays a key role in Greek policy, both domestic and foreign. The Greek case is also similar in that the religious identity is a result of a political conflict. The Greek War of Independence arose from the ideals of the French Revolution, but wrapped itself in the garb of the Orthodox Church simply because of the differentiating power of religious identity. As a result, the Greek relationship between nation and religion is strong. As Adamantia Pollis claims:

> ... the Enlightenment and its tenets of modernity, reason and secularism, largely bypassed modern Greece. The national identity that was constructed became coterminous with ethnic identity, in which religion, specifically Eastern Orthodoxy, became an essential ingredient.
>
> Pollis (2003: 156)

The Greek story, like that of Poland, is complicated by the fact that a variety of "others" were important throughout the past several centuries. The Islamic threat was not the only threat. In the twentieth century, the escapades of the Balkans have reshaped Greek identity in a variety of ways. As a result, the fellow Orthodox peoples of the area have had an interesting and significant impact on Greek-ness. All of this will be revealed as we delve into the history of the modern Greek nation.

Another reason for examining the Greek situation is the fact that, more than in the other cases, there is some dispute about the nature of the Church and its historical role in society. This is possibly because, as Theofanos Stavrou points out, "Strange as it may seem, the study of the Orthodox Church in modern Greece has been by far the most neglected area of scholarly inquiry" (Stavrou 1995: 35). This chapter will seek to reconcile some of these differing views and will lay out my own claims regarding the reasons for the church–state–nation relationship in today's Greece. But first, the religious nature of the Greek nation must be sufficiently established.

Religion and the Greek identity

Greece is easily recognized as a religious nation, although its specific manifestation of religious identity is a little different than either Ireland or Poland. The importance of Orthodoxy in Greek society is reflected in both of this study's criteria – religious identity and political religion. The link between Church and state is so strong in Greece that it evokes the occasional accusation of "theocracy," and Orthodoxy is central to Greek culture – in symbols, celebrations, holidays, and more.

Religious identity

The level of religious identification in Greece is as strong as in any state in Europe, East or West. The linkage can be seen in the standard statistics of religiosity. David Close indicates that "Despite the inroads of secularization, Greeks ranked as the most religious people in western Europe on various indices" (Close 2002: 219). A survey of 15- to 24-year olds (a group not known for strong religious ties) revealed an interesting relationship between the Greek people and the Orthodox Church. Over 97 percent of the youth interviewed in Greece claimed to belong to the Orthodox Church, a figure higher than in any other country surveyed. Even Ireland was lower, at just under 93 percent. Less than 3 percent of those surveyed claimed that they *never* went to church – again the lowest in the survey. However, when asked about how often they did go to church, less than 10 percent actually claimed to attend at least once a week. Only France was lower (at 8 percent) (ISSP 1998: li). Part of this anomaly can be explained by the differences between Catholicism (which requires regular attendance) and Orthodoxy (which is much more lenient). "Orthodoxy ... is able by its very nature to contain a greater degree of diversity within itself than is Catholicism; this is one reason for its relative success in a changing moral climate" (Davie 2000: 20).

What is important is the level to which people identify with the Church. In this sense, Greece is among the most religious states in Europe. "Greece was apparently the only country in capitalist Europe in which the proportion of the population claiming that God was important in their lives increased: from 58 per cent in 1985 to 77 per cent in 1994 ... " (Close 2002: 220). And the linkage extends to political beliefs as well. Close points out that " ... a Eurobarometer poll of the late 1990s found Greek youth to be more opposed than any others in Europe to euthanasia (68.5 per cent) and to gay marriages (47.7 per cent)" (Close 2002: 219).

Like Ireland and Poland, the linkage between religion and national identity extends beyond simple measures of religious belief and attendance. In Greece, Orthodoxy is central to Greek-ness. Returning again to our criteria, Orthodoxy is a central factor in recognizing another Greek. Adamantia Pollis makes this point well: "Since religion is a central tenet in Greek ethnonational identity, a person who is not Greek Orthodox is not considered an authentic Greek and can face legal and social barriers" (Pollis 2003: 162). This is because "In Greece, the church permeates every layer of life" (Gage 1986: 95). In the twentieth century, "Historical descent, language, culture and *religion* were triumphant in circumscribing the parameters of the reconstructed Greek ethnonational identity ...; religious minorities, as well as ethnic minorities, were marginalized" (emphasis original) (Pollis 2003: 157). It is not necessarily the case that the Greek people are simply more religious. Rather, Orthodoxy is a central and basic constitutive element in Greek identity. Although language and descent have played roles at various points in Greek history, Orthodoxy has always remained fundamental. "Orthodoxy, as the Greek people see it today, is a national religion, indissolubly woven with the customs and character of these people ..." (Theotokis 1961).

Political religion

Religion is clearly central to the Greek national identity. Significantly, this linkage carries over into the political realm even more vigorously than in the two previous cases. The Orthodox Church is constitutionally tied to the Greek state. Stavrou points out that Greece:

> ... is the only Orthodox country in which official state recognition of the church continued uninterrupted during the twentieth century, at a time when Orthodoxy elsewhere experienced a general retreat either through indifference or through assaults, sometimes by the state itself.
>
> Stavrou (1995: 36)

"All Greek constitutions from the first in 1844, to those of 1863, 1911, 1927, 1952, 1968, through the most recent one in 1975, in one way or another specify that Greek Orthodoxy is the state religion ..." (Pollis 2003: 157).

The official ties between the Greek Orthodox Church and the Greek state far exceed the types of linkages seen in Poland and Ireland, strong as they are. Whereas the previous two cases each had some official constitutional recognition of the Church, the Greek case reveals that recognition in action. In Greece, "The Orthodox Church is a legal person incorporated under public law, whereby, although a separate legal entity, it is part of the state administration ... " (Pollis 2003: 158). The Church is an official state institution run by the Ministry of National Education and Religious Affairs. Members of the clergy are public servants and their salary is paid by the Greek state. "The President formally appoints the bishops and archbishop, while the state, including the police, is expected to enforce church decisions" (Pollis 2003: 158). Proselytism is illegal in Greece. Although this restriction also extends to those seeking to convert people to the Greek Church, the actualities of enforcement reveal a much clearer pro-Orthodox bias. Until fairly recently, the Orthodox Church was solely responsible for the institution of marriage in Greece. A recent law created civil unions, but popular support led to the recognition of civil and religious marriages as equal, as opposed to the intended sole recognition of civil unions. In addition, as Rémond indicates, "Of the ... fifteen members of the European Union [before the recent expansion], Greece is the only one that still mentions religion on its citizens' identity card" (Rémond 1999: 138). Pollis goes on to argue that:

> The centrality of the Eastern Orthodox religion as a marker of Greekness, the legal status of the Greek Orthodox Church and its symbiotic relationship with the state, the remaining restrictions on religious freedom for minority religions, all attest to Greece's divergence from the secular principles of the Enlightenment and the basic tenets of most West European states.
>
> Pollis (2003: 164)

Evidence of "political religion" is abundant in today's Greece.

The combination of a national identity strongly tied to the Orthodox Church and the recognizable implications of that linkage in politics makes the religious nature of Greek nationalism apparent. How Greece came to be so is the more interesting issue. Considering the fact that Greece has had a number of experiences similar to both Ireland and Poland, we are able to draw some valuable conclusions. Insomuch as the Greek case has also been quite unique, we can also eliminate a few potential explanations. To do so, we must once again examine the historic development of the Greek nation. As our examination will be limited to modern Greek nationalism (as opposed to Classical Greece), we will begin with a brief overview of Byzantium.

Byzantium

Greece's history is fascinating in that it has, even more than Ireland or Poland, been central to European history and culture for thousands of years. Greek culture has been admired, studied, and imitated throughout modern Europe. Ironically, Greece did not exist as a unitary state until 1832. As Curtis points out, "In antiquity, hundreds of states were inhabited by Greeks, so the Greek national identity transcended any one state. For much of their history, Greeks have been part of large, multiethnic states" (Curtis 1995: 4). This was true not only in Ancient Greece, but also under the Roman Empire, which conquered the Greeks in the first century BC. The Roman era in Greece had longlasting implications for politics, religion, and the Greek nation. In 330, the Roman Emperor Constantine shifted his capital from Rome to Byzantium, renaming it Constantinople. In 364, the Roman Empire was officially divided into the West, ruled from Rome, and the East, ruled from Constantinople. As the Western Empire fell to barbarian invasions, the importance of Constantinople grew. In addition, a schism began to emerge between the Western Church in Rome and the Eastern Church in Constantinople – a schism that would only grow in subsequent years. Ultimately, Greek Orthodoxy became the official religion of Byzantium after the fall of Rome in the fifth century.

The Byzantine Empire faced new dilemmas in the sixth and seventh centuries. The Slavs and Muslims began to have an influence in the region at approximately the same time. The Slavic peoples began immigrating into the Balkan Peninsula in the seventh century and, although they were eventually "Hellenized", they would have an impact on Greek politics from that point forward. Similarly, the establishment of the Islamic faith in the early seventh century signaled the beginning of an ongoing rivalry between Orthodoxy and Islam. The Islamic expansion would be the justification for the infamous Crusades of the eleventh, twelfth, and fourteenth centuries. Significantly, it was the Fourth Crusade that may have cemented the East–West schism forever. In 1204, the European crusaders, in need of money and influenced by the Venetians, sacked Constantinople. Any ideas of a unified stance against Islamic invasion were destroyed (Moynahan 2002). The decline of Byzantium was irreversible. In 1453, the Ottoman Turks captured Constantinople, establishing it as the center of a new empire that spread across the Mediterranean and loomed large for the Christian states of Europe.

Although this discussion of Byzantine Greece is brief, it is important for a number of reasons. To begin with, the Roman cleavage and the later, and more significant, division between the Eastern Church and the Western Church had major repercussions in the formation of a unique religious identity in Greece. Hans Kohn points out the importance of this divide for later Greek culture: the Greeks "regarded the Greek Orthodox Church as their national heritage and soul. This had been the established church of the Byzantine Empire, an empire Greek in language, with a Greek as Patriarch at Constantinople its highest religious dignitary" (Kohn 1944: 535). The sack of Constantinople in 1204 was particularly significant in the creation of an East–West divide. "The Crusades and Latin and Ottoman rule turned [the Church] into a truly Greek institution, a repository of traditional Greek values and a vehicle of Greek identity immune to Western incursions" (Koliopoulos and Veremis 2002: 145). To this day, Greece maintains an identity distinct from the other Western European states with which it is so often included.

The second point that needs to be made focuses on Ottoman rule. Although this topic will be discussed extensively in the next section, it is important to note that the threat from the Islamic world was strangely Janus faced. In one way, the Muslim invasion represented an inherent threat to Orthodox identity. There was a great deal of pride in Byzantium, and the fall of Byzantine sovereignty was disheartening and frightening. However, the Muslims had also earned a reputation as rulers who were, in many ways, preferable to Christians. The papal attacks on heresy had created an atmosphere of low tolerance and strict expectations. The Muslims, on the other hand, allowed a great deal of religious diversity, provided that non-Muslims paid the appropriate taxes and were not subversive (Moynahan 2002). "In the words of one Orthodox Christian of the period, 'Even the Saracens are merciful and kind compared with these men who bear the cross of Christ on their shoulders'" (Gage 1986: 100). The result was a divided loyalty under Ottoman rule – a tug-of-war between the prominent position of the Orthodox Church in the empire and the desire for the glorious days when Byzantium was a world power.

The Ottoman experience

Once Constantinople fell to the Ottoman Turks in 1453, the remaining enclaves of Greek culture followed shortly. Those areas that were not incorporated into the Ottoman state were instead absorbed by the expanding Venetian Empire. The Greek people would remain part of the Ottoman Empire until the early nineteenth century (or later, depending on geographic location). Like the Byzantine Empire, Ottoman rule had a strong impact on the formation of modern Greek nationalism.

As the Ottoman Empire expanded deeper and deeper into Europe, a wider range of people became integrated under Turkish rule. The subjects of the empire were divided into Muslims, or the "domain of the faithful," and non-Muslims, or the "domain of war" (Curtis 1995: 25). As mentioned previously, non-Muslims were not required to convert to Islam, and the non-Muslim religious subdivisions, or "millets," were used by leaders to govern the Ottoman subjects. There were four key millets – Armenian, Jewish, Catholic, and Orthodox, which was by far the largest and most influential. "The millets enjoyed a fair amount of autonomy. At the head of each was a religious leader responsible for the welfare of the millet and for its obedience to the sultan" (Curtis 1995: 25). As a result, the ecumenical patriarch, as he was known, became integrated into the governing structure of the empire and was granted fairly extensive secular powers in addition to his traditional religious powers. "For many Greeks, therefore, the important matters of everyday life were governed, not by a corrupt Turkish governor or *hodjibashi*, but by the priests and primates of the Orthodox church" (Boatswain and Nicolson 1995: 141). As Curtis points out, "This combination meant that the institution of the Orthodox Church played a vital role in the development of Greek society during the Ottoman era" (Curtis 1995).

In spite of the relative autonomy granted to the various religious groups under Ottoman rule, Orthodox life was far from ideal. Although non-Muslims had general religious independence, politically speaking they were still subject to a foreign and oppressive power. Orthodox Christians were granted some political rights, but there was no doubt that they were considered inferior subjects. "The victorious Moslems allowed the Christians to continue to practice their religion, but they were forced to pay heavy taxes and were forbidden to serve in the army or to marry Moslems" (Gage 1986: 101). Similarly, "the non-Muslim inhabitants of the Sultan's territories were not regarded as his subjects but as cattle (*rayah*), a resource to be tapped for manpower and cash in pursuit of the endless Holy War" (Boatswain and Nicolson 1995: 140). Greeks were not allowed to bear arms, ride horses, or wear Muslim garb, and Orthodox churches were banned from ringing their church bells. Although many of these rules were enforced with decreasing regularity, the notion of Greek inferiority was always apparent, as was the case in Ireland under English rule or Poland during partition. In addition, Greeks were routinely used as galley slaves in the various Turkish wars, and "in court, testimony of a Muslim would always be accepted over that of a non-Muslim" (Curtis 1995: 26).

The situation was something of a paradox. On one hand, the Orthodox Church (and, as a result, the Greek population) held a position of power and privilege under Ottoman rule. On the other, the Greek people were treated in an inferior manner, a situation that certainly aroused animosity in the Orthodox people. Stavrou explains:

The arrangement was paradoxical ... : it basically championed preservation and continuation of the political and religious status quo on which so much else depended; yet consciously and unconsciously, it fostered nationalist aspirations, which ultimately contributed to the dissolution of the Ottoman Empire and the undermining of religion itself as the main point of reference.

Stavrou (1995: 42)

Stavrou has the first part of the equation correct. The second is untrue to a point. Religion may not have been the source of revolution in the nineteenth century, but it was certainly the focus of identity once the war had begun.

What is important to realize is that, for many influential national and Church leaders, the Ottoman system was beneficial. As Colin Nicolson argues, " ... on the whole, the Greeks did not challenge Turkish domination (until the nineteenth century), and remained the most favoured and cooperative of the Sultan's non-Muslim subjects" (Boatswain and Nicolson 1995: 143–4). This is a crucial factor in our understanding of Greek nationalism. At this time, the Ottoman Turks had incorporated the Orthodox Greeks into their empire while still allowing a significant degree of religious sovereignty. The result was a Greek nation that existed at a religious frontier, *but was not threatened with assimilation.* The nature of the millet system meant that the Orthodox Greeks were allowed to carry on their traditions and customs without fear, as opposed to Poland under partition or Ireland under the Union, where national customs, languages, and religions were banned and attacked relentlessly. In the Ottoman Empire, the Greeks "lived reasonably settled and prosperous lives, subject to discriminatory treatment, but living under the laws of their own religion and community" (Boatswain and Nicolson 1995: 144). Nicolson also makes a valid point by indicating that life in the Ottoman Empire was a dream compared with contemporary Europe. "Despite the hardship and uncertainty of Turkish rule, it is doubtful whether the many Greeks would have preferred the life of the millions of Christians who lived as serfs or feudal tenants in Central Europe, Russia or France ..." (Boatswain and Nicolson 1995: 144). The result was an existence that, although not ideal, was certainly acceptable to the wider population of Greek Orthodox subjects.

Although Turkish rule did not necessarily incite religious nationalism in the Greek people, it certainly laid the groundwork for its future incarnation. The privileged position of the Church meant that it became the central focus of Greek identity. The Church was responsible for the education of Orthodox subjects, and it helped to maintain Greek culture and language. As Koliopoulos and Veremis indicate, "The Orthodox Church ... preserved Greek identity and kept the Greek nation from being assimilated [culturally] by the nations of its foreign rulers" (Koliopoulos and Veremis 2002: 142). This identification of the Church as a guardian of Greek-ness would have major implications as the War of Independence evolved in the nineteenth century. Renée Hirschon argues that "The congruence of religion with national identity is a legacy of the Byzantine Empire as a theocratic state and that of the Ottoman administrative system where the *millet*, or 'nation', was defined by religious criteria" (Hirschon 1999: 160–1). In many ways, she is correct. The circumstances of Ottoman rule allowed the Church to preserve Greek-ness in a position of privilege. However, the religious frontier is what made the Orthodox Church the focus of national identity. Had the Church been repressed (as opposed to supported) by the Ottoman Empire, the linkage between Church and nation would have actually progressed much faster. The national tie to religion is not a result of the "theocratic" nature of Turkish rule. Rather, Greek identity is intricately tied to Orthodoxy because the Ottoman Empire existed in the first place. In other words, it was not a strong church–state relationship that tied Greek-ness to Orthodoxy; rather, it was the constant presence of the Muslim Turks that encouraged the Greek identification with the Orthodox Church.

Approaching revolution

The convenient nature of Ottoman rule began to change in the late 1700s and early 1800s. Although a string of powerful and successful leaders had ruled the Ottoman Empire, a series of internecine struggles had seen a serious decay in the quality of the Sultans who ruled over an increasingly overextended realm. As Colin Nicolson indicates, "Once Turkish military expansion stopped, the whole system, depending as it did upon plunder and conquest to reward its élites, began to fall apart" (Boatswain and Nicolson 1995: 145). The consequence, as Nicolson goes on to explain, was an increase in the demands on the Orthodox population. The highest quality lands were redistributed to a Turkish upper class. Ultimately, there were two key influences (in addition to Ottoman decline) that shifted sentiment away from Turkish rule and towards an independent Greece. The first was perceived Russian support. The second was the French Revolution.

The role of Russia

During the reign of Catherine, Russia began to foster notions of a "Third Rome" – a new center of Christian civilization centered on the Orthodox Church. The plight of the Greek people took on a special significance for her. A link had already begun to emerge between the Greek and the Russian peoples. As Hans Kohn points out, "Greece and Russia were united by faith; Russia acted as the protector of the Orthodox Church and of the Greeks in the Ottoman Empire; Greek ships sailed frequently under the Russian flag; Greeks served as Russian consuls" (Kohn 1944). The need to intervene on the behalf of fellow Orthodox Christians also provided a convenient excuse for imperial expansion, as it had for the Russians in Poland. Whatever the reason, the desire to see Constantinople in Orthodox hands once again featured prominently in the foreign policy of the Russian state throughout Catherine's and, subsequently, Alexander II's reigns.

Russian involvement in Greek politics was most clearly demonstrated by the Orlov brothers' uprising. In 1768, the Ottoman Empire sought to take advantage of Russia's involvement in Poland and declared war. In order to gain an advantage, Catherine dispatched the Orlov brothers to Greece in an attempt to spark a general rebellion, but the brothers were unsuccessful. As indicated previously, the general population of Greece was content with Ottoman rule. However, some support did exist. "Inspired by the belief that Russia's war with the Turks signaled that country's readiness to liberate all the Christians in the Ottoman Empire, a short-lived uprising took place in the Peloponnesus beginning in February 1778" (Curtis 1995: 29). Although the uprising was a disaster, it brought down harsh reprisals from the Ottoman rulers, which only served to solidify a more general sense of resentment and opposition. The response of the Ottoman Turks was not unlike that of the British towards Irish uprisings. A population that may have been supportive was pushed away by harsh reprisals and discriminatory legislation.

The French Revolution

More significant for Greek nationalism was the French Revolution. A great deal of support for the War of Independence came from the members of the Greek diaspora. Greeks, without a country of their own for hundreds of years, had migrated throughout the Ottoman Empire and to a wide variety of foreign countries. When the French Revolution brought the concept of modern nationalism to the world scene, intellectual Greeks around the world latched on to the ideas inherent in it. Groups such as the *Etairia Philike* (Friendly Society) began to push for Greek independence.

The fact that these groups were centered outside Greece was very significant. First, the *Etairia Philike* was founded in Russia and was encouraged by the perception that the Russians would support a Greek uprising in the Ottoman Empire. Even more significant was the fact that these diaspora groups suffered from a disconnect with the Ottoman Greeks. Specifically, those Greeks living outside the Empire could not conceive of the level of satisfaction that the average Greek had with their situation under Ottoman rule. As Nicolson indicates, the movement "underestimated the reluctance of many Greeks within the Empire to disturb the status quo from which they were benefiting" (Boatswain and Nicolson 1995: 151). Relatively satisfied with their economic and political position, the Ottoman Greeks were not ready to rise up in revolution. Because of this, the War of Independence, when it did occur, was largely an intellectual movement that was not centered on the Orthodox Church. The Greek War of Independence is considered by many to be the first modern nationalist movement. Hans Kohn points out the reasons for this characterization: the Greeks "were the first [modern nationalist movement], not because they suffered too heavily under

Turkish oppression, but because the ideas of the French Revolution had found among them a well prepared field … " (Kohn 1944: 537). Therefore, the " … conception of Greek nationalism was violently opposed by the conservative forces, especially in the Church. They saw in it a revolutionary attempt to undermine the faith and order" (Kohn 1944: 541).

Although this will be discussed in more depth later, it is important to make clear that the Greek War of Independence arose from secular and intellectual circles. It was not, in the beginning, a war of religious identity. The fact that religion was the easiest tool for Greek differentiation meant that Orthodoxy was quickly adopted as a rallying point for the revolution. In the end, "What transpired … was a revolt based on religious divisions led primarily by liberals with the intent of creating a secular state" (Gallant 2001: 68). Religion was used as a tool. It was not the goal. However, as in the previous cases, nationalist movements are based on differentiation, and religion could not be avoided in the Greek case.

The War of Independence

Although the decline of the Ottoman Empire, the perceived support of Russia, and the encouragement of diaspora groups set the stage for revolution, a very specific series of events actually set the war in motion. In the early 1800s, an Albanian leader known as Ali of Ioannina began establishing himself as a regional force in the Balkan Peninsula. As he gathered an increasingly large power base, Ali began to prove threatening to the Sultan's power. As a result, in 1820, the Sultan sent a major force to crush Ali. The *Etairia Philike* saw this confrontation between two potential Muslim oppressors as an opportunity to stake their own claim to self-rule. In 1821, the leader of the *Etairia Philike*, a Russian military officer, launched an attack on Ottoman forces across the Russian–Turkish border.

Although the insurgents were quickly defeated, the attack of Alexander Ypsilatis (the *Etairia* leader) inspired a wide assortment of uprisings across the Greek community. There were a number of reasons for this newfound support. Significantly, the Turkish leaders had called an assortment of Greek leaders to a meeting in Tripolitsa, and many may have preferred rebellion to what might have lain in store for them following an attempted Greek insurgency. In addition, a persistent belief that Russia would intervene on behalf of their fellow Orthodox brethren may have encouraged stronger popular support for war. Perhaps most significant of all were the "long-standing feelings of religious antagonism" (Boatswain and Nicolson 1995: 155). The decline of the Ottoman Empire had brought with it a significant reduction in religious liberties under the Sultan. All these factors contributed to the occurrence of an initial uprising, although it was widely dispersed and relatively weak. The various Greek factions that were involved each had their own goals, and there was not much of a unified front against the Turkish response.

The chief goal of the Greek upper classes was to rid society of the Turks, the military classes sought independent enclaves for themselves in imitation of Ali Pasha, and the lower orders simply desired to escape taxation, increase their property, and move up the social scale. Diaspora Greeks also returned home with dreams of a resurrected democratic past. Keeping these competing and disparate interests together proved one of the greatest challenges of the war.

Curtis (1995: 31)

Luckily for the Greeks, the Sultan was still focused on defeating Ali of Ioannina, and his distractions meant initial success for the Greeks, who were able to take several strategic points in the Peloponnese.

Because of the privileged position of the Orthodox Church and the modern nationalist inspirations behind the Greek War of Independence, religion was not central to the initial movement. In fact, the Church had many reasons to oppose a Greek uprising. As Koliopoulis and Veremis argue,

It is now established that Church leaders were not more – indeed they were much less – enthusiastic freedom fighters than most other representatives of Greek elite groups with a vested interest in preserving the Ottoman Sultan's decrepit but still formidable empire.

Koliopoulos and Veremis (2002: 143)

They go on to point out that "the movement for Greek national independence, and the consequent launching of the Greek nation-state, could not possibly have been welcome to church leaders in the way that it has subsequently been portrayed" (Koliopoulos and Veremis 2002: 144). In spite of the Church's reluctance, the fact that the Ottoman Empire was an Islamic state and the Greek people were Orthodox meant that the revolution would eventually adopt a religious tone. Once again, this is because religion provided the easiest tool for mass mobilization in support of the Greek cause, particularly considering the diverse interests that were swept up into the war.

The Ottoman Empire would unintentionally encourage this shift as well. The Sultan did not look kindly upon the Greek revolt, and he moved to repress it with tremendous force.

The traditional Ottoman response to rebellion was to crush it by intimidation and terror. The Greek revolt was not seen as an expression of national self-determination, a concept that was meaningless to the Sultan, but as an attempt by greedy individuals to usurp power for their own ends. Above all, it was seen as a religious phenomenon: all Christians within the Empire were judged responsible for the excesses of the Peloponnesian chieftains and were liable to communal punishment.

Boatswain and Nicolson (1995: 157)

As a result, the dispositions of the Church changed quickly. Attitudes shifted with "the summary execution of all the metropolitans and bishops whom the Ottoman authorities could lay their haunds [sic] upon. The survivors understandably threw in their lot with the revolutionaries, raised the flag of insurrection and blessed their arms" (Koliopoulos and Veremis 2002: 144). The religious nature of the revolution was cemented with the subsequent execution of the Ecumenical Patriarch outside his church in Constantinople on Easter Sunday. His body was hung in the street for three days before being turned over to the local population, who proceeded to drag the body through the streets. A series of brutal executions throughout the Greek territories followed. The massacres precipitated two important shifts in the war: a solidification of the Greek populace behind the Orthodox identity and a swing in foreign sentiment towards the Greek cause.

In 1822, Ali Pasha (Ali of Ioannina) was defeated by the Turkish forces, and the Sultan was able to stage a full-scale assault on the Greek insurgents. Although the Ottoman advance south into the Balkans seemed destined for victory, a series of mistakes allowed the Greeks to achieve some success, resulting in a stalemate between the rebels and the regime. Unsatisfied with this outcome, but unwilling to lose control over the Balkans, the Ottoman Sultan turned to Mehemet Ali, an Egyptian vassal who had created a powerful military state under Ottoman rule. While the Greek forces were squabbling among themselves, Turkish forces launched a new offensive from the north coordinated with a landing of Egyptian forces under Mehemet Ali in the south. The unity of the Muslim forces reinforced the religious dimension of the conflict. " ... A trail of burned crops, slaughtered livestock and empty villages marked the progress of [Mehemet Ali's] advance, and in Modon a slave market was opened where Greeks were sold as galley-slaves or forced to work in labour gangs" (Boatswain and Nicolson 1995: 164). Once again, religion was the single most effective device for differentiating the Greek cause from the Ottoman Empire and the affiliated Islamic troops of Mehemet Ali's Egypt.

The Greek cause was soon on the brink of disaster. The Great Powers of the day had done little or nothing to support the Greek insurgency. The Napoleonic Wars were still fresh in the memories of British, French, and Russian leaders, and their main concern was stability rather than Greek self-determination. However, as the war endured (it would last for twelve years), the powers became more willing to support Greek efforts. The massacre of Orthodox Christians had led to Russian support for some level of Greek autonomy, and Egyptian involvement had aroused concern in Britain and France. Together, the three Great Powers signed the Treaty of London in 1827. Far from fulfilling the Greek desire for national sovereignty, the treaty merely established a Greek principality that was to continue under Ottoman rule. The battered Greek forces accepted. There was, however, an important stipulation in the treaty that allowed the Great Powers to intervene if the Sultan violated the agreement in any way. Already on the brink of victory, the Egyptian forces were not sure how to respond. In October, a confrontation between the Egyptian fleet and a combined Russian, French, and British fleet erupted into chaos when one of the Muslim ships opened fire. The combined fleet of the Great Powers quickly destroyed the Ottoman fleet, and Greece's fate was changed forever. In May 1832, the Great Powers established a protectorate over the independent Kingdom of Greece and named a Bavarian prince King Otho of Greece.

The impact of the war on national identity

Greek nationalism could not be described as religious nationalism prior to the War of Independence. The Greek nation existed at a religious frontier with the Islamic world, but the threat of assimilation from the Ottoman Empire was relatively minimal. Specifically, the Greeks had established a prominent position in the Empire, and the Orthodox Church was actually part of the Ottoman administration. The fact that Greeks were free to practice their own religion and educate their own children meant that the fear of absorption into Islamic culture was minimized. However, as the Ottoman Empire entered a period of decline, the Sultans responded by placing increased pressure on Greeks, and the ultimate massacre of Greek Orthodox subjects at the onset of the War of Independence created an indubitable threat to the Greek nation.

As a result of these changes, Greek national identity at the end of the War of Independence was securely centered on the uniqueness of the Orthodox tradition. Although language would later enter into the Greek understanding of nationhood, initially Orthodoxy was primary.

> As Greece took up the struggle for national independence in the nineteenth century, however, "Greek-ness" was still primarily defined by Orthodox Christianity. The primacy of religion as *the* criterion of Greek identity is noteworthy. It continued overriding the distinctions of language and dialect which had become increasingly significant in the growth of Balkan nationalism (emphasis original).
>
> Hirschon (1999: 161)

Veremis and Koliopoulos emphasize this point: "Religion was *the one determinant on which everyone agreed*, while residence was accepted only in determining citizenship. Language was only grudgingly conceded for spreading Greek education to all the Orthodox subjects" (emphasis mine) (Veremis and Koliopoulos 2003: 13).

It is also important to note that the conception of Greek-ness was still largely focused on all the Orthodox subjects under Ottoman rule. After Greek independence was established, a new "Greek" Orthodox church had to be established, as the Ecumenical Patriarch was still part of the Ottoman regime, and Greek allegiance could never be sworn to a Turkish official.

"The 'nationalization' of Orthodoxy signified the abandonment of ecumenical Eastern Orthodoxy and the projection of a nationalist Greek Orthodoxy" (Pollis 2003: 156). Although the two churches (Greek and Eastern) were reconciled in 1850, the Greek Church remains autocephalous to this day. In spite of this split, and as a result of the Orthodox conception of Greek-ness, all Orthodox subjects of Ottoman rule were viewed as part of the Greek nation. In other words, as Greek-ness was defined in terms of religion, all Orthodox subjects in the Ottoman Empire were considered "Greek." "At the time of Greek independence in 1829, the Greek nation was conceptualized as a resuscitated Byzantium – a Christianized Ottoman Empire – that would incorporate a multiplicity of religions, cultures, and ethnicities" (Pollis 2003: 156). When the first constitution was established, it defined Greeks in a very specific way. Greeks were "those indigenous inhabitants of the domain of Greece *who believe in Christ* …" (emphasis mine). As Veremis and Koliopoulos point out, "Religion, or more accurately, Eastern Christianity, was the principal qualification and criterion of Greek national identity. Residence in the 'Greek domain' was the second qualification" (Veremis and Koliopoulos 2003: 20). This imagined linkage to all Orthodox Christians in the Empire would have profound effects on independent Greece, specifically through the concept of the Great Idea.

The Megali Idea

After the war ended, Greeks had earned their independence, but they faced a series of major challenges. The Greek economy had been devastated by the decade-long war, and many of the most prosperous areas had been left outside the newly formed Greek state. In addition, the newly crowned King Otho was a seventeen-year old Bavarian Catholic who quickly established an authoritarian regime. Both his Catholicism and his absolutism were areas of contention for the Orthodox Greeks who had just fought a war against authoritarianism. When the National Church split with the Ecumenical Patriarch in 1833, Otho was named as the head of the Church. The concept of a Catholic head of the Orthodox Church was not well received. As a result, Otho was never fully accepted. In 1844, he was forced to accept constitutional rule and, in 1862, he abdicated the throne. Part of Otho's failure can be explained by his failure to successfully implement the Megali Idea, a concept that would play a critical role in Greek history throughout the nineteenth and early twentieth century.

The Megali Idea, or Great Idea, was the belief that "Greeks must be reunited by annexing Ottoman territory adjacent to the republic" (Curtis 1995). In other words, the Greeks did not see the War of Independence as complete until all Orthodox Greeks were united under the new Greek state. The very nature of the Megali Idea indicates the level to which religion and nation had become inseparable. The War of Independence had been fought by a wide range of Orthodox Christians, a fact that undermined linguistic bases of nationalism. "Albanian-speaking Suliots and Hydriots, Vlach-speaking Thessalians and Epirots and Slav-speaking Macedonians had fought in revolutionary Greece with the other Greeks, and no one had thought that non-Greek speakers were any less Greek than Greek speakers" (Veremis and Koliopoulos 2003: 15). The Church was called on to support the cause of the Megali Idea.

> Greek state pressure to mobilize all efforts in the drive to push the nation's frontier into the Balkans, while reclaiming lands and peoples that had come under Slavic influence in previous centuries, was also felt by the Church establishment, which was called upon not only to bless the national effort but also to contribute to the drive to reinforce the educational and ecclesiastical status of Greeks in the contested lands.
>
> Koliopoulos and Veremis (2002: 147)

Thus, a relatively weak state that had only recently been brought into existence set out to expand its frontiers in order to rescue fellow Orthodox Christians from Ottoman rule.

The Megali Idea was encouraged by Greeks throughout the Ottoman Empire who persisted in calling for unification with the new Greek state. In the 1830s, there were insurgent movements by the Greek populations in Thessaly, Macedonia, and Epirus. More significantly, Cretan Greeks rose up in revolt in 1839. Crete held a particular significance because of its economic stature and its political importance. By the late 1840s, Greece and the Ottoman Empire were on the brink of war over territorial issues. In 1853, Russia invaded Ottoman territory – an action that provoked the Crimean War. The Greeks saw the Russian advance as an opportunity to implement the Megali Idea and quickly launched an attack on the Ottoman territories of Thessaly and Epirus in order to "protect" the Christian populations there. The Turks quickly defeated the Greek advance. In addition, neither Britain nor France wanted to see increased Russian power in the region, and both countries had allied themselves with the Ottoman Empire. Upset at the Greek attack on their ally, the British and French "landed troops at Piraeus and forced the King to accept a pro-British administration, occupation by British and French troops, and supervision of Greek affairs that continued for several years" (Boatswain and Nicolson 1995: 178).

Greek fortunes continued to suffer in the nineteenth century. Economic growth continued to be dismal, and the new country's foreign debt grew at a remarkable pace, largely because of the costly wars it continued to fight over "Greek" lands. In addition, the Ottoman Sultan established an independent Bulgarian Church in 1870 – an action that posed a major threat to Greek claims to all of Orthodoxy. "It marked the start of a Turkish strategy of 'divide and rule', but above all it heralded the challenge of Slav nationalism" (Boatswain and Nicolson 1995: 183). In the 1870s, Serbians and Montenegrins attacked the Ottoman Empire, and Russia moved within striking distance of Constantinople. Insurrections erupted once again through-out the Greek populations of the Empire – from Crete to Thessaly to Epirus. Before Greece could move to annex new territories, a peace treaty was agreed upon. Although the Greeks did gain some territories in Thessaly and Epirus, it became apparent that Russian support had fallen on the side of a large Bulgaria. Outraged by the treaty, Greece began to mobilize its troops in order to take contested territories by force, but was once again prevented from doing so by the French and British, who installed a naval blockade and forced the Greeks to step down the confrontation with Bulgaria. In the 1890s, a renewed call for unification with Crete released an outpouring of Greek nationalism, resulting in a military confrontation between the Greeks and the Turks, ultimately leaving the Greeks defeated once more.

The creation of Balkan nationalism was profound for Greek identity. When the Sultan allowed the establishment of a Bulgarian Exarchate, it challenged the Greek national claim to all the Orthodox people of the Ottoman Empire. No longer would a simple religious definition of Greek nationalism suffice. Later, the Balkan Wars of 1912 and 1913 further revealed the Bulgarian threat to Greek nationalism. For the first time in modern Greek history, a significant "other" took the form of an Orthodox state. The question of Greek-ness again became central to politics:

> Religious differentiation from the Turks was no longer sufficient in the new political framework. It was, above all, essential to define modern Greek identity in relation to the other Orthodox peoples in the Balkans, Bulgars, Albanians and Vlachs, with claims to the same lands. What was the relation of the Greeks to these "others", and who were the Greeks?
>
> Veremis and Koliopoulos (2003: 14)

This redefinition took the form of a reinforced emphasis on Greek Orthodoxy.

> Religion ... as a determining factor was no longer a convincing argu-ment and had to be redefined. In the new situation what was important was not Orthodoxy as such, but adherence to the Ecumenical Patriarch; and the Bulgars and all those who adhered to the Bulgarian Exarch were "schismatics."
>
> Veremis and Koliopoulos (2003: 23)

In addition to the new threat from Bulgaria, the Russian decision to support Bulgarian claims in the region reinforced the fact that Russia was not the strong supporter of the Greek nation that it was once believed to be. "With Constantinople as the goal of Greek and of Russian national aspirations, Greece had to look for other titles than the religious one for her claim to Byzantium" (Kohn 1944: 536). The result was an added emphasis on his-torical and cultural ties to Ancient Greece as well as the Greek language.

For the first time, Greek nationalism truly emphasized several factors. Although religion was no longer the single most important factor in religious nationalism, it was *as important* as the other factors, if not more so.

It was at this point that language entered the equation. Previously, language had been

> ... a less important factor than religion in defining national identity. Certainly this was less so than it is in contemporary Greece, where competence with the language may often lead to assumptions that a national or ethnic link exists while lack of it is a major source of doubt or disqualification.
>
> Hirschon (1999: 161)

The duality can be witnessed in a Greek textbook published in 1908, which stated that "Greeks are those who speak Turkish but profess the Christian religion of their ancestors. Greeks are also the Greek speaking Muslims of Asia Minor, who lost their ancestral religion but kept their ancestral tongue" (Veremis and Koliopoulos 2003: 25). Greek nationalism had not yet become truly exclusive.

Adamantia Pollis makes an argument that differs from this. According to her, "Even as late as the Balkan Wars ... and immediately after World War I, official Greece defined itself as a territorial nation intent on reclaiming its historical lands. The ethnicity or religion of the people in the territories it coveted was of little significance" (Pollis 2003: 156). I argue that Pollis has missed the key point. The Greek concept of territory was based on historical Byzantine claims that were, at their core, based on religion. The indifference of the Greeks to the inhabitants of former Greek territories (if any existed) was directed at the non-Orthodox citizens who lived alongside the Orthodox Greeks. In fact, the goal of the Megali Idea was the unification of the Orthodox people under a new Byzantine Empire. If doing so meant the incorporation of others as well, then so be it. Pollis goes on to argue that:

> A confluence of historical factors in the early 1920s, most importantly, Kemal Atatürk's Turkish nationalist revolution as the Ottoman Empire was collapsing forcefully ended the dream of a reconstituted Byzantium ... The Greek nation was gradually reconceptualized and reconstructed in terms of an exclusive ethnicity in which "Greek-ness" manifested several indelible attributes. In this gradually reconstituted nation, religion played an increasingly central role.
>
> Pollis (2003: 156)

The influence of religion had always been present. Under Ottoman rule, the Greeks were defined by their Orthodoxy, both by themselves and by the Sultan himself. In addition, the Orthodox identity was central to mobilization in the War of Independence, as well as the motivation (or excuse) for the

Megali Idea. Religion had been central to Greek identity long before the Balkan Wars, and it would continue to play an important role in Greek-ness despite the incorporation of language and cultural heritage into Greek nationalism. As Makrides indicates, during this era, " ... religion in Greece was more a way of life. Thus, any 'attempts to proselytize are looked upon as attempts to denationalize.' Moreover, there was no question of 'deposing the time-honored [Orthodox] dogma', which was deeply embedded in Greek consciousness" (Makrides 1997: 179).

The continued importance of Orthodoxy in the Greek identity was also influenced by Turkish actions. In spite of the increasing Bulgarian threat, the Turkish threat remained the most influential factor in Greek nationalism. When, in 1908, Kemal Atatürk came to power through the Young Turk movement, he did so by emphasizing a unitary nation. Huntington points out that "Rejecting the idea of a multinational empire, Kemal aimed to produce a homogeneous nation state, expelling and killing Armenians and Greeks in the process" (Huntington 1996: 144). Although there would be a number of threats to the Greek nation in the twentieth century, the Turkish threat would remain central to Greek consciousness, which is why Orthodoxy continued to play a central role in Greek identity.

The World Wars

As European tensions began to rise in the early twentieth century, Greece was once again caught in the fervor. When the European powers began to separate themselves into two key alliances, Greece found itself divided as well. The Greek King was married to Queen Sofia – the sister of Kaiser Wilhelm of Germany, a key member of the Central Powers. He also felt that Greek neutrality would be rewarded by the German state after the war was complete. On the other hand, Prime Minister Venizelos supported Greek involvement on behalf of the Triple Entente of Russia, France, and Britain. This line of thought was supported by the fact that the Ottoman Empire was allied with the Central Powers, as was Bulgaria, which Greece had recently fought over territorial ambitions in Macedonia. Furthermore, the Greeks had a treaty with Serbia, which was at war with Austria–Hungary over territorial disputes. In the end, these split loyalties would divide all Greek society in what became known as the National Schism.

In the end, the Greeks were spurred on by the Megali Idea and the thought that an alliance with the Entente would result in territorial expansion at the end of the war. This would, in fact, be the case. After the war, Greece was awarded territory in Thrace and Macedonia, the Dardanelles and, most significantly, Smyrna, which was in Asia Minor and what is now Turkey. Greek leaders decided that, in order to create a defensible territory, Greek claims in Asia Minor must be expanded. In 1921, Greece launched a war against Turkey, now led by Atatürk. Although the Greek advance initially proved very successful, Atatürk launched a massive counterattack once the Greek forces had penetrated deep into Asia Minor and spread them-selves much too thin. The Greek retreat was rapid and humiliating. In the end, over 30,000 Greeks were killed.

The defeat of the Greeks in the Greco-Turkish War ultimately signaled the death of the Great Idea. The Treaty of Lausanne in 1923 established the terms that ended the war. Turkey regained its control of territory around Smyrna, but overall the treaty was relatively light on Greece with one exception: as a stipulation of the treaty, Greece and Turkey were to exchange a large number of Muslim and Orthodox populations.

> All Muslims living in Greece, except for the Slavic Pomaks in Thrace and the Dodecanese, and Turkish Muslims in Thrace, were to be evac-uated to Turkey; they numbered nearly 400,000. In return approximately 1,300,000 Greeks were expelled to Greece. *The determining factor for this shift was religion, not language or culture* (emphasis mine).
>
> Curtis (1995: 50–1)

This shift in population had several key implications for Greek nationalism. First, the subsequent refugee crisis further strained the political and eco-nomic situation of the Greek state. Second, the expulsion of non-Orthodox populations made the Greek identification with Orthodoxy even stronger. "With the removal of Turkish and Bulgarian minorities, Greece became for the first time an ethnically [homogeneous] state with few of the problems of national minorities that plagued her northern neighbors" (Boatswain and Nicolson 1995: 213). This transformed the notion of Greek-ness into a more homogeneous concept as well. As Veremis and Koliopoulos indicate:

> The Greeks of the interwar period were led to believe that all people inhabiting Greece were or ought to have been Greek, not only in sharing the same culture, but also in speech. Greek national ideology and assumptions about the Greek nation were led, under the influence of the threat from Bulgaria and international communist sedition, into a narrow path which did not allow differences in speech or in any other way.
>
> Veremis and Koliopoulos (2003)

Furthermore, the movement of large Orthodox populations from Turkish territory finally destroyed any romantic notions of territorial expansion in the name of Orthodoxy or Greek-ness. Ethnic and Orthodox Greeks had been removed from Turkish territory and returned "home." There was no longer a need to launch an expansionist campaign against the Turkish state.

The content of Greek nationalism was transformed during the interwar period. The Asia Minor debacle of 1922 that put an end to the largest

Greek community outside the realm, signified the end of Greek irredentism and the beginning of a parochial definition of "Greekness."

Veremis and Koliopoulos (2003: 16)

World War II also had a significant impact on Greek history, although it was
less important for nationalist sentiments. Although Greece desired to remain
neutral in this war, the aspirations of Mussolini in Italy proved too strong. In
1941, Italy invaded Greece. An Italian victory proved much more difficult
than expected, and when the Greeks invited British involvement in their war
against Italy, it provoked Hitler's anger. Greece and Crete each fell rapidly to
the German advance, and it was the brutal German occupation that proved
important in the future of Greek politics. The key antagonists in World War
II – Germany and, more significantly, Italy – were both non-Orthodox states.
The fact that the war was relatively short (in comparison to Ottoman Rule)
meant that the religious national implications were minimized. But there was
some impact. Specifically, the Jewish population was virtually eliminated in
the Greek state, as it was in Poland, only continuing the homogenization
process that began after the Greek defeat in Asia Minor a few years previously.

In addition, the era of occupation led to one of the more drastic schisms
in Greek history – the Communist resistance versus the anti-Communists.
The fact that the Russians and British had agreed that Greece would be a
British sphere of influence meant little to the various factions, other than the
fact that the British only supplied arms and support to pro-Monarchist
groups. In the end, the schism resulted in a brutal civil war that lasted from
1946 until 1949. The economic and social toll of World War II and the
subsequent civil war on Greece were enormous, but in terms of national
sentiment (particularly religious nationalism), events in the decades following the wars would prove more critical.

The Turkey issue

Perhaps the most influential post-war issue in Greek society was, and continues to be, the issue of Turkey and the related issue of Cyprus. As has been
indicated, "The Greek attitude to Islam is coloured by the country's more or
less antagonistic relations with Turkey ..." (Safran 2003: 6). That antagonism, which arose out of the Ottoman dominance of Greece, continued after
Greek independence and in spite of the population exchanges following
World War I. As Thanos Dokos argues,

In the post-Cold War era Greece is faced with what she considers as a
major security threat and a number of risks: the threat is perceived to
emanate from her eastern neighbor (Turkey) and the risks are seen as
resulting from Balkan and Mediterranean instability.

Dokos (2003: 46)

The Turkish threat has had and continues to have a more significant impact on Greek identity than Balkan instability. As a result, it makes sense to address it first, beginning with Cyprus.

Cyprus was created as an independent state in 1960. Previously a British colony, Cyprus had a majority Greek population and a large Turkish minority – around 20 percent of the population. The international agreements that established the independence of the state also stipulated that certain guarantees be made for the Muslim minority. However, animosities between the two groups led to escalated tensions which, in turn, led to escalated interest by the Turkish and Greek states. This can be partially explained by the longstanding tensions between the two populations on the island. Specifically, the Ethnarch, a political and spiritual leader of the Greek peoples on the island, had led a strong call for unification with the Greek state in the 1950s. Turkish leaders asserted that, if Cyprus were ever to become independent of British rule, it would have to revert to Turkish control, as had been the case during Ottoman rule. Growing weary of the issue, international leaders were able to reach an agreement in 1959 that resulted in independence.

Animosities in Cyprus continued to run strong. The early 1960s proved to be a very contentious time for Cypriots, Greeks, and Turks.

> In the years immediately following independence ... the relative welfare and the interaction of the two ethnic groups in Cyprus became the object of constant quarrels ... A series of crises and armed conflicts, capped by the interventions of United Nations peacekeeping forces in mid-1964, forced the Turkish Cypriot population into enclaves that were circumscribed by the increasingly active Greek Cypriot National Guard.
>
> Curtis (1995: 274)

Soon, only Greeks were included in the government and, in 1964 and 1967, Turkey began implementing plans to invade Cyprus. As a result of the creation of religious enclaves, the religious frontier was once again made abundantly clear in Cyprus, just as it was clear along the mainland borders of Greece and Turkey. The tensions between Turkey and Greece meant that Cyprus became central to Greek foreign policy during this era.

The issue came to a head in 1974. Greece was under the control of a military dictatorship. The junta backed a coup by Greek Cypriot groups that overthrew the reigning Cypriot Ethnarch who was opposed to union with Greece. The Turkish reaction was swift and dramatic. Turkish troops quickly launched an invasion in order to secure the northeastern portions of the island – home of the Turkish minority. Shortly thereafter, the military junta in Greece came to an end, and the new Greek leader, Karamanlis, was forced to deal with a rapidly escalating issue in Cyprus. Curtis argues that Karamanlis had three basic options in Cyprus: (1) launch a war against Turkey, an option that would have likely not gone well for Greece, as it was not militarily prepared for such an action; (2) delay a war until Greece was more prepared, an option that "likely would have initiated a chain reaction of revanchist wars similar to those that occurred between Israel and its Arab neighbors"; or (3) use political and economic pressure on Turkey while preparing for future Turkish deterrence (Curtis 1995: 275). Karamanlis opted for the third option, a course of action that avoided immediate war at the cost of Greek national aspirations, but at the same time failed to fully step down tensions between the two states.

In subsequent years, Greco-Turkish relations continued to decline. As Boatswain and Nicolson point out:

> The festering crisis over Cyprus had poisoned relations between Greece and Turkey. Greek complaints about the treatment of their minority in Istanbul (now less than 10,000, compared to 70,000 in 1960, 100,000 in 1920, and nearly 300,000 in 1820) were matched by Turkish anxieties about the Turks of Eastern Thrace. Complex geographical problems over ownership of mineral rights in the Aegean, which could only be solved by compromise, led instead to military confrontations. In July 1976 the two countries nearly went to war over the activities of the Turkish survey vessel Sismik in the Aegean.
>
> Boatswain and Nicolson (1995: 256)

The issue of Aegean water rights continued to strain relations between the states, bringing them to the brink of war again in 1987 and in 1994. These tensions were encouraged by nationalist rhetoric in both nations. "Since the invasion, periodic nationalist declarations by radical factions in Turkey, which usually make headlines in Greek newspapers, have intensified Greek fears" (Curtis 1995: 280). Turkey continued to be perceived by Greeks as having aspirations in Cyprus, several Aegean islands, and in Thrace, where the Muslim minority is most substantial.

> In the first half of 1995, nationalist rhetoric in Greece continued to describe Turkish plots to stir irredentism in the Turkish minority in western Thrace as a base for a Turkish invasion and capture of that Greek province. That strategy was seen as one of three elements of Turkey's offensive position toward Greece, the other two being Cyprus and the Aegean Islands.
>
> Curtis (1995: li)

In addition, Turkey undertook a program of modernizing and building its military in the 1990s, an action that was understandably disturbing to the Greeks. As Dokos points out, "Geography and its small population in comparison to that of Turkey further increased Greek insecurity" (Dokos 2003: 46).

The significance of the Greco-Turkish tensions is clear for this investigation. By the beginning of the twentieth century, Greek national identity had become firmly ensconced in Greek Orthodoxy. The Balkan Wars and the Greco-Turkish war that followed World War I only furthered this linkage. In post-World War Greece, the animosity to Turkey was still strong, and the foreign policy issues of both states only reinforced the Turkish threat to Greek identity. Cyprus was a particularly obvious example of the ongoing tensions between the Greeks and Turks, but the states came frighteningly close to war over several other issues, including control of water and air space in the Aegean. The fact that these tensions occurred at a religious frontier meant that, once again, religion provided the easiest form of self-identification and differentiation for the Greek people. The religious identities helped to reinforce the tensions between the groups in a cyclical pattern, but the religious frontier and its associated threat were the initial catalysts for religious nationalism among the Greek people.

The Balkans issue

Cyprus and Turkey were not the only significant issues for the Greek nation in post-World War Greece. The other major influence on Greek identity was the dissolution of Yugoslavia and the turmoil in the Balkans. Greek foreign policy understandably took a particular interest in the newly formed countries on its doorstep, and its interactions with Serbia, Bosnia, Albania, Kosovo, etc. had a significant impact on Greek identity. As Couloumbis, Kariotis, and Bellou argue, "Unlike the rest of our EU partners ... we [the Greeks] are still surrounded by a fragile and dangerous region" (Couloumbis *et al.* 2003: 2). The Balkan threat is important in any understanding of modern Greek identity.

The linkages between Greece and the other states in the Balkan Peninsula extend back to Ottoman rule. When Greece achieved its independence from the Turks, they turned to the Megali Idea and its plan for extending Greek hegemony throughout the Orthodox regions of the Ottoman kingdom. While support for the Great Idea was strong in the new Greek state, elsewhere in the Ottoman world, it proved problematic. "Some Greek patriots dreamt of Greek leadership throughout the Orthodox world ... while the non-Greek Orthodox peoples had to assert their rising nationality as much against the Greek Church as against the Turkish overlord" (Kohn 1944: 535). As a result, a variety of states in the region followed the Bulgarian lead by establishing independent Orthodox Churches. The Balkan Wars of the early twentieth century further strained relations between Bulgaria and Greece.

All these issues came to the fore in the 1990s with the dissolution of the Yugoslav state. At the time, Greco-Turkish relations were still very strained. Turkey had played a key role in the Gulf War and had achieved a level of Western approval that threatened Greece's favored relationship with Europe and the United States. As Communism ended and Yugoslavia began dissolving into a variety of independent republics, Greece became increasingly concerned for a variety of reasons. First, Yugoslavia had been central to Greek trade, both as a trade partner and as an overland route to Western Europe. Second, and more important, Greeks were concerned that a vacuum of power in the area would open the door for Turkish involvement justified by the Muslim populations of the region, a prospect that was unappealing on a variety of fronts. Finally, the issues that arose out of the crisis were important because they clearly demarcated the Greeks from their perceived allies in the West. Two such issues were particularly important: the creation of the Former Yugoslav Republic of Macedonia and Greek support for the Orthodox Serbs.

When Slobodan Milosevic came to power in the early 1990s and began a program of ethnic cleansing in the former Yugoslav state, the Western world fell, almost unanimously, against him. The Greek state, on the other hand, continued to support Serbia in defiance of pressure from the European powers. When, in 1992, the UN declared a full embargo on Serbia, Greek exports reportedly continued to flow into Serb territory. Again in 1994, Greece voted against North Atlantic Treaty Organization (NATO) airstrikes against Serb forces, and it was the only state to support the claim that Serbian forces were responding to Bosnian aggression. These actions are significant for two reasons. First, it demonstrates again the strength of the Greek association with the Orthodox Church. Although the strong economic ties between Serbia and Greece have some explanatory power, there is little doubt that Orthodox ties were behind Greek support of the Serbs against the Croatian Catholics and Bosnian Muslims, who were likewise vigorously supported by Turkey. Second, the defiance of the overwhelming Western policy against Serbia reemphasized the uniqueness of the Greek identity. Greeks had perceived themselves as distinctly different from "Europe," especially as Greece was the only predominantly Orthodox member of NATO and the European Union (EU) until the end of the Cold War and the subsequent expansion of each of these two groups. Not only was Greece distinct from Turkey in Balkan policy, but also from the Protestant and Catholic states of Europe, who tended to support the Croatian people.

The second issue in the Balkans – one that proved more important for Greek nationalism – was the formation of the Former Yugoslav Republic of Macedonia (FYROM). As Yugoslavia was dissolving in 1991, the Macedonian Republic declared its independence, an action that, to the surprise of most non-Greeks, produced outrage in the Greek nation. To those unfamiliar with Greek history, it was difficult to understand the ire that had erupted from Greek nationalists. But, as Curtis points out:

> The use of the term Macedonia in the name of the new nation that emerged from Yugoslavia to Greece's north is objectionable to Greece because that name … is associated with the Greek empire of Alexander

the Great and the present-day northern province of Greece. ... [T]he name usage has conjured fears of irredentist expansionism into Greek territory.

Curtis (1995)

The Macedonian name held strong ties with ideas of the Greek nation. Alexander the Great's reign was associated with the term "Macedonia" and Alexander himself was Macedonian. In addition, a Macedonian movement in the ninth century had been largely successful in repelling Islamic expansion into the Byzantine Empire. All this means that the term "Macedonia" was understood by Greeks to be an important part of their heritage. In addition, the new Macedonian constitution seemed to allude to Macedonian territory in northern Greece, a claim that aroused a great deal of suspicion and insecurity in the Greek population. The Greeks responded by implementing a trade embargo on "Skopje" – a somewhat derogatory term used by the Greeks, who refused to acknowledge the Macedonian name. This approach again bewildered Western observers who could not comprehend the Greek stance.

The Balkan issues of the 1990s have had an indubitable impact on Greek nationalism. The creation of the FYROM aroused a fear of irredentist expansion into Greek territory, and the general dissolution of the Yugoslav Republic meant that Greece once again faced the prospect of general instability on its doorstep. Significantly, the Macedonian claims to parts of Greek culture renewed or emphasized a cultural interpretation of Greekness. However, although these issues have been important for Greek nationalism over the last decade or so, they must be understood in the larger context of Greco-Turkish relations. The great threat of Balkan instability was the prospect of expanded Turkish influence in the region through Islamic populations. The long antagonistic relationship between the Greeks and the Turks made this unacceptable. The bigger issue was, and continues to be, Turkish power and the related threat it presents – and that clearly fits into a pattern of religious frontiers, threats, and subsequent religious nationalism. As a result, Greek policy in the Balkans was structured by this relationship. As Close points out "The Church continued to be regarded by most people as essential to national identity; so that for example religious ties with Serbia and other Balkan states were invoked by governments in the 1990s to justify their policies towards them" (Close 2002).

Greece today

Greece today is a thoroughly Orthodox country. In terms of religious practice and religious institutions, Greece appears to be secularizing, as is the case in both Ireland and Poland. As Kourvetaris and Dobratz argue, "Owing to secularization, industrialization, urbanization, and political change the influence of the Orthodox church is declining in Greece"

(Kourvetaris and Dobratz 1987). Very few Greeks attend church on a weekly basis. In fact, attendance numbers are among the lowest in all Europe. However, a closer look reveals that the relationship between religion and nation is one of the strongest in Europe. In spite of low regular attendance figures, the number of Greek citizens who claim to belong to the Orthodox Church is incredibly high (over 97 percent), and almost all Greeks participate in religious festivals and holy days.

In addition, the linkages between Church and state remain strong. The presence of the archbishop at the inauguration ceremonies of the President in 1985 "reinforced the impressions shared by many visitors to Greece that despite increasing secularization, the presence of the Orthodox Church is real, at times even lending that small Mediterranean country a 'theocratic' aura" (Stavrou 1995: 38). Although its membership in the EU has forced Greece to make some reforms, the Orthodox Church still maintains a strong hold on policy, and non-Orthodox minorities still experience discrimination, particularly in the case of Turkish Muslims. In his discussion of minorities at risk, Ted Gurr points out that the Turkish minority in Greece is unique in all Europe in that it is has not "benefited from some public effort to come to grips with the group's differential status." He points out that "the reasons lie in the historical enmity between the Greeks and Turks and the exigencies of the Cyprus conflict, not in some special failing of Greek democracy" (Gurr 1993: 169). The minority issues in Greece are not the result of some general democratic deficiency. Rather, the historic tensions between the two populations mean that Greek-ness is still defined in terms of religion, and Muslim populations by extension are not truly Greek or welcome. Samuel Huntington points to the same minority issues: "The Albanian and Greek governments are at loggerheads over the rights of their minorities in each other's countries. Turks and Greeks are historically at each others' throats. On Cyprus, Muslim Turks and Orthodox Greeks maintain hostile adjoining states" (Huntington 1996: 225). These animosities are a result of the religiously based national identities in these regions. Although Huntington would like to claim that the animosities are a result of religion, it would be much more accurate to point out that the religious identities emerged because of historical animosities. Today they are mutually reinforcing, but the threat came before the identity.

Greek nationalism today continues to be shaped primarily by Greco-Turkish tensions. As a result, any shifts in Greek nationalism away from the Orthodox Church have been generally muted. As long as the Turkish state continues to threaten the Greek people in Cyprus, the Aegean, and on the mainland, Orthodoxy will continue to play a central role in the differentiation of the Greek people. Stavrou makes an important point in his examination of the Greek Church: "The church may be a sleeping giant, as some have suggested, but a giant institution it still is ..." (Stavrou 1995: 53).

Conclusions

Once again, the basic argument is that national identity is shaped in reaction to key forces and threats. When these threats carry the potential for national assimilation or destruction, national identity becomes particularly strong. As a result, existential threats that happen to cross religious frontiers result in strong religious nationalism. Whether or not the conflict is truly religious is unimportant. What matters is religion's ability to differentiate the nation from the threat. Greece, although deviating from the example of Ireland and Poland, fits this model well.

Greek identity, like that of Ireland and Poland, has rallied around its religious uniqueness. This is because Greece has long existed at a religious frontier with Catholicism and then Islam – from the Byzantine Empire's struggles with its Roman counterpart through the rise of Islamic invaders and into Ottoman rule. To this day, the religious frontier with Turkey continues to play a prominent role in Greek national identity. Significantly, the linkage between the Orthodox Church and the modern Greek people did not become fully developed until the War of Independence. In many ways, the linkage was a result of the war, not a cause. This can be explained by the fact that, although there was a clear religious frontier in the Ottoman Empire, the threat to the Greek people was minimized by the privileged position they held in the Ottoman administration. However, once the war began, Orthodoxy quickly became a rallying point for the Greek movement because it was the most obvious tool for differentiation between the Turkish and Greek peoples. In Poland, religion entered the realm of nationalism when the Polish state began its economic and political collapse that ultimately ended in partition. The frontier was ever present, but the threat waxed and waned – and national sentiment followed. The same was true in Greece. As the War of Independence climaxed, the threat from the Ottoman Empire waxed, as did religious sentiment.

An emphasis on the "other"

Greece, like Poland, provides a good case for examining the role of the "other" in identity formation. In Ireland, the threat was a relatively constant British "other," and the resulting Irish identity was relatively constant as well. In Poland, the importance of a variety of others ebbed and flowed – from Orthodox Russia, to Protestant Prussia and Germany, to Islamic invaders. Although Polish identity remained focused on Catholicism throughout these shifts, minor adjustments in what it meant to be Polish can be seen based on who the primary "other" is at any given time. The same is true in Greece. Although the Ottoman Empire/Turkey has been and continues to be the primary other in Greek identity, the problems created by Great Power involvement (particularly Russia) and Balkan collapse have meant that Greek-ness has been reformulated almost constantly. The creation of

Bulgaria in the nineteenth century, the movement of large Orthodox and Muslim populations after World War I, and Russian desires for control of Istanbul all led to narrower definitions of Greek-ness. The shift took Greek identity from a wide focus on all the Orthodox subjects of the Ottoman Empire to a much narrower focus on Greek Orthodoxy, Greek language, and Hellenistic culture and descent. "The non-Greek Orthodox Christians, the Latin or Western Christians and the Muslims have been the three principal 'others' for the Greeks ..." (Koliopoulos and Veremis 2002). Each has been important in shaping modern Greek identity.

It is important to reiterate that Greek Orthodoxy has remained central to Greek identity because the Islamic threat has been and continues to be the primary "other" for Greeks. As Nicholas Gage points out:

> It is not surprising that religion is so important in Greece. During the hundreds of years when the Turks ruled the country, only their church provided Greeks with a sense of unity and national identity. The music, art, literature, and oral history that survived the Turkish occupation were conserved by the churches and monasteries.
>
> Gage (1986: 96)

Ioannis Konidaris makes a similar point: "The existence of special bonds between the Orthodox Church of Greece and the State is explained by the fact that this Church helped the nation survive through 400 years of Ottoman occupation, by maintaining the faith, the language and the culture" (Konidaris 2003: 225). The Orthodox Church preserved Greek culture while under the control of the Ottoman Empire and, as such, it became a repository for Greek identity. It did so partly because of its privileged position, but more so because of its ability to differentiate the Greeks from their Turkish oppressors.

An emphasis on politics

It is also worth returning again to the issue of religion versus politics. As in the previous two cases, religion in Greece was used in an instrumentalist fashion. The ultimate divide between the Turks and Greeks was not theological or liturgical; it was instead about issues of land control, sovereignty, and equality. Even after independence, the Megali Idea – the key driving force for nearly 100 years of Greek foreign policy – was inspired by territorial ambitions. It was, however, justified with religious rhetoric. The calls for *enosis*, or unity, were driven first and foremost by political goals and aspirations.

This same trend continues today in Greece. There is no doubt that Orthodoxy is central to Greek identity and culture, perhaps even more so than in Poland or Ireland, but much of the association can be explained by culture rather than theology. For instance, Adamantia Pollis illustrates how most Greeks view Orthodoxy as crucial to Greek-ness, but with limited relevance for an individual's personal spiritual life.

> Although there are no firm data, indirect evidence seems to indicate that religiosity qua religiosity is weak. Despite the centrality of Orthodoxy as a marker of Greekness, Greeks on the whole, by contrast to practicing Catholics, are notorious for the absence of theological conformity or spirituality ... [T]he predominant Greek attitude remains one of conformity to Church rites and rituals but minimal adherence to doctrine and dogma.
>
> Pollis (2003: 163–4)

Hirschon discusses the same phenomenon in relation to Greeks living abroad:

> The continuing, even if residual, saliency of religious identity is shown clearly in the diaspora context, for example at the Easter celebrations where many non-religious Greeks attend church services and participate in the celebrations. As one explained to me, "I'm not a believer, but to be Greek is to be Orthodox. That's why I go."
>
> Hirschon (1999: 162)

In today's Greece, as in Ireland or Poland, the willingness to tolerate church involvement in politics is on the decline. David Close argues that Greeks, similar to the Irish, would like to see the Church take a more informal role in politics. The Church is viewed as having priorities that are "out of tune with social needs. The evidence, direct and indirect, is that most people wanted the clergy to act more as social workers, and take a greater interest in pressing social problems" (Close 2002: 221).

The fact that Greeks are less religious does not mean that they are less Orthodox. In other words, Greeks may view the institutional church with increasing skepticism, but they generally continue to think of themselves as Orthodox; and in terms of nationalism, it is self-identification that is critical. What does it mean to be Greek? There is little doubt that Orthodoxy is still a key part of that definition.

The importance of Orthodoxy has been a near constant in Greek history – certainly since the 1800s. This is due to the constant threat posed by the Islamic Ottoman Turks to the Greek people. Orthodoxy came center stage because of its ability to differentiate the Greeks from those who provided the most significant threat to their existence. Although Greece earned its independence nearly 200 years ago, the Turkish threat has continued to reinforce the Greek association with the Orthodox Church. Some are rather quick to dismiss the depth of this relationship. Adamantia Pollis claims that " ... Eastern Orthodoxy could have been disassociated from the state and become part of civil society were it not for the power of the church institutions in everyday life, the clergy's participation in the revolution and the defeat of the Greek troops in Asia Minor after World War I" (Pollis 2003: 157). While Pollis may be correct, her "ifs" are enormous stipulations. The argument is a bit like claiming that secularization would not have happened in Europe if the church had remained important. The fact of the matter is that reliance on Orthodoxy was unavoidable due to the contrast with Islam dating back to Byzantium. This animosity explains all of Pollis' stipulations – from a linkage between church and state to clerical participation in the War of Independence. As long as Turkey continues to be the key antagonist in Greek foreign policy, Greek-ness will continue to be defined in terms of religion.

7 The broader context

Although it would be ideal to examine all European nations and their historic relationships with religion in as much depth as the previous cases, it cannot be done in any concentrated form. Therefore, this book has examined the relationship between religion and national identity in three of the most prominent cases of religious nationalism in Europe. Because this case selection has limitations (as does any case selection), it is worth taking some time, albeit more briefly, to examine the other nations in Europe that might prove relevant to the question at hand. Although this discussion must be limited, it does allow for some context to be included. This approach allows us to examine the theory in a wider context and to see whether the proposed combination of factors fits in secular nations as well. It also isolates outliers, which can then be investigated for further clarification.

Several issues must be addressed before dealing with the cases themselves. First, the choice of cases needs clarification. Although this is an examination of nationalism, I have opted for a state-by-state analysis. This allows for a clearer demarcation of cases. In other words, the inclusion of "nations" at either the substate or the interstate level would add a significant number of cases and would lead to a great deal of debate regarding what constitutes a nation. In addition, the previous three cases have all been examined at the state level. Doing so in this chapter allows for continuity. Studying substate groups can help to illuminate the puzzle, and they will be referred to throughout this chapter (in Switzerland, Germany, Spain, etc.). A future study could also examine the power of this theory at the substate level.

Second, not all states will be included. Those states with a population of less than 100,000 (Andorra, San Marino, Monaco, Vatican City, Liechtenstein) will be excluded, because these states lack much of a nationalist movement. Also, the investigation will be limited to the traditional conception of Europe. So, Russia will be included, but Turkey will be excluded. There is no conflict of interest in this decision as Turkey does not challenge the general formula laid out in this book. The states will be examined by relevant groupings, beginning with confirming cases of religious nationalism, then proceeding to confirming cases of secular nationalism (states that lacked one or both of the causal factors of religious frontiers and threats). Finally, potential outliers and clear outliers will be examined.

Confirming cases

Other cases of religious nationalism

There are, in addition to the three examined thus far, a number of nationalist movements in Europe that qualify as religious nationalisms. Several of these are fairly obvious and straightforward: Cyprus, Malta, and the states of the former Yugoslavia. There are also a number of less obvious examples of religious nationalism, including Lithuania, Moldova, Romania, Bulgaria, the Slovak Republic, and Belarus. As diverse as these cases may be, they each fit the general pattern of a threatening religious frontier leading to religious nationalism. A brief look at each further reveals the role of threatening religious "others" in the formation of a religiously based national identity. Perhaps no case makes this linkage more clearly than the former Yugoslav states.

The former Yugoslavia

The former Yugoslavia is perhaps the most notorious example of modern religious nationalism in Europe. It fits the pattern of religious nationalism perfectly. The Balkans have, for over 1,000 years, been home to a distinct religious frontier (between the Catholic and Orthodox Churches, as well as between Christianity in general and the spread of Islam from the Middle East). There have also been threats across these religious frontiers. When conflicts have arisen between ethnic groups on the peninsula, religion has played a central role in identity formation. This is evident when one looks at the individual nationalities in the former Yugoslav state.

The Orthodox Serbs, perhaps more so than any of the other former Yugoslav nations, were threatened by their religious frontier. This is because the Serbs were controlled by a religious "other," whereas the Slovenes and Croats were ruled by Catholic Austria–Hungary and the Albanians and Bosnian Muslims were ruled by the Ottoman Turks. Similar to the other nations under Ottoman control, the Serb story was a mixed blessing of sorts. Although the Orthodox faith was allowed, the Serbs were clearly an inferior class – Serbs were conscripted into the military and church land was confiscated throughout Serbian territories. The Serbs rebelled several times, often citing religious ties to Russia or an objection to Greek control of the Orthodox Church. Serb power grew as Ottoman power waned, and although independence was achieved in the late nineteenth century, religious issues have continued to plague Serbia. The Balkan Wars of the early twentieth century saw a number of nations unite to throw off Ottoman rule, but divisions between the groups soon arose. The formation of one Yugoslav state seemed to weaken the links between nation and religion on the surface but, as was proven in the past two decades, these divides continued to play an important role. Historic divides between Catholic Croats and Orthodox Serbs (i.e., the killing of two million Serbs, Jews, and Gypsies by Croatian Ustaše during World War II) proved to be useful tools for mobilization under Slobodan Milosevic's rule. As Curtis indicates, "Ethnic hatred, religious rivalry, language barriers, and cultural conflicts plagued the Kingdom of the Serbs, Croats, and Slovenes ... from its inception ..." (Curtis 1990: 29). When Milosevic needed a tool to gain more power during the disintegration of the Yugoslav state, religion was easily accessible. The result was clear, and the religious threat from a "power-hungry" Croatia proved clear enough for a national identity shift. Even today, the issue of Kosovar nationalism provides a rallying point for Serb nationalism.

Currently, over 80 percent of the Serbian people belong to the Serbian Orthodox Church, and this figure is further inflated if the scope is narrowed to ethnic Serbs. Although few attend church regularly (only about 7 percent weekly), this pattern is consistent with other Orthodox nations. Because of its history, the Serbian nation had long been associated with religion. In fact, "the connection between religious belief and nationality posed a special threat to the postwar communist government's official policies of national unity and a federal state structure" (Curtis 1990: 107). This linkage was enhanced through events during the existence of Yugoslavia – including the atrocities of World War II. As a result, "Religious affiliation ...was closely linked with the politics of nationality; centuries-old animosities among [Yugoslavia's] three main religions ...remained a divisive factor in 1990" (Curtis 1990: 106). The rhetoric that emerged during the 1990s from the Serbian leadership clearly linked nation and religion. As Adrian Hastings points out: The Serbs ...

> portrayed the seizure of power in Kosovo and the attack on Bosnia as little less than a crusade against Muslims, the long-awaited revenge for 1389, and wherever they gained control in Bosnia they destroyed every mosque and every Muslim tombstone, while hastily building Orthodox churches to replace them.
>
> Hastings (1997: 146)

Much of the literature on the former Yugoslavia argues that religion serves a very superficial role, and that the conflict of the nineties was about other issues – specifically political ambitions. This is true; however, the tie to religion is clear. Although the fighting was not about religion *per se*, religion did provide the best tool for national mobilization. As such, Serbian nationalism has been centered quite obviously on Orthodoxy, and it fits the pattern of religious mobilization against threatening "others" perfectly.

Like the Serbian case, the Croatian case is fairly straightforward. Originally, the area that is now Croatia was at the very center of the Catholic–Orthodox divide. Later, as the Byzantine Empire collapsed, the

Croatians were originally overrun by the Ottoman Empire and subsequently taken under the crown of Austria–Hungary (a Catholic state). Although the Austrians were also Catholic, Croatia was a part of the Military Frontier Province, and the presence of the Islamic Ottoman Empire was very obvious. The threat from this religious frontier has been clear throughout Croatian history. Most significantly, the threat from the Ottoman Empire shaped national identity in Croatia. The threat, which emerged in the sixteenth century after the Christian defeat at the Battle of Mohács, led to the declaration in 1609 that the Catholic faith was the only legal faith in Croatia. The religious threat waned in the eighteenth century and, by the 1800s, language reentered the national debate, as it provided a better means of differentiating the Croats from the Hungarian rulers than religion. As Hastings indicates, "Indeed, as hostility to Hungary grew in the nineteenth century, the Catholic Church could be seen at times in almost hostile terms" (Hastings 1997: 137). However, by 1868, Croatia gained some level of political autonomy from Hungary, and soon after national identity once again focused on religion – this time in response to growing Serbian minorities. The advent of World War I meant that Austrian-ruled Croats fought against the Russian-aligned Serbs, further exacerbating ethnic animosities. Although the two peoples were integrated into one Yugoslav state, the ethnic tensions continued over perceived Serb dominance in the country. In addition, the Nazi use of the Croatian Ustaše to destroy Serbian and Jewish populations increased tensions. These tensions would prevail until they exploded in ethnic conflict in the 1990s, conflict that clearly presented a threat to the Croatian nation, as was made clear by Serb rhetoric at the time.

Although religious statistics are difficult to find because of the secular emphasis of Communist rule and subsequent social turmoil over the past decade, it is still easy to recognize the religious nature of Croatian nationalism. It is important to note that the issues involved in the conflict were not religious in nature – rather, they were political goals veiled in religious rhetoric. However, the national sentiment was clearly tied to religion in the various nation groups of the former Yugoslavia. The conflict was fought along religious lines, and religion became the key differentiator between groups so that "Bosnian Muslims," "Orthodox Serbs," and "Catholic Croats" became the common phrases used to describe the participants. Regardless of issues of church attendance or political religion (both of which are difficult to assess in a period of civil war), religion was and continues to be an obvious factor in national identity in Croatia.

Bosnia also lies at the historic fissure between Orthodoxy, Catholicism, and Islam. However, the fact that Bosnia was both predominantly Muslim and a part of the Ottoman Empire for centuries meant that the religious frontier was not threatening in any significant way. In fact, Bosnian identity was based on a geographical conception, as opposed to the neighboring Serb and Croat nations which had distinct ethnic and religious linkages. It was not until the nineteenth century that Bosnian national identity began to emerge with a religious element. This was due to two main features: (1) the growth of Serb and Croat nationalism and (2) the subjugation of Bosnia to Habsburg rule (Hastings 1997: 139). As Pedro Ramet indicates, the Bosnian "position within the Ottoman Empire had been a privileged one and it was only with the imposition of rule by Catholic Austria that collective identity was stimulated by cultural threat" (Ramet 1984: 156). This threat continued to develop throughout the World Wars and into the Yugoslav era. Most significant is the threat that has been abundantly clear in the past two decades. The growth of Serb nationalism clearly targeted Bosnian Muslims and led to the declaration of Bosnian independence. The transition was far from peaceful, and the nature of Serb rhetoric meant that Bosnia and Islam became linked together in the minds of the world and in the minds of Bosnians.

Ultimately, Bosnia and Herzegovina was established as a federal state with a division between Serb-dominated areas and Bosnian-dominated areas. Each of these groups continues to emphasize religious ties in their push for autonomy and power. There is no doubt that Bosnia and Herzegovina is a religiously heterogeneous state. Approximately 40 percent of its citizens are Islamic, 30 percent are Orthodox, and 15 percent are Catholic. However, much of this heterogeneity can be explained by the multinational nature of the state. Bosnia contains a large percentage of ethnic Serbs, which accounts for the high percentage of Orthodox citizens. If one considers simply the Bosnian nation, the Islamic percentage increases. Like the other former Yugoslav states, the importance of religion within Bosnia is clear. It is important to point out that religion may not necessarily serve religious purposes, but it is undoubtedly important for purposes of self- and national identification. The wars in the Balkans have portrayed religion as an important element and, in elections since the Dayton Accords, there has been a clear division between Serb nationalists and Bosnian nationalists, each emphasizing religion as one key national identifier. Bosnia clearly meets the dual criteria of religious identity and political religion.

Religious frontiers have played a much more minor role in Slovenia than in the other former Yugoslav states. The Slovenes were converted to Catholicism in the tenth century and fell under the dominion of the Habsburg Empire in the thirteenth century. Therefore, as Slovene identity began to strengthen in the nineteenth century, it did so in response to Hungarian and Austrian identity. The presence of the Ottoman Turks was always apparent and often disrupted Slovenian life. As a result, the religious dimension never fully subsided. Once Slovenia was integrated into the Yugoslav state, the Serbian efforts at dominance created tension within the Slovenian community as it did in the Croat community. Ultimately, this tension proved less severe than the Serb–Croat tension. Although there is no current religious frontier for Slovenia, the frontier created by a Serb-dominated Yugoslavia in the latter part of the twentieth century did lead to Catholic ties to Slovenian nationalism. Therefore, nationalism in Slovenia is partially linked to religion and partially secularized. In terms of demographics, the Slovenian people are largely Catholic – over 71 percent in the 1990 census. Interestingly, in the subsequent decade, the rate of self-identification dropped drastically to slightly over 57 percent (Slovenia 2002). It is no coincidence that the significantly higher figure occurred during a time of national struggle for independence from a religiously differentiated group, the Orthodox Serbs. This shift to secularism has continued, but it has been accompanied by a continued emphasis on religious identity in society. In addition, there is a formal separation of religion and state, and this is reflected in policies such as abortion (Slovenia allows abortion in most cases). Religion played an important part in Slovenian nationalism for a relatively brief period of time. However, as time passes, Slovenia will likely continue its return to secular notions of nationality.

Finally, the Macedonians also provide an interesting example of religious nationalism. Although the Macedonians have a long history of subjugation, it was not until Ottoman rule that the subjugation took place along a religious dimension. Subsequent history led to the development of tensions between the Macedonians and their Greek Orthodox superiors in the Ottoman kingdom. When Bulgaria gained independence in the late nineteenth century, the resulting feud over Macedonian territory led to the Balkan Wars. Tensions erupted again in the 1990s over the new Macedonian state, inflaming rhetoric throughout the Balkans. Therefore, in addition to the obvious religious frontier with Islamic Albania, there is also a significant national/religious frontier with Greece. Approximately one-third of Macedonian citizens are Muslim, so Macedonia is dissected by the religious frontier.

The contested nature of the Macedonian state since the early nineties has meant that the Macedonian situation has remained tenuous. The various disputes over who has the historic claim to the Macedonian name (Greeks due to linkages with Alexander the Great, etc.; Bulgarians because of the historic and ethnic links; Serbia because of Yugoslavia, etc.) have made the insecurity of Macedonia clear. The Greek intransigence over the issue surprised many who were not familiar with the situation. In addition, attacks have occurred across the Albanian border. Add to this the fact that there has been unrest among the Islamic Albanian minorities in the state, and it is apparent that these religious frontiers are threatening.

As a result, Macedonia is a mixed case of religious nationalism. Because of the dual nature of national threats (Greece, Serbia, etc. represent ethnic as well as religious divides), national identity incorporates the importance of the Macedonian Orthodox Church. This is particularly evident in matters involving Albania and the divide between Orthodoxy and Islam. The ethnic divides that exist between Macedonia and their Greek and Serbian neighbors tend to moderate the influence of religion. In many ways, cultural and ethnic distinctions are more useful in national differentiation. There have been shifts in recent years away from strongly nationalistic and religious rhetoric. The 2002 parliamentary elections saw a disappointing result for the pro-nationalist VMRO-DPMNE, winning only thirty-three of the Sobranje's 120 seats (C.I.A. 2004). In addition, the constitution was recently amended so that the Orthodox Church is no longer the only church mentioned. The threat to Macedonian nationhood comes from a very complex mix of religious, ethnic, cultural, and historic frontiers. As a result, Macedonian nationalism has adopted a similarly complex nature.

Cyprus

Cyprus presents a unique situation among the European cases. Specifically, there is a very predominant religious frontier that cuts Cyprus in half. This division has weakened religious ties to Cypriot nationalism, but it has created very strong substate national identities based largely on religion. Cyprus can be better classified as a bi-national state (Greek and Turkish Cypriots). The presence of a religious frontier has been significant throughout the history of Cyprus, as Cyprus has been under the control of Ottoman Muslims, Venetian Catholics, British Protestants, and several other groups. Throughout this period, (Greek) Cypriots have relied on their religion and culture in their strivings for *enosis* with Greece.

This religious frontier is significant largely because it separates ethnic Greeks from ethnic Turks, two groups that have a significant history of threat and conflict (Solsten 1993). The Green Line – the divide between the Orthodox Greek Cypriots and the Muslim Turkish Cypriots – is a constant reminder of this violent history. There is little doubt that the main concern of Greek Cypriots is the Turkish presence, and the main concern of Turkish citizens is the threat of Orthodox dominance. Both communities rally around their religious identities. The result is that both Greek and Turkish Cypriot nationalism are heavily influenced by religion. Greek Cypriots are sometimes referred to interchangeably as Orthodox Cypriots. As is the case in Greece, the Orthodox Cypriots are strongly religious – over 80 percent consider themselves religious, although less than 5 percent attend church weekly. In addition, when asked about belief in God, only Poland had a higher percentage of positive respondents. Religious festivals are a key part of national culture, and to be a member of the nation one must be a member of the religious group (both Greek and Turkish). When turning to religion's role in politics, the link is clear. The first President of independent Cyprus was a former monk. In addition, legislation parallels church beliefs – for instance, abortion is not allowed on demand. The Cypriot case is one of the clearer examples of religious nationalism in Europe. Although the state is divided into two "nations," each clearly demonstrates a pattern of religious frontiers and threats resulting in religious nationalism.

Malta

Similarly, Malta demonstrates the role of historic animosities and threats in shaping modern identity. Although there is no current religious frontier

(Malta is an island nation), Malta has been subject to the control of several religious others throughout its history, most significantly the Arabs and most recently the British. Much of the religious heritage of Malta can be traced back to the Order of the Knights of the Hospital of St. John of Jerusalem. The Knights of Malta, as they became known, were given control of the island in 1530 as a reward for their service in the Crusades. The islands have been strongly Catholic ever since, and attacks by the Turks and domination by the British have reinforced this identity over time.

The result is a clear link between Catholicism and Maltese identity. The population of Malta is almost entirely Roman Catholic (98 percent), and Catholicism is central to national self-perception. As Godfrey Baldacchino states:

> The Catholic Church and its ethos and ceremonies remain today the closest to a national Maltese symbol. In spite of evident secularisation, around 70 per cent of the population attend weekly mass regularly; a third of all young Maltese complete their schooling in church schools; and most young Maltese have to attend long hours of "doctrine" to qualify for the sacrament of confirmation. There is one church or chapel for every square kilometre on the small archipelago, and many remain in use.
>
> Baldacchino (2002)

Religion also plays an important role in politics. Abortion is completely banned (only Ireland has laws as strict), the church plays a crucial role in education, and religion is formally established via the constitution. Although religious freedom is technically granted, the Maltese constitution states that:

(1) The religion of Malta is the Roman Catholic Apostolic Religion.
(2) The authorities of the Roman Catholic Apostolic Church have the duty and the right to teach which principles are right and which are wrong.
(3) Religious teaching of the Roman Catholic Apostolic Faith shall be provided in all State schools as part of compulsory education.

There is little doubt that religion is a vital part of Maltese nationalism. British control has meant that language is less useful for national identity, and Catholicism easily filled the gap.

Lithuania

In many ways, the Lithuanian case parallels that of Poland. Both represent largely Catholic states at the frontier with Orthodox Russia. Lithuania, even more so than Poland, is and was threatened by Russian dominance. Unlike the other Baltic States, Lithuania's religion was not imposed upon it by outsiders, but was a key focus of Lithuania's golden age. Catholicism was adopted in the thirteenth century by King Jagiello when the Polish–Lithuanian commonwealth was formed. It was this association that led to the most prosperous and powerful era in Lithuanian history. The subsequent partition of Poland left Lithuania under Russian control and, due to Russian attempts at assimilation, the Lithuanians fell back on their Catholic identity in an effort at differentiation. This religious focus of national identity flourished until the end of World War I, when Lithuania achieved independence. During the interwar period, clashes broke out between the Poles and the Lithuanians over territorial concerns, and there was a remarkable push towards anti-clericalism, but the subsequent return to Russian control after World War II encouraged a shift back to religious identities. As Kolsto indicates:

> Now Lithuanian nationalists were confronted not by Polish cultural domination but by Soviet Communism. The Moscow Communists were atheists and were also in the popular understanding associated with the Orthodox Russian nation. All at once, then, the Catholic faith became a rallying point of Lithuanian national consolidation. Under perestroyka, the re-opening of the Vilnius cathedral was seen not only as an important religious event but also as a milestone in the struggle for the re-establishment of Lithuanian national independence.
>
> Kolsto (2000)

Lithuania follows the pattern of religious nationalism perfectly. Today, Lithuania is a predominantly Catholic state with over 80 percent of the population belonging to the Roman Catholic Church. A mere 9 percent claim no religious affiliation, a remarkably low number for a former Communist state. When examining only ethnic Lithuanians, the percentage of Catholics grows even larger. As a whole, the Lithuanian nation considers Catholicism as a key part of national identity. As Iwaskiw states:

> The Roman Catholic Church is the oldest continuously surviving Lithuanian institution. As such, it has played a dominant role in the development of Lithuanian society, especially crucial during those long stretches of time when Lithuanians had no state of their own.
>
> Iwaskiw (1995)

As a result, religion is strongly associated with Lithuanian-ness. " ...The Catholic religion in many respects is associated with the Lithuanian nation, and an attack on religion is an attack on national existence" (Remeikis 1972). John Coakley states that "It could be argued that being Irish, Polish or Lithuanian implies being Catholic ..." (Coakley 2002: 218). He continues:

> Can one be a Protestant Pole, a Protestant Lithuanian, an Orthodox Estonian or a Muslim Bulgarian provided one's mother tongue is that of the majority? Not, apparently, in all cases. Thus we find a tendency, at least in the past, for Protestants in Polish Masuria to identify as

"Masurs" or even as Prussians or Germans rather than Poles (Blanke 1999); for Protestants in Lithuanian Klaipeda to identify as "Memellanders" rather than Lithuanians (Misiunas 1968);

Coakley (2002: 218)

This religious identity translates into the political realm less clearly than in Poland, Ireland, or Greece. Specifically, there is no state religion, abortion is allowed on demand, and the church plays a more minor role in formal politics. However, there is a strong link between Lithuanian identity and religion, explained by the historic presence of the Russian/Soviet threat.

Other post-Communist states (Romania, Bulgaria, Belarus, Slovak Republic)

In a number of other post-Communist countries, the importance of religion as a national identifier is reemerging. Many of these states have seen a resurgence of religious practice as well as an increase in the role of religion in government in the 1990s and beyond. However, the links between national identity and religion tend to be weaker than in the more prominent examples of religiously nationalistic states, such as those discussed in previous chapters. This is sometimes because these states are still in transition. In other cases, the religious threats are simply not as drastic.

In Romania, the various regions of the state were not unified until the twentieth century. Until that point, Romania had been divided between a number of foreign conquerors. Transylvania had been subject to Catholic Habsburg rule, which included repression of cultural and religious expression, and the regions of Walachia and Moldavia had been ruled by the Ottoman Empire under similar circumstances. This domination by Austria, Hungary, and the Ottoman Empire led to the unification of national identity and religion: "The importance of religion and the Orthodox church for the maintenance of national consciousness in Moldavia and Wallachia was matched by a similar function in Transylvania, which was under Habsburg rule for centuries" (Gilberg 1984: 170). In addition: "It seems clear that religion in general, and in particular Orthodoxy, represented a vital element of national defense for the Romanians in Moldavia and Wallachia, and also Transylvania, in the face of severe repression suffered in all three provinces by the Romanian peasant masses" (Gilberg 1984: 171). The threats from Romania's neighbors continued into the twentieth century, at which point Romania was " ... sandwiched militantly between Russia itself and pro-Russian Bulgaria" (Martin 1978: 105). After World War II, Romania "faced Hungarian, Soviet, and Bulgarian demands for restoration of territories lost under the treaties ... " (Bachman 1989: 36).

The result was an ongoing insecurity regarding the Romanian nation and a religiously based nationalism. Approximately 87 percent of the population is Orthodox, and the number increases when ethnic minorities (i.e.,

Hungarians) are excluded. In addition, 94 percent claim to believe in God and 42 percent claim that religion is very important – both remarkably high for a former Communist country (ISSP 1998). Although church and state are officially separated, the government does have extensive power over the Romanian Orthodox Church. In addition, the treatment of religious minorities reflects the ongoing view that Orthodoxy is an important part of Romanian identity. Although the linkage between religion and nation may be weaker in Romania than in other countries (Greece, Poland, Ireland), there is little doubt that the Romanian Orthodox Church factors into national identity.

Bulgaria, another Orthodox state, had a similar experience to that of Greece. Like Greece, it was subject to Ottoman rule for centuries. The Bulgarians were allowed to practice their religion and benefited reasonably from Ottoman rule, but their position within the Empire was not as prominent as that of the Greeks. There was a clear threat to the Bulgarian nation from Islam, and the Bulgarians responded with a strong religious identity in much the same way that the Greeks did. This antagonism against the Turks is still prominent today, although recent developments have led to something of a détente. The Bulgarians have received a great deal of support from the Russians throughout their history, a fact that would have important consequences during the Soviet era. In fact, Russian support of the Bulgarian nationalist movement led to strong ties (culturally and politically) between the two states. As a result, when the Soviets occupied Bulgaria during World War II, they were hailed as liberators – a stark contrast to the greeting received in Poland. The amicable relationship between Bulgaria and the Soviets can be explained by the religious links (Orthodoxy) and the historic ties between the states. Therefore, Soviet power was not viewed as threatening to the Bulgarian nation, but supportive. This meant that Bulgarian identity was not formed in opposition to the Soviets (as in Poland), but rather in opposition to Turkey and the surrounding Balkan states (as in Greece).

As a result, the Church was repressed during the Soviet era, but not to the extent that it was in other Communist states. In addition, the security provided by the Soviet alliance seriously diminished the Turkish threat to the Bulgarian nation. This did not drastically alter the fact that Orthodoxy is a key element of Bulgarian identity. Even under Communism, "civil baptism" remained an important Bulgarian rite (Curtis 1992: 88). With the end of religious suppression, there has been a boom in Orthodox identity and practice. Although Bulgaria is not at the level of Poland, it is important to point out that the Orthodox/Catholic difference may play a key role. Also, in terms of post-Communist states, Bulgaria is one of the most active in the religious realm. Only a few years after the end of Communism, three-quarters of the population claimed to belong to the Orthodox Church, and over half claimed to be religious – only Poland has higher rates among the post-Communist states. This linkage also translates into political action –

religious tolerance is official state policy, but the constitution declares Orthodoxy to be the "traditional religion" and Islam maintains an inferior status owing to its link with Ottoman oppression. Although this political clout is not as evident in social laws (i.e., abortion), it should be noted that Orthodox views on abortion differ significantly from those of the Catholic Church. It is fair to argue that Bulgaria is, in fact, a religious nation. As Petya Nitzova points out:

> The concept of the modem Bulgarian nation which crystallized in the nineteenth century was defined along linguistic as well as religious lines. According to it, to be Bulgarian is to speak Bulgarian and to belong in faith to the Bulgarian Orthodox church.
>
> Nitzova (1997)

The Belarusian case is less clear cut than either Romania or Bulgaria. Throughout Belarusian history, conflict between religions has played a central role. The Belarusians were initially introduced to Christianity via the Orthodox Church. They were integrated into the Polish kingdom from the fourteenth through the eighteenth century, a union that was marked by the conversion of the Lithuanian king to Catholicism, which in turn led the nobility to convert as well. The peasantry maintained its tie to Orthodoxy. Ultimately, the Uniate Church was created, which recognized Rome as its head, but still maintained traditional Orthodox liturgy and practices. By the eighteenth century, over two-thirds of the Belarusian people were members. The partition of the Polish–Lithuanian state by Russia, Prussia, and Austria in the late 1700s meant that Belarus was almost entirely integrated into the Russian Empire. Russian rule was very harsh. Orthodoxy was forced on the people, the Belarusian language was banned, and the term Belarus itself was outlawed. This harsh treatment led to a rise in nationalist sentiment directed at reunification with Poland, which had been less brutal in its administration.

Later, under Soviet rule, the Belarusian people were divided between the Belarusian SSR, Poland, and direct Soviet rule. The Polish state proved to be repressive, going so far as to confine Belarusians to concentration camps in the 1930s. The Soviets were hostile to religion in general. Today, Belarus finds itself still sandwiched between two powerful neighbors – Catholic Poland and Orthodox Russia. As a result, Belarus is attempting to maintain a delicate balance between separation from Russian influence and integration with the regional power. Therefore, Belarusian nationalism is still fairly difficult to categorize. The movement itself has a long history, but the end of Soviet domination has led to resurgence in the past fifteen years that is still playing out. Belarusian nationalism to this point has been largely based on linguistic elements. This is because the Belarusian language was useful in differentiation from both Poles and Russians. The fact that Russia is also predominantly Orthodox likely factored into the focus on language over religion. It is worth noting, however, that a Belarusian Exarchate has been established, which lends some religious uniqueness to the Belarusian people. There has been a strong movement to associate the Orthodox Church with the Belarusian people in the past five years. In 2002, a law was passed that ended religious freedom and granted special privileges to the Orthodox Church. President Lukashenko addressed the issue by saying that "The State has always stayed and will stay beside the church, which brings good to the people." This religious rhetoric is manifested as a conflict over power between Polish-influenced nationalists and Russian-influenced nationalists.

In terms of nationalism itself, the majority of Belarusians still identify with the Orthodox Church (between 60 and 80 percent, depending on the source). They are, however, largely apathetic in the religious realm. This identity has started to grow stronger as new laws have restricted religious practice and religious minorities have been increasingly persecuted. This can be explained to some extent by the unique religious identity of Belarus (Catholic/Orthodox) and the prominence of its political neighbors.

The Slovak republic, like Belarus, provides an interesting case of religious nationalism. Unlike the previous three cases, the Slovak Republic is predominantly Catholic. The only traditional religious frontier that it has is with Ukraine, which is largely Orthodox. Slovakia's remaining neighbors are all primarily Catholic – Poland, the Czech Republic, Hungary, and Austria. The unique nature of Czech identity has meant that the Slovak/Czech divide has played the role of a pseudo-religious frontier. When the two states were unified in the early part of the twentieth century, the Czechs dominated the new Czechoslovakia. At the time, these Czech leaders emphasized the rhetoric of the Czech Hussite tradition. As a result:

> The third source of national awareness [in addition to economic and political under-representation] was religion: Slovaks distrusted the Hussite and atheist traditions of the Czechs. So when the Slovak People's Party was founded in 1913 it was led by a priest Hlinka and it expressed religious and status and economic devaluations. It declared itself "For God and People" ...
>
> Martin (1978: 146)

Alan Scarfe makes a similar point: " ... in Slovakia Catholicism dominated the social life of the people to the extent that when, in 1918, the leadership of the new Republic of Czechoslovakia identified its national ideology with the Hussite rebellion of the fifteenth century ..., Slovakia was estranged" (Scarfe 1984: 34). Whereas Slovak identity had formed in opposition to Hungarian domination, the new unification of Czechoslovakia turned national focus towards the Czechs, and the secular/Protestant heritage of their sister nation led to a new emphasis on the Catholic nature of Slovak identity. In this way, the Slovak case parallels the Polish resistance to secular Russia, although the extent of association between religion and nation was more limited in Slovakia.

The result can be seen in the fact that the Slovak Republic is largely religious – nearly 70 percent claim to belong to the Catholic Church. Interestingly, the number of people who claimed a religious affiliation increased from 1991 to 2001 – from 73 percent to 84 percent (U.S. Dept of State 2003). Catholicism does play an important part in society, and this relationship transfers into the political arena to some extent. Specifically, there has been a heated debate regarding abortion in recent years. In fact, there were attempts to pass a Constitutional Amendment that would drastically curtail the availability of abortions. The bill was vetoed by the president, but the amount of popular support is indicative of the role that Catholicism plays in the state.

Slovakia provides an interesting example of the give and take of religious nationalism. Unlike many of the nations in this study, the importance of a religious frontier in the Slovak case is relatively new. Most of its history was spent focusing on the other dominant Catholic states in its region (Germany, Austria, Hungary). It was only in the twentieth century that the Czech border became truly significant for Slovak nationalism. Even then, the frontier was not a true religious frontier. Although there were religious divides, the Czechs are also predominantly Catholic. As such, the frontier focused on historic heritage (Jan Hus and later atheism) more than on current religious realities. It is important to note that, during the Communist era, the Slovaks had been targeted by the Soviets and Czechs for their sustained religiosity. All of this combined (brief significance of the frontier, emphasis on historic rather than current religiosity, economic and political threat as opposed to existential) means that Slovak nationalism does in fact emphasize the importance of the Catholic Church. As Alan Scarfe indicates, "The symbiosis of nation and church is also well advanced in ... Slovakia" (Scarfe 1984: 35). However, the importance of religion is more minor than in Poland or Ireland where the frontier is clear and so is the threat.

Secular nationalisms (absence of a religious frontier)

Europe provides abundant cases of secular nationalism as well. For instance, a significant number of countries simply do not exist at a religious frontier. They turn to other factors (i.e., language and culture) that are better able to differentiate them from their neighbors, focusing on those "others" that are most threatening. Austria, the Czech Republic, Denmark, France, Norway, Iceland, Luxembourg, and Sweden all fall into this category.

The epitome of secular nationalism (France)

France is often seen as the ultimate example of the culmination of secularization in Europe. It provides a model for many political scientists looking to understand the process of secularization, rationalization, and modernization. However, France is truly an exception, rather than the norm. In terms of our current model, France has no major modern religious frontiers. Because Germany and Switzerland are divided countries, neither places much emphasis on religion in their national identity. The fact that both are internally divided weakens the power of religion in the interstate relationship. In other words, a Franco-German conflict would be difficult to frame in religious terms.

Throughout history, there have been numerous significant religious frontiers for France – with the English (internationally) and with Calvinists (domestically and in Switzerland). As a result, in the earlier stages of the formation of French identity, both the English and the Huguenots proved threatening and pushed France towards a Catholic self-conception. Therefore, "Until the Revolution of 1789 ..., 'Frenchness' was defined so thoroughly in terms of Catholicism that France was considered 'the eldest daughter of the Church'" (Safran 2003: 1). However, the French Revolution proved to be the most significant turning point in the relationship between religion and nation in France. During the Revolution, the Church was so strongly allied with the monarchy that an overthrow of the political order necessitated an overthrow of the social and religious order as well. As Steve Bruce points out:

> [The French Revolution] saw the Church ally itself with the old regime and the social elite against the forces of social reform. For the many who espoused the Revolution, the Church was discredited by its anti-revolutionary stance, and these countries have since the late eighteenth century been largely divided between believers – often the more rural people – and secularists, who often concentrated in the more urbanized and industrialized areas.
>
> Bruce (1996b: 59)

This meant that the most significant threat to the French nation was the monarchy itself, and the monarchy derived its power from the Church. The Church, therefore, was not useful in defining the nation. Rather, it had to be done away with for the sake of French-ness.

> The French Revolution, unlike the American, had seemed a mortal foe to the faith. At the height of the Jacobin terror, an effort was made to dechristianize the nation. The Christian year was abolished on October 5, 1793; time was no longer measured from the birth of Christ, but from the declaration of the French Republic, so that 1793 became Year One. Sundays and saints' days disappeared; the poet Fabre d'Églantine, who renamed the months, said proudly that the new calendar no longer commemorated "some skeletons found in the catacombs of Rome." Christian festivals and holidays were to be replaced by five days dedicated to virtue, genius, labor, opinion, and rewards.
>
> Moynahan (2002: 593)

There are other significant points in the relationship between Church and nation in France, but none had an impact as severe as the French Revolution. The Church itself became the key threat to the French nation and was severed from the national concept.

As a result, the French nation has made a concerted effort to separate itself from the Catholic Church. This relationship is revealed in statistics of religiosity: only 29 percent of the French population claims to be religious, as opposed to over 80 percent in Poland and Cyprus and more than 70 percent in Ireland. The French figure is also markedly lower than the European average of 49 percent. In addition, a mere 12 percent of the population claims to attend church weekly; this, too, is below the European average. When asked about their religious principles in a recent poll, 45 percent of French respondents claimed that they held no such religious principles. Only 6 percent of the Irish and less than 9 percent of the Polish responded similarly.

Statistics regarding the clergy are equally drastic: "France in 1948 had almost 43,000 Roman Catholic clergy; by 1987 this had declined to 28,000. Since 1975 there have been fewer than 100 ordinations a year" (Bruce 1996b: 31). But perhaps even more telling than the statistics on Church attendance are the following statistics on cultural identification:

> A poll taken several years ago revealed that for 63 percent of the respondents, French national identity was symbolized by French cuisine; for 62 percent, by human rights; for 42 percent, by the French woman; for 34 percent, by church steeples; and for 22 percent, by betting on horse races.
>
> Safran (1998: 65)

As opposed to the Polish, Irish and Greek cases, French citizens identify with French women and cuisine at starkly higher rates than religion, which is more comparable to horse racing. Clearly, France is a secular state.

When turning to the issue of political religion, it is difficult to find a European state that is more aggressive in its pursuit of secular governance. Separation of Church and state is a mainstay of French society, as is currently being demonstrated by the feud over the rights of Islamic minorities to wear traditional head scarves in French schools, a practice that the government has made clear is unacceptable. As William Safran indicates:

> On the one hand, France is officially committed to laïcité (secularity); on the other hand, it is committed to religious pluralism. The former is reflected in the continuing de-Christianization of French society, the latter in the fact that France has become a multiethnic and multi-religious mosaic.
>
> Safran (2003: 8)

In either case, the differences between the French approach and that of religious nationalistic states are evident.

As in a number of other European states, the role of growing Muslim minorities may well reshape nationalism in France. The recent political scuffles over the *hidjab* show that a Catholic identity still lurks below the surface. Although it is true that much of the reaction to Muslim minorities can be labeled "secularism," it is also true that the national holidays in France all fall on traditional Catholic dates, and the national heroes still often relate to France's Catholic heritage. An increasing Muslim threat may bring a Catholic identity to the forefront.

Austria

A religious frontier has also been largely absent in Austria's history. All Austria's neighbors are primarily Catholic (Czech Republic, Slovakia, Hungary, Slovenia, Italy) with the exception of Switzerland and Germany, both of which are divided between Catholicism and Protestantism. Significantly, southern Germany is strongly Catholic, meaning that the actual religious frontier extends deeper into German territory. In addition, for much of its history, Austria (as the Habsburg Empire) played the role of dominant (or threatening) power. The Habsburg Empire, at its peak, extended across much of Europe. The one significant religious threat that did emerge came from the expansionist Ottoman Empire in the sixteenth century. The Habsburg leaders recognized this threat and arranged an extended peace that diminished any peril from Islam. Later wars (fought with the support of other European states) pushed the Ottomans out of Hungary and weakened the Turkish threat further. During World War I, the Austro-Hungarian Empire faced significant threats from Russia in the Balkans, but these were relieved when Russia withdrew from the conflict. In current politics, the only true religious frontiers are with Switzerland (a neutral state) and Germany, with which the Austrian people have long maintained a close identification, based primarily on linguistic ties. In addition, Austria has made a concerted effort to remain neutral in European politics since the end of World War II. Although there are minor religious frontiers in the Austrian case, none has been truly threatening, at least not in the past century.

As a result, Austria, like many predominantly Catholic states, features an interesting mixed relationship between religion and nationalism. Over half of Austrians (63 percent) claim to be religious, although less than 20 percent actually attend church weekly. These figures are close to the European average. In addition,

> The form of nominal Roman Catholicism many Austrians practice is called "baptismal certificate Catholicism." In other words, most Roman Catholics observe traditional religious holidays, such as Christmas and

Easter, and rely on the church to celebrate rites of passage, such as baptisms, confirmations, weddings, and funerals, but do not participate actively in parish life or follow the teachings of the Roman Catholic Church on central issues.

Solsten and McClave (1993: 103)

In terms of political religion, the secular nature of Austrian politics is evident. Although there is a history of linkages between the Austrian state and the Catholic Church during the Habsburg era, religious freedom was official policy beginning with the 1867 constitution. Religion today is officially separated from government, and policy reflects its independence from church influence, specifically on issues such as abortion. Therefore, although a large percentage of Austrians still consider themselves religious, the role of the church in national politics is limited. Instead, nationalism in Austria is largely based on heritage and language, as opposed to religion.

Imposed religion, part 1 (Czech Republic)

The Czech Republic, like Austria, has no true modern religious frontier. Poland, Slovakia, and Austria are all primarily Catholic states, and Germany to the west is a divided country. Again, the religious division goes deeper into the German state. This has not always been the case in Czech history. The Czechs were converted to Catholicism in 950 by the Holy Roman Empire. It was not until the Reformation that a true religious frontier emerged in Czech politics. When it did emerge, it did so under the leadership of Jan Hus, a pre-Reformation political reformer. During the Reformation, much of the Czech population converted to Hussitism, but the Holy Roman Empire reacted quickly and powerfully, destroying the movement and exiling all non-Catholic clergy. The result was a nation that was largely Catholic, but also associated Catholicism with oppression and foreign menace.

The nation was born in the proto-Protestant Hussite movement and persistently in Czech history the baneful influence of Germans and of the Catholic Church were linked together ... Hence the success of the Counter-Reformation, though finally assured by the Battle of White Mountain in 1620, rested uneasily on a base which gave it little support. Since Protestantism was largely eliminated by the Counter-Reformation the national feeling found it difficult to root itself in loyalty to religion whether Catholic or Protestant. Catholicism was disqualified by its associations; Protestantism was largely destroyed.

Martin (1978: 103)

Therefore, when Soviet-influenced Communism entered the arena, the Czech nation was already largely secular and the secular aspects of the Communist ideology were much less threatening than in Poland. Therefore, Communism did not represent a religious frontier/threat in the Czech case.

The result is a secular form of nationalism. In terms of religious identification, less than 26 percent of the Czech population consider themselves religious, even lower than in France and among the lowest in Europe (ISSP 1998). In addition, only 8 percent of the population attends church weekly, and nearly half of the population (45 percent) does not belong to any church, regardless of denomination. This very secular approach to nationalism is also reflected in the political realm. Unlike many other states in Europe, the Czech state guarantees freedom of religion in the constitution, and "all religious groups officially registered with the Ministry of Culture are eligible to receive subsidies from the State ... " (U.S. Dept of State 2003). This is in sharp contrast to Ireland, Poland, or Greece.

Essentially, the trauma of the Counter-Reformation tore the Czechs from their religious heritage. Because the Protestant Church had been forcibly separated from Czech nationalism and the Catholic Church had been associated with a foreign power, secularism became a logical choice for the nation. In the end, this meant that the anti-religious sentiments of the Communist regime were much more easily swallowed in Czechoslovakia than in Poland. In fact, the Slovak people, who had traditionally maintained a closer relationship with the Church, had a more difficult time than their Czech brethren. When the religious frontier faded (as a result of the Counter-Reformation), the other constitutive elements of nationalism that had previously stood alongside religion filled the void. As a result, Czech nationalism became centered on language, culture, and ethnicity. Meanwhile, religion was subjugated to an awkward position – the Czech people were no longer Protestant, but Protestantism remained part of their national heritage. This relationship holds true today.

The Scandinavian states

Most of the Scandinavian countries also feature no true religious frontiers, as they are surrounded by similarly Lutheran states. The one exception is Finland (discussed later). As a result, this region has recently been free from religious threats. There are exceptions, but most of these date back hundreds of years – most notably during the Thirty Years' War. More recently, the most significant "others" for each of these counties have primarily been the other Scandinavian states and Germany, each of which is also Lutheran. The result is clearly secular nationalism. Despite the establishment of state churches, religion plays only a minor role in governance. In fact, Sweden disestablished its church in 2000. In addition, religious practice has fallen to remarkably low levels – only 3–4 percent attend weekly in Denmark, less than 15 percent actually attend services regularly in Norway and, in Sweden, less than 10 percent attend church monthly (ISSP 1998).

As a result, language and culture have played more prominent roles in Scandinavian identities. In Norway, for instance, nationalism was primarily formed in opposition to the Danes and Swedes, and the nation has focused on non-religious factors as a result. A Norwegian language was more or less created in the nineteenth century and made the focus of Norwegian identity. There have been some shifts in Norwegian identity over the years, but religion continues to play a minor role at best. Similarly, Iceland was part of the Norwegian and Danish states for much of its existence. It was under Danish rule that the Icelanders were converted to Lutheranism, and it was against Denmark that Iceland eventually strove for its independence. Ironically, the conversion of the Icelanders to Lutheranism had a strong impact on the secular nature of Icelandic nationalism. By the time that modern Icelandic nationalism emerged in the nineteenth century, Lutheranism had become a solid part of Icelandic identity. Therefore, religion served little purpose in the quest for independence from Denmark, a fellow Lutheran state. However, the Icelandic language and literature (a proud part of the Icelandic heritage) was useful. Subsequent threats have come from Britain (over fishing rights) and the United States (over military bases). Neither country provides any real threat to the Icelandic nation, nor are they differentiated by religion. As a result, the Icelandic approach to religion is similar to that of other states wherein religion is a cultural signifier to which many people relate (baptism, weddings, and funerals), but the relationship is not reflective of the actual religiosity of the people.

> Religion is neither an issue in the everyday life of the Icelanders, nor a political one. Major political and ethical issues are debated without reference to religion. However, the man in the street is keenly interested in various questions about religious experience, life after death, and so on, as a private matter and without reference to official doctrine. There is an almost total absence of a fully fledged atheistic world view, or anti-clericalism.
>
> Nordal and Kristinsson (1996)

Icelandic nationalism, though infused with a bit of religion, is clearly secular.

Secular nationalisms (absence of a threat)

A number of other countries demonstrate the fact that both causal factors are necessary rather than sufficient. Specifically, it is not uncommon in Europe to find states that do exist at a religious frontier, but are not (or have not historically been) threatened by that frontier. In such cases, national identity is more often formed in opposition to some other, more threatening or meaningful other. Russia and Germany provide the best examples of this.

Germany and other divided states

Germany lies along one of the great religious frontiers in European history. It was here that Luther set in motion the Reformation and established an entirely new division between Catholic and Protestant. Significantly, this frontier splits the modern German state in two: the north and east is primarily Protestant while the south and west tend towards Catholicism. Germany is, as a result, a divided nation in terms of religion. This frontier extends beyond the German borders – the southern and eastern neighbors (Austria, Czech Republic, Poland, and France) are largely Catholic and the northern neighbors (Denmark and the Netherlands) are predominantly Protestant. As such, Germany exists at a religious frontier. However, the fact that the German nation is bisected by this frontier has limited its uses for nation building.

Despite the presence of this frontier, the threat that ultimately led to the formation of a unified German state in the nineteenth century was France. The Germans had been defeated by Napoleon, and the reaction was to create a stronger Germany in order to prevent this from happening again. As the German people were divided by religion, language and descent were emphasized. As Adrian Hastings points out, this is the classic *jus sanguinis* of German nationalism: " ... the Germans have defined themselves ethno-centrically in terms of a community of descent (in theory), of language (in practice), which is then productive of a state" (Hastings 1997: 13). Religion played a part during this era, specifically through Bismarck's distrust of Catholics and the resulting *Kulturkampf* – the results of which can still be seen to some extent in the stronger religious identity among Catholics than Protestants (threat leads to religious identity). As a whole, religion has been less useful in building German identity than has language and descent. The Holocaust, for instance, was justified based on Jewish race or ethnicity more than Jewish faith.

In terms of current threats to the German state, there are few of significant importance – certainly few that fall along a religious dimension. The one exception that is worth following is the broad distrust of Islamic workers, specifically from Turkey. As in France, the increasing significance of Islamic minorities may potentially cause a shift back towards a more religiously based conception of nationhood.

This lack of a threatening frontier ultimately means that German nationalism has consistently been defined according to heritage and language. Religion, other than in regional identities (i.e., Bavaria), plays a much more minor role in nationalism. As Hastings indicates: Germany's "division between Catholic and Protestant, and its remoteness from the front line with Islam, removed from it the principle religious factors discoverable elsewhere in the construction of a national identity" (Hastings 1997: 112). As a result, Germany is a relatively secular state (only 58 percent claim to be religious) that appears to be headed in the same direction in the future. Only 14 percent of the German people claim that religion is "very important" and the number of unaffiliated persons is rising (ISSP 1998).

Several other states in Europe are similarly divided. Both Belgium and the Netherlands fit the general pattern of religious nationalism throughout much of their history. Both states were part of the Spanish empire, and the spread of Protestantism throughout the northern Netherlands introduced a religious frontier between the Dutch, their Spanish rulers, and the Belgians to the south (who remained largely Catholic). The subsequent battle for Dutch independence meant that a threat clearly accompanied the religious frontier, and both the Belgians and the Dutch turned to religion as a key factor in national identity. However, after independence, the Netherlands quickly became an international and colonial power, rapidly expanding their influence throughout the world. The threat from Belgium and Spain diminished dramatically. Similarly, independence for Belgium resulted in a shift in threat for the Belgians. Specifically, attempts to enter the colonial race, the two World Wars, and the rise of Flemish nationalism shifted the focus of Belgian identity.

David Martin points out the importance of both the decrease in threat and the amount of time that has passed since the early era of Dutch nation building: " ... in nations like Britain or Holland where the myth of origins is some four centuries old, where the external threats once associated with it have long since receded and where nationhood is not experiencing any contemporary threat, there the sense of linkage between nation and religion lies dormant" (Martin 1978: 106). Adrian Hastings makes a similar point: "Holland was created in its separatedness by a religious struggle, but, once established, nationalism largely took over from religion" (Hastings 1997: 28). The threat today from the religious frontier in Holland is very minor. Dutch identity has a historic link to religion, but no modern tie. The result is a highly secular population – 40 percent claim to be atheist or agnostic. Religion and state have been separated since 1798 and there is little discrimination.

As in Germany, recent rises in Muslim populations have led to an upsurge in religious rhetoric in the Netherlands, including the killing of Pim Fortuyn who had espoused controversial anti-Islamic views. Should the growth of Islamic populations continue to be seen as threatening, it is likely that religion could reenter the national debate in the Netherlands.

In Belgium, Catholicism remains relatively important. It would be difficult to ignore the impact of Catholicism in the early nineteenth century (following independence). As Rezsohazy states, " ... during the 19th century and until the end of World War II no other single institution or party could rival the church's ubiquity and influence" (Rezsohazy *et al.* 1990: 45). However, as the specter of the Protestant Netherlands has diminished, other factors have taken over. Specifically, because of linguistic divides within Belgium, national identity has shifted to the substate level in order to focus on the divisions between the Flemish (who started the movement) and the Walloons (who are reacting). The result is a largely secular nationalism that still links to religion in certain contexts, but the relationship is largely a façade. As a result, the majority of Belgians are Catholic and 68 percent claim to be religious; however, only 15 percent claim that religion is very important. The role of religion in politics has been greatly diminished. Rezsohazy indicates that "The bishops and the clergy no longer intervene in political life, and the faithful have become completely independent in choosing their political commitments" (Rezsohazy *et al.* 1990: 47). In Belgium today, the divide between the Flemish and Walloons has taken center stage (partly because of the absence of other threats) and has resulted in emphases on language, as both are predominantly Catholic. In other words, the primary religious frontier for Belgium (the Netherlands) is no longer an existential or assimilative threat for the Belgian nation.

Switzerland follows a similar pattern of internal religious cleavages weakening the role of religion in nation building. The Reformation had a major impact on Switzerland through the impact of such leaders as Zwingli and Calvin and, as a result, Switzerland's only religious frontier is internal. The strong role of Protestantism in Swiss history is still evident today in certain cantons. Switzerland today is divided about equally between Catholics (46.1 percent) and Protestants (40 percent).

Because of its unique circumstances, Switzerland has an interesting relationship between nationalism and religion. The Swiss cantons united with the goal of mutual defense in mind, so there has been a national adoption of the federal and neutral mindset. Add to this the fact that Switzerland is divided religiously, and the result is a largely secular national identity. However, prominent religious divisions and some level of self-rule for the cantons have led to a noticeable amount of religiously based regional identity. This identity has been rather overwhelmed by linguistic divisions, but there is no doubt that Catholicism and Protestantism play into regional awareness. This is clearly reflected in the fact that Switzerland is one of the more religious states (51 percent claim to attend weekly) and yet does not truly qualify as a religious nationalism. As such, the formula for religious identity holds true at both the national and subnational level in Switzerland.

Russia and Finland

In the Russian case, the religious frontier is very apparent and does not divide the nation, as is the case in Germany. Specifically, the Orthodox nature of Russia contrasts with numerous Protestant (Baltics) and Catholic (Poland) states to Russia's west. There is also a very large and very significant religious frontier with Islam to the south of Russia. Ever since its conversion to Orthodoxy in the tenth century, Russia has dealt with significant religious frontiers.

However, for much of its history, the Russian Empire was sufficiently strong as to minimize the threats from its religious frontiers. This is not to say that religious frontiers have been entirely non-threatening. The Islamic threat from the Ottoman Empire led the Russians to take a particular interest in their Orthodox brethren in the Balkans. In addition, Afghanistan and, even more recently, Chechnya have provided significant threats, particularly because of the terrorist tactics used by the Chechen rebels. Of particular importance are events such as the recent Beslan massacre. With the fall of Communism, Russia's prominence and security have also been challenged. The added impact of economic devastation has enabled religion to return to the center of national sentiment.

Although the lack of threat has historically meant a non-religious nationalism, these recent events show that Russian nationalism may, in fact, be transforming along the lines laid out in earlier chapters. Although it is not yet possible to declare that Russian nationalism is a religious nationalism, it is clear that Russian nationalism has made a remarkable shift in that direction over the past decade and a half. Although statistics are not widely available, the majority of ethnic Russians associate with the Orthodox Church. "According to polls, in the first half of the 1990s the church inspired greater trust among the Russian population than most other social and political institutions" (Curtis 1998: 210). This relationship has strengthened since the fall of Communism, as has the relationship between church and state. As Curtis indicates, "After enduring the Soviet era as a state-controlled religious façade, the church quickly regained both membership and political influence in the early 1990s" (Curtis 1998: 203). He concludes:

> In the 1990s, the Russian citizenry has shown that the traditional, deeply felt linkage between Russian Orthodoxy and the Russian state remains intact. That linkage has a palpable effect on Russian secular attitudes towards religious minorities, and hence on the degree to which the new constitutional guarantee of religious liberty is honored.
>
> Curtis (1998: 210)

This sentiment is shared by others. In describing the newly emerging nationalist sentiment in the early 1990s, Walter Laqueur made the following assertion:

> Who belongs to the nation? Only ethnic Russians who belong to the Orthodox Church. Catholics, Muslims, Protestants or Jews can be Russian subjects, they can be tolerated and given freedom of religious practice, they can even be given certain civic rights. But since "Holy Russia" is meaningless for them, they cannot be true Russians.
>
> Laqueur (1992: 111)

To be fair, Laqueur was discussing the more radical fringes of Russian nationalism, but the U.S. State Department tends to agree:

Religious matters are not a source of societal hostility for most citizens; however, many citizens firmly believe that at least nominal adherence to the Russian Orthodox Church is at the heart of what it means to be Russian. Popular attitudes toward traditionally Muslim ethnic groups are negative in many regions, and there are manifestations of anti-Semitism as well as societal hostility toward Catholics and newer, non-Orthodox, religions.

U.S. Dept of State (2003)

Although Russia may not exhibit true religious nationalism yet, it has made significant steps in that direction. This is likely because Russian religious frontiers have become increasingly threatening due to the weakening of the Russian position. Of course, the reduction in governmental restrictions on religion has contributed as well.

The Finnish case is related to the Russian case. Because Russia is predominantly Orthodox and Finland Protestant, there is a clear religious frontier between the two states. It is also clear that the religious frontier has been threatening to the Finns for much of their history. However, the Swedes have provided as significant an "other" for Finland as have the Russians. Linguistic ties served a more important function in national identity, as the Swedes and Finns were both Protestant. However, once Finland fell under the control of the Russian Empire in 1809, the threat from the religious frontier was significantly elevated. Interestingly, the Russians encouraged a linguistic national identity because it was useful in separating the Finns from the Swedes and diminishing the possibility of a return to the Swedish–Finnish union. Whereas the Swedish union had been largely beneficial to the Finns, the Russian situation was more tenuous and, indeed, threatening. By the late nineteenth century, a policy of Russification was pursued. The Finns, however, gained their independence in 1917, and the Russian threat was still present, but diminished. The two states went to war several times in the subsequent century, but the Finns were able to maintain a delicate balance that allowed some Russian control in Finnish politics while still preserving national sovereignty. The Finns set out to change the nature of Soviet relations after World War II and were largely successful – creating a new, more constructive link. Ultimately, the fall of the Soviet Union meant an end to the Russian threat.

As a result, Finnish nationalism is a mixed case. The vast majority of Finns (nearly 90 percent) belong to the official Lutheran Church of Finland (C.I.A. 2004). In addition, 59 percent consider themselves religious. However, only 15 percent consider religion to be very important, and even fewer attend church regularly (Inglehart *et al.* 1997). There is some official linkage between Church and state, but the constitution guarantees religious freedom. Religious instruction is incorporated into the public schools, but students are allowed to opt out. As Solsten and Meditz point out, "Much of this religious influence was based in Finland's past, however, and did not correspond with attitudes of most Finns, because by the 1980s the country had become a highly secularized society" (Solsten and Meditz 1990: 104). Religion is a significant part of identity for the Finnish people, but it is largely ceremonial.

> The role the state churches played in life's key moments made them, for reasons of tradition, important to most Finns, even to those who were not religious. More Finns were baptized, married, and buried with church rites than were members of the churches. A very important rite of passage for adolescents was confirmation, which signified a coming of age even for those from freethinking families. For this reason, more than 90 percent of 15-year-olds were confirmed, despite the several weeks of lessons this entailed.
>
> Solsten and Meditz (1990: 104)

The nationalist views tend to center more on linguistic ties because language proved useful in Finnish differentiation from both the Russians and the Swedes. Religion's importance is present but limited, and it certainly plays a more limited role in politics than in more religious nations. Although a religious frontier has been present in Finland for nearly a millennium, the threat from that frontier has been limited. In the past fifty years, the Finns have pursued a policy of conciliation with the Russians, and the result has been a tenuous, but peaceful existence, at least since the Treaty of Friendship, Cooperation, and Mutual Assistance was signed in 1948. The result has been a secular nationalism with hints of religious influence.

Hungary

Hungary follows a similar pattern to the Czech Republic (discussed previously) and Latvia and Estonia (discussed later). It is a divided, although prominently Catholic, country that exists at a number of religious frontiers – with Orthodox Serbia, Romania, and Ukraine. Historically, the Hungarian nation has been part of several other frontiers of even greater significance. For instance, throughout much of its history, Hungary was subject to either Ottoman or Austrian dominance, and the twentieth century introduced the Soviet "frontier" as well. The Austrian frontier was also significant because, for a significant period, Hungary had submitted to the Reformation and was nearly 90 percent Protestant, in contrast to Austria's strong Catholic heritage.

A number of these religious frontiers did pose a threat to the Hungarian nation. The Ottoman domination of Hungary during the sixteenth and seventeenth centuries presented a clear cut example of a religiously based national threat. In addition, the Reformation was simultaneously spreading throughout the Hungarian population. As a result, the subsequent domination by Habsburg Austria from the end of the seventeenth century through the beginning of the twentieth century also presented a situation of religiously based national threat. The Protestant tie to Hungarian identity was quite strong. However, the strength of the Austrian-led Counter-Reformation led to a slow reconquest of the Hungarian people. The result was a situation similar to the Czech example in which the Hungarian heritage was linked to Protestantism but the people had been forcibly separated from that national heritage. Therefore, subsequent national movements could not rely on Catholicism because it was associated with Austrian dominance, and Protestantism had lost its usefulness because the population was predominantly Catholic. In the past fifty years, the most significant others for Hungarians have been the Soviets and the Slavic peoples to Hungary's south and east. By the twentieth century, Hungarian identity had become entrenched in the Magyar culture and language, and that identity remained useful and central in twentieth-century differentiation. All this contributed to the fact that the Catholic Church was not central to resistance during Soviet rule. As Burant states:

> Western observers concluded that although the country possessed about 5 million practicing believers, religion did not provide a viable alternative value system that could compete with the predominant secularism and materialism promoted both by the government and by trends within an increasingly modern society. Thus, religion was unlikely to become a vehicle for dissent as in Poland ...
>
> Burant (1989: 94)

Potential outliers

Although most European countries do fit the general pattern of religiously threatening frontiers leading to religious nationalism (and the absence of either a frontier or a threat leading to secular nationalism), there are a handful of states that seem to buck the trend. Three such states (Italy, Spain, and Portugal) appear to be states in transition. So they are not true outliers. It is debatable whether or not these states are secular in their national conceptions. However, a brief examination of each allows for a better understanding of the general relationship between threatening others and religious nationalism.

The birthplace of Catholicism (Italy)

Italy appears to defy the broader trend in that there are no major religious frontiers for the Italian nation (all its direct neighbors are strongly Catholic as well, with the exception of Switzerland). The most significant others for the Italians since the dawn of modern national consciousness have been other Catholic states (i.e., Austria during the *Risorgimento*). Yet Catholicism still plays a significant role for the Italian nation.

As there have been no major religious frontiers in modern Italy, neither have there have been significant associated threats. Significantly, one of the major threats to Italian nation building came from the Catholic Church itself. During the *Risorgimento* in the nineteenth century, the Neo-Guelph movement pressed for an Italian state with the Pope at its head. The Church was unwilling to go to war with Austria, another Catholic state, in order to fulfill the Italian idea. In the years that followed, the Catholic Church continued to be one of the strongest opponents of Italian unification. Thus, we see a pattern almost opposite to the Polish, Irish, or Greek cases. In each of those instances, the Church supported the nation in opposition to the state. In Italy, the Church represented opposition to the Italian nation, whereas the state symbolized the idea of unification.

Despite this, the Italian nation is clearly influenced by Catholicism. Around 90 percent of Italians are Catholic and 65 percent claim to be religious. These numbers are higher than average, but significantly lower than in Ireland, Poland, or even the United States. Attendance is also relatively high. At the same time, there is a marked shift towards secularization. A new concordat between the Church and the state was agreed upon in 1984 which drastically altered the relationship. "According to the 1984 concordat, Roman Catholicism is no longer the established state religion ... Rome is no longer a 'sacred city' but its 'particular significance' was acknowledged" (Shinn 1985: 118). In addition, in the last two decades, major changes have occurred with regard to abortion and divorce laws, both being liberalized extensively. This rather odd relationship can be explained by Italy's unique situation. On one hand, the Catholic Church has lost its power over the nation because of (1) its actions during Italian unification and (2) its inability to distinguish Italy from its neighbors. Whereas these conditions would almost certainly lead to secular nationalism in any other state, the unique relationship between Catholicism and Italy has slowed this process. Although Catholicism does not differentiate Italy from Austria or France, it is undeniable that the Catholic Church is an Italian institution. The predominance of the Catholic Church has led to an odd situation in terms of national identity. Because it is the home of Catholicism, Italian identity has continued to emphasize its special relationship with the Church. However, as Adrian Hastings argues:

> Rome was the obvious capital of Italy but it was also, even more obviously, the city of the Pope and the papacy could never be a merely Italian matter. Even in the nineteenth century Italian nationalism would be profoundly embarrassed about how it should relate to the Popes. In the fifteenth the political, international and religious importance of the papacy was such that it placed the construction of Italian nationalism in a category all its own.
>
> Hastings (1997: 117)

The result is a mixed case. David Martin claims that "Presumably the Italian pattern is influenced for Catholicism in that the Papacy is Italian, but against it in that the Pope was a temporal ruler and opposed to Italian nationalism" (Martin 1978: 11). In the end, the Italian nation can best be described as a secular nation that is highly religious. Although the people of Italy hold religion in high esteem, they tend to turn to other factors when describing what it means to be Italian. As time passes, secularization is likely to make further inroads.

Conservative Mediterranean dictatorships (Spain and Portugal)

Spain and Portugal also provide examples of potential outliers. Both states have a long history of religious frontiers and threats from their Moorish neighbors to the south. In addition, a strongly conservative dictatorship ruled for much of the twentieth century in both states. Both Franco and Salazar actively pursued a traditional agenda that aimed to keep the Church central to Iberian society. As a result, secularization has been attenuated, but not stopped. In fact, rapid change has occurred in the past two decades, particularly in Spain.

In the case of Spain, there are no true modern religious frontiers. Spain shares only two borders of any significance (Portugal and France), and both are strongly Catholic. However, it is also important to note that, although there are no current religious frontiers, religious frontiers played a crucial role in Spanish nation building for over 1,000 years. In the 700s, Islamic forces began spreading across the Iberian Peninsula, and the subsequent *Reconquista* would not be completed until the turn of the sixteenth century. In the meantime, Muslim rule meant a delicate balance between Islamic, Jewish, and Catholic communities, often with negative consequences for the Catholic Spaniards. The *Reconquista* did not end with the recapture of Spanish lands. Rather, the war against the religious "other" continued internally under the guise of the Inquisition, which was not fully abolished until the 1830s (Kohn 1944). The internal threat from Islam was demonstrated many times – for instance, an uprising in Andalusia in 1568 in which an appeal was sent to the Ottoman Empire for aid. As Hastings indicates:

> Because the conquest of the Moorish kingdoms achieved in the thirteenth century came to be seen both as a national war of liberation there was a special holiness, a special Christianness and Catholicism, in Spain's very existence ... That holiness and therefore national identity too seemed inherently threatened by the survival of Muslim or Jew in the kingdom and especially by secret Jews or Muslims ...
>
> Hastings (1997: 111)

By the sixteenth century, Spanish identity had become fully linked to Catholicism, and the subsequent international religious threats continued to solidify the bond. Over the following centuries, conflict between Spain and newly Protestant England (the rise and fall of Mary, the defeat of the Armada, colonial expansion in North America) led to a strengthened Catholic identity. The Spanish also fought against the Turks several times in the sixteenth century (Lepanto and Malta). In the seventeenth century, wars in the Spanish Netherlands were fought along religious lines, resulting in the independence of the Protestant Netherlands. The subsequent decline in Spanish power meant a withdrawal from international politics and a resulting attempt at Enlightenment and reform under Charles III in the late 1700s. Although secularism was gaining some ground, the French Revolution and the Napoleonic invasion of Spain had major repercussions. What had previously been an organic push for secularism now became a foreign-imposed shift, and the Spanish reacted harshly against the secularism of the French Revolution.

Secularism again gained ground in the second half of the nineteenth century and would likely have continued had it not been for the rise of Franco. A serious of conflicts over reform of society and religion brought about the Civil War and Fascist control of Spain. In 1931, "the secular constitution of the Second Republic imposed a series of anticlerical measures that threatened the church's very existence in Spain and provoked its support for the Franco uprising five years later" (Solsten and Meditz 1988: 111). Franco's dominance put the religious nature of Spanish society on life support if you will, essentially extending its life artificially. After the fall of Franco in the 1970s, Spain returned to its secularizing pattern and quickly implemented reforms in Church–state relations, education, social policies, and more.

Today, there are no true religious frontiers and no serious threats to the Spanish nation. The past fifty years have shown a remarkable shift towards secularization, which will likely continue unless the threat from Islam (as demonstrated in the Madrid train bombings) increases significantly. There is no doubt that modern Spanish identity is linked to Catholicism. Estimates put the percentage of Catholics in Spain at between 85 and 98 percent (C.I.A. 2004; ISSP 1998; Solsten and Meditz 1988). In addition, a significant number of Spaniards claim to be religious, including nearly 65 percent of youth between the ages of 15 and 24 (ISSP 1998). However, "Being a Catholic in Spain had less and less to do with regular attendance at Mass and more to do with the routine observance of important rituals such as baptism, marriage, and burial of the dead" (Solsten and Meditz 1988: 113). In addition, the numbers of Spaniards entering the clergy has dropped drastically in the past thirty years. Although the Spanish ties between national identity and religion may not be as strong as in Ireland, Poland, or Greece, they do not lag far behind. The conception of Spanish-ness as Catholic is in many ways accurate. In terms of politics, however, the differences can be seen. The buffer between religion and politics is more established in Spain than in other true religious nationalisms. Church and state are officially separated, but the Catholic Church does receive certain privileges. For instance, religious education, albeit optional, is provided in public schools. Abortion is allowed, but the limitations are stricter than in many European states. There is a clear religious influence on politics in Spain, but the influence is diminishing and has certainly progressed further than the other examples of religious nationalism discussed. As a result, it would be wrong to categorize Spain as a fully religious nation, but it would also be erroneous to describe it as secular. The best way to describe Spanish nationalism would be as a secularizing, partially religious nation. This is due to the long historic ties between religion and nation in a part of the world where religions collided for centuries. This link has been carried over into modern times and is now being loosened, although the process is gradual. Adrian Hastings summarizes the situation well:

> Spanish nationhood … was shaped by its position on the frontier with Islam. Here religion was more continually decisive than for any other in western Europe, decisive through the character of the medieval wars which initially established it, decisive through the activity of the Inquisition in ensuring its continuance, decisive in the highly and narrowly religious ideal which became nationally normative. Spanishness and Catholicism, the Catholicism of Isabella, "La Catolica", seemed for centuries inseparable and only a very agonized modern history would tear them, partially, apart.
>
> Hastings (1997: 112)

Portugal mimics the pattern of Spain to a large extent. Although there are no religious frontiers for Portugal today, Portuguese history has been heavily influenced by the Moorish expansion into Iberia and the subsequent *Reconquista* that retook Spain and Portugal for Catholicism. The threat from Islam was clear for much of Portugal's history. From the eighth century, Muslim forces from North Africa began invading and conquering territory that had previously been Christianized under the Visigoths. The fight against Islam continued for the Portuguese until 1250. For the subsequent 300 years, the power of the church was diminished somewhat as the threat from Islam subsided (the Spanish did not complete the expulsion of Islam until the turn of the sixteenth century). During this period, the monarchy was able to exert a great deal of control over the Church, and Portugal began to extend its influence around the globe. In the era of colonialism, Catholicism provided a useful tool in the rhetoric of imperial growth (i.e., the white man's burden). The Reformation brought religion back to the forefront at home, and the Inquisition was established in Portugal under the model of Spain. Catholicism provided a tool for expansionism against local and foreign heretics and an excuse for imperial ambitions. The "other" for Portugal during this time was Spain – in the Americas and Iberia. "In 1640 Portugal revolted against this Spanishization, but the long-drawn struggle brought no political awakening of the masses nor any quickening of the intellectual and social life of the leading classes" (Kohn 1944: 494). In the seventeenth century, Portugal was briefly united with Spain and, during the Napoleonic Wars, Spain and France allied together against the Portuguese and the English. An emphasis on the Portuguese language accompanied this era. The French Revolution brought ideas of liberalism and modern nationalism which took root in Portugal (and Spain) during the nineteenth century. However, Portugal fell under the rule of an absolutist regime that was strongly allied with the Church in the early twentieth century. Salazar's regime falsely maintained religion's influence in Portugal much as Franco did in Spain. Since the fall of Salazar, religion's role has declined rapidly.

As a result, Portuguese nationalism, like Spanish nationalism, represents a strange mixed case. The Portuguese history of anti-Islamic sentiment has shaped national identity. As Hastings points out, the Portuguese nation:

> grew out of religious war, this time the Crusades. Portuguese nationhood was characterized in consequence for centuries by a particularly militant type of Catholicism, aggressive, nationalist, anti-Islamic. The commitment to Christian reconquest of the Iberian peninsula was no less crucial in the construction of Spanish nationhood. For both a militant nationalist Catholicism remained a significant force well into the twentieth century.
>
> Hastings (1997: 190)

As in Spain, a pro-Catholic authoritarian regime maintained the influence of religion artificially. In terms of population, Portugal is over 95 percent Catholic (nominally), and 76 percent claim to be religious. Catholic rituals are a key part of Portuguese culture and history. However, these numbers have been falling sharply in recent years. The age gap is wide, with younger populations attending less frequently than older generations. In addition, the number of individuals entering the priesthood is in decline. Although these numbers are significant, it is worth noting that this pattern is also evident in Ireland, Poland, Greece, etc. It is fairly straightforward to claim that Portuguese national identity is still strongly associated with religion. Politics are also closely linked to religion. Portugal is one of the few European states in which abortion is prohibited under nearly all circumstances. However, Church and state are officially separated and freedom of religion is constitutionally guaranteed.

Portugal and Spain can be viewed as anomalies of sorts. They are, in many ways, nations in transition. It will be of great interest to watch as Portuguese and Spanish identities continue to shift in the coming years. For now, Portugal and Spain can be classified as weak religious nationalisms in transition.

Outliers

Four European states serve as clear outliers to the general trends. Albania, Ukraine, Estonia, and Latvia all feature prominent, threatening religious frontiers. In three cases, Russia has served as the significant "other," much as was the case in Poland. However, in none of these four states has the presence of such a religious frontier resulted in religious nationalism. In Latvia and Estonia, this is because the prominent national religion (Lutheranism) was associated with foreign dominance and threat (from Germany). As such, it was not a useful tool for nation building. Albania and Ukraine, on the other hand, are divided internally along religious lines, therefore weakening the power of religion as a nationally unifying force.

Religiously divided states (Albania and Ukraine)

Albania, like its Balkan neighbors, has existed at a religious frontier between Catholicism and Orthodoxy for hundreds of years. Unlike its neighbors, Albania was largely converted to Islam during the rule of the Ottoman Empire. Interestingly, these conversions did not happen on a large scale until the Russo-Turkish wars, when the Ottomans were threatened by the Orthodox links between the Russians and Albanians. The conversion was largely successful. Today, nearly 70 percent of the Albanian people are Muslim. Significantly, the religious frontier divides the Albanian people, not only between the Muslim majority and the Catholic and Orthodox minority, but also between diverging sects of Islam (Sunni versus Bektashi). Thus, religion has proved less useful than other tools for uniting the Albanians in their various national movements throughout history.

Because the Ottoman Empire was also Islamic, the Albanian people were largely content to remain subject to its rule (as was true of many Orthodox Greeks). The ultimate rise of Albanian nationalism came as the Ottoman Empire crumbled and the threat of integration into the neighboring states increased. Although this threat did occur across a religious frontier, the religious fragmentation of Albania meant that an ethnic approach to identity was adopted.

> The Albanians' religious differences forced nationalist leaders to give the national movement a purely secular character that alienated religious leaders. The most significant factor uniting the Albanians, their spoken language, lacked a standard literary form and even a standard alphabet. Each of the three available choices, the Latin, Cyrillic, and Arabic scripts, implied different political and religious orientations opposed by one or another element of the population.
>
> Zickel and Iwaskiw (1994)

The subsequent adoption of Communism in Albania brought with it extensive attacks on religion, which ultimately had a mixed effect. Although some Albanians were reluctant to pass their religion on to their children, others responded by identifying more strongly with their traditional religious ties.

As a result of these historic divisions, nationalism in Albania today is largely secular. Although some of this secularism can be attributed to the Communist attacks on organized religion under Hoxha from the 1940s onward, more significant are the religious divides within the Albanian nation, most notably the schism within Islam itself. The result is a state that features a strong separation of Church and state – there is no official religion, no religious symbols are allowed in school, and the link between the people and their various religions is still tenuous after the Communist era. Official state holidays are drawn from all four predominant religions. There are few statistics of church attendance because of restrictions on religion that have only recently been lifted, but the secular attitude of the people is largely accepted. This disjoint between Church and people has also meant that religion has had little influence in the political sphere in recent years.

Similarly, Ukraine exists at a number of religious frontiers, one of which is the prominent divide between Catholicism and Eastern Orthodoxy. Ukraine is largely Orthodox (although there is a significant Uniate population), and this contrasts with the highly Catholic populations of Poland, Slovakia, and Hungary. Ukraine's subjugation to Catholic Poland and Lithuania for a substantial period of history did have the effect of creating a religiously minded national movement. However, it also led to the formation of the Uniate faith – a hybrid between Catholicism and Orthodoxy. In addition to the Orthodox/Uniate/Catholic divides, there are also significant intra-Orthodox divides, the most substantial of which is the distinction between the Ukrainian Orthodox and Russian Orthodox churches. Despite the fact that the Ukrainian Orthodox church was founded as a response to Russian domination, the end result is that Ukraine features two significant religions (Uniate and Orthodox), both of which are successful in differentiating them from their most threatening neighbor, Russia.

In the broader picture, Ukraine fits the overall argument that threatening religious frontiers create a national emphasis on religion. Religion did, in fact, play an important part in the nation-building stages of Ukrainian development. It was useful in establishing independence from Poland, Lithuania, Austria, and Russia (although a new Ukrainian Orthodox identity had to be established in the last case). As a result, there is a linkage between nation and Church. As David Martin indicates, "In Lithuania, the Ukraine and Armenia, the church has deep roots in national awareness and is relatively strong" (Martin 1978: 222). Similarly, Vasyl Markus argues that in the Ukraine, " … national culture has been inspired by religion for over one thousand years and therefore a symbiosis of religion and nationality is taken for granted" (Markus 1984: 79). The Ukrainian case is more complicated than most. Although most citizens are Orthodox, a fair number still ascribe to the Uniate faith. Therefore, religion was useful in a variety of nationalist independence movements in that it separated the Ukrainians from their oppressors. Interestingly, the different regions of Ukraine provide an additional test of the theory, much as the partitions of Poland did. The

Western Uniate regions of the Ukraine were more stubborn in their resistance to foreign domination than were the Eastern Orthodox regions. The
west also proved to be more religiously minded. Adrian Hastings points out
that "It is noticeable how different it was [for the Russians] to try to incorporate Catholic Poles or Armenians from incorporating Ukrainians, most of
whom were Orthodox Christians" (Hastings 1997: 120). Markus points to
the differing roles played by clergy in each location: "The nineteenth century
witnessed almost a complete alienation of the Russianized Ukrainian clergy
from the emerging modern national movement in Eastern Ukraine ... In
contrast, the Galician (West Ukrainian) revival largely was promoted and
led by the Uniate clergy" (Markus 1984). The aftermath was more complicated. Religion has not been as useful in the national unification process.
The Ukraine, as a result, is an interesting case in that religion proved highly
useful in national differentiation, but much less so in building a unified
national identity. As a result, religion is strong in the country, but its links to
the nation are weaker than in true religiously based nations.

States with an imposed religion (Latvia and Estonia)

Latvia and Lithuania, on the other hand, provide a slightly different pattern
of nation building. Germany played a significant role in the history of both
states and, as a result, both are predominantly Lutheran. However, this is
because Lutheranism was imposed on both states by conquering Germans
and maintained by foreign German elites. So the predominant religion in
both states (and the Czech Republic as well) is associated with foreign
dominance. The willingness of the nation to rely on this foreign artifact was
therefore greatly diminished.

Significantly, there were a number of threats across religious frontiers in
both cases. Estonia has been more or less under the control of outside
powers since the thirteenth century. Sweden controlled Estonia until the
1700s, at which point Russia conquered the territory. Russia controlled
Estonia up to the Bolshevik Revolution, when Estonians fought for and won
their independence. It was a short-lived independence, however, and Estonia
once again fell under Russian control during the Soviet era after World War
II. As a result, Estonia's primary threat has come from Russia, an Orthodox
state. Of course, the other key threat to the Estonian nation came from the
Germanic nobles who ruled over the Estonians throughout the Germanic,
Swedish, and Russian eras. This factor also contributed significantly to a
secular identity for the Estonian people.

Russia also served as the primary threat to the Latvian nation through
much of its history, especially during the twentieth century. The Russian role
began in the eighteenth century when Peter the Great conquered Latvia. For
the next two centuries, Latvians were under the control of German elites in
the economic sphere (feudalism) and Russian elites in the political sphere.
Significantly, Lutheranism was relatively useless in nation formation because

of the German factor. Although the Latvians earned their independence after World War I, the Molotov–Ribbentrop pact in World War II meant that the Germans and Russians once again conspired to end Latvian independence, and the Latvians fell under Russian control once more. Russian interference in Latvian politics for the next fifty years was central to Latvian identity. The date of the Molotov–Ribbentrop pact is still recognized in Latvia and was a key part of the Helsinki '86 movement in the 1970s and 1980s. The large ethnic Russian minority in Latvia has meant that the threat of Russian interference remained high even after independence (especially when compared with the other Baltic states). However, as in Estonia, the presence of German Lutheran elites has been central in diminishing the role of religion in Latvian nationalism.

The impact of a foreign-imposed religion is clear in both states. In Estonia, only 21 percent claim to be religious and only 5 percent claim that religion is "very important." In addition, although Lutheranism is the historically dominant religion, the level of atheism has risen to a point at which Estonia should be classified as religiously heterogeneous (Orthodox, Catholic, Jewish minorities). Religious freedom is guaranteed, and the people tend to associate Estonia with cultural or linguistic ties more than with religion. Thus, the Estonian case closely parallels the Czech case, in which religion has been severed from the national story. Lutheranism, the primary religion of the people, is associated with an outside cultural influence – in this case, Germanic. Because of the oppression of the Germanic nobility, Lutheranism was weakened as a national mobilizer. As Raun indicates, "Because of the Baltic German domination of the Lutheran Church, the religious factor was muted in Estonian nationalism" (Raun 2003). Iwaskiw indicates the same: " ... Estonians tend not to be very religious, because religion through the nineteenth century was associated with German feudal rule" (Iwaskiw 1995: 34). As a result, religion during the Communist era was repressed fairly easily, but there has been an upsurge in activity since the fall of Communism. In addition, nation and religion had been separated prior to the introduction of the Russian threat. This meant that other tools were used in modern Estonian nationalism.

The Latvian case follows the same pattern. Although Lutheranism is predominant among ethnic Latvians (approximately 55 percent), ethnic Latvians only comprise about two-thirds of the population. Roman Catholicism and Orthodoxy are also prominent – particularly in the Russian minorities. In addition, only 38 percent of the population claims to be religious and less than 5 percent attend church weekly. This pattern can be explained by the same relationship between Lutheranism and German influence in Latvian affairs. As Walter Iwaskiw indicates: "For centuries Latvian attachment to Lutheranism was rather tepid, in part because this religion had been brought by the Baltic barons and German-speaking clergy" (Iwaskiw 1995: 122). Latvian resistance to Russian control began at a time when Lutheranism was not central to Latvian identity, but was instead associated with foreign dominance. Ethnic factors have been useful for nation building, although the large Russian minority (30+ percent) weakens the power of ethnic ties. Cultural and linguistic ties have proven useful in national differentiation and remain central to Latvian nationalism. The role of the church in politics is relatively weak, and national self-identi-fication does not center on religious elements.

Conclusions

The results of this cross-Europe analysis are displayed in Table 7.1, which provides a general summary of the relationship between religious frontiers, threats, and religious nationalism in all thirty-nine European states exam-ined. The categorization into dichotomous sets is problematic for many of these states (Italy, Macedonia, Finland, etc.) because they often fall closer to the dividing point than to either end of the spectrum. This loss of context means that Table 7.1 is not as effective as the discussions above, but the summary below does provide the reader with a basic glimpse of religious nationalism across the continent. Table 7.2 shows the breakdown of all thirty-nine states into those cases that do fit the broader pattern of religious and secular nationalism and those that are outliers.

Tables 7.1 and 7.2 show that thirty-two of the thirty-nine cases (82 per-cent) examined fit the broader pattern of religious-based national identity. In those thirty-two cases, religious frontiers and threats (or their absence) played a key role in determining the religious or secular nature of national-ism. Only seven of the thirty-nine cases proved to be outliers. A brief look at these seven cases shows that each had particular reasons for deviating from the general path. Of these outliers, Albania, Latvia, and the Ukraine are internally divided in terms of religion (i.e., the religious frontier runs through the nation), thereby weakening the nation-building power of religion. Estonia and Latvia both feature a religion that is associated with foreign oppression (Germany) and therefore is separated from the national heritage, again weakening its nation-building abilities. Italy is an exceptional case in that religion is virtually impossible to separate from national heritage. There is little doubt that the Catholic Church is an Italian institution and, despite the fact that Catholicism has stood in the way of national consolidation, the Catholic heritage of Italy cannot be easily dismissed. The two Iberian cases, Spain and Portugal, both demonstrate the power of religiously based dicta-torships. In both cases, national identity began to form in a time of religious war. In both cases, an authoritarian government maintained strong ties between Church and state and, in both cases, there has been a noticeable shift towards the secular since the 1970s. It is likely that each will continue to secularize in the coming years and will soon fit the broader pattern of reli-gious nationalism in Europe.

These outliers should not be minimized. They are significant and must be explained if the broader theory is to hold. However, each can be explained

Table 7.1 Religious frontiers, threats, and nationalism across Europe

Country	Religious frontier?	Threat?	Religious nationalism?
Albania	Yes	Yes	No
Austria	No	No	No
Belarus	Yes	Yes	Yes
Belgium	Yes	No	No
Bosnia and Herzegovina	Yes	Yes	Yes
Bulgaria	Yes	Yes	Yes
Croatia	Yes	Yes	Yes
Cyprus	Yes	Yes	Yes
Czech Republic	No	No	No
Denmark	No	No	No
Estonia	Yes	Yes	No
Finland	Yes	No	No
France	No	No	No
Germany	Yes	No	No
Greece	Yes	Yes	Yes
Hungary	Yes	No	No
Iceland	No	No	No
Ireland	Yes	Yes	Yes
Italy	No	No	Yes
Latvia	Yes	Yes	No
Lithuania	Yes	Yes	Yes
Luxembourg	No	No	No
Macedonia, FYR	Yes	Yes	Yes
Malta	Yes	Yes	Yes
Moldova	Yes	Yes	Yes
Netherlands	Yes	No	No
Norway	No	No	No
Poland	Yes	Yes	Yes
Portugal	No	No	Yes
Romania	Yes	Yes	Yes
Russia	Yes	No	No
Serbia and Montenegro	Yes	Yes	Yes
Slovak Republic	Yes	Yes	Yes
Slovenia	Yes	No	No
Spain	No	No	Yes
Sweden	No	No	No
Switzerland	Yes	No	No
Ukraine	Yes	Yes	No
United Kingdom	Yes	No	No

FYR, Former Yugoslav Republic.

based on its own unique circumstances. The final chapter will attempt to do just that: synthesize the findings of this chapter (and those previous to it) into a broader understanding of religious nationalism in Europe today. However, it is clear that, as a whole, religious frontiers have an indubitable role in the formation of religiously minded nationalisms.

Table 7.2 Categorization of cases

	Confirming cases (32)	Potential outliers (3)	Outliers (4)
Religious nationalisms	***Secular nations (no religious frontier)***	***Catholic homeland*** Italy	***Religiously divided states***
Belarus	Austria		Albania
Bosnia	Czech Republic	***Religious dictators***	Ukraine
Bulgaria	Denmark	Portugal	
Croatia	France	Spain	***Imposed religion***
Cyprus	Iceland		Estonia
Greece	Luxembourg		Latvia
Ireland	Norway		
Lithuania	Sweden		
Macedonia			
Malta	***Secular nations***		
Moldova	***(no threat)***		
Poland	Belgium		
Romania	Finland		
Serbia	Germany		
Slovak	Hungary		
Republic	Netherlands		
Slovenia	Russia		
	Switzerland		
	United Kingdom		

Note: The three "potential outliers" are categorized as such due to their transitional nature. Spain, for instance, has demonstrated a fairly clear shift towards the secular in the most recent elections. The "outliers" can also be disputed to some extent. Both Albania and Ukraine exist at a religious frontier, and both demonstrate a resultant religious nationalism, but at a subnational level. This, too, can be demonstrated by the most recent Ukrainian elections.

8 Conclusions

The basic argument of this book is that religious frontiers, when threatening, lead to the formation of a religiously based national identity. As identity is based largely on what distinguishes something from its primary "others," religion enters into the equation only when the nation is significantly different from its neighbors in this arena. For the most part, this argument has been proven true. Through the in-depth examination of several key religious nationalisms, the historic role of religious frontiers in nation building has become clear. In addition, the examination of counter-cases allows the theory to be further clarified and strengthened. The previous chapter accomplished that goal. However, some clarification is still necessary.

This chapter will begin by looking at the main theory and its general applicability in the European context. It will then proceed to lay out several clarifying stipulations which serve to elaborate on the relationship between religion and modern nationalism. In doing so, the deviation of the various outlying cases (i.e., Portugal) will be explained. The chapter will then take a brief look at several of the competing theories that were discussed in Chapter two, such as modernization theories, explanations regarding the church–state relationship, and rational choice arguments. Thus, it will be possible to synthesize the findings of the various approaches into as accurate an understanding of religious nationalism as possible. To begin, however, we should take a step back to the general idea laid out in the earliest chapters.

The argument

In this book, it is argued that religious nationalism is primarily shaped by two key factors: religious frontiers and threats. Neither is sufficient to produce a religiously based national identity. Both must be present in order for a linkage to form between religion and nation. In general, this theory has proven to be remarkably accurate in explaining nationalist movements. In each of the three primary cases, religious frontiers and threats played a crucial role in nation building.

In Ireland, the Norman invasion brought an alien culture to the island. The Irish nation began to identify itself in opposition to this new threat, but

Irish sentiment did not begin to take on religious tones until after the English Reformation, at which point the English became not just a threatening other, but a religious other as well. To this day, the British have proven to be the most significant and threatening "other" for the Irish nation. The result has been a strongly Catholic national identity.

In Poland, the threat from religious frontiers has also been clear. The religious divide between Poland and its non-Catholic neighbors (Russia and Germany) has been one of the more prominent features in the history of the Polish nation. Significantly, the role of threat is also demonstrated through the diminishing power of the Polish state following the "Golden Age." The subjugation of the Poles to Russian and Soviet rule further enhanced the nation-building power of the Catholic Church.

In Greece, as in many nations formerly under Ottoman rule, the Orthodox Church played a critical role in national differentiation. This was because Greeks were most clearly differentiated from their oppressors by religion – the Ottomans were Islamic. The threat from Turkey continues today on a variety of fronts, perhaps most notably in Cyprus. As a result, the Greeks continue to emphasize the importance of Orthodoxy in their national concept.

In each of these cases, it is clear that the interplay between religious frontiers and national threats had important ramifications for national development. The English case reinforced this understanding by demonstrating that the threatening nature of a religious frontier can change, and with it the religious links to nationalism. As British power expanded, the Irish threat diminished, and Protestantism was no longer essential in national differentiation.

The findings in Chapter seven reinforce the general argument. The vast majority of cases fit the broad pattern. Thirty-two of thirty-nine states examined support the claim of this book. The seven that do not are therefore critical to our further understanding. Many of these cases are on the borderline. Italy, for instance, is difficult to categorize. Is it a secular nation that is very religious? In other words, are the Italian people largely religious, although the linkage does not carry over into nationalism? Or is Italy a case of a weak religious nationalism, where there is a linkage between religion and nation, albeit weaker than in Ireland, Poland, or Greece? An argument could be made either way. Regardless, it is worth examining this and other outliers in order to: (1) clarify the causal processes involved in the formation of religious nationalism today; and (2) more thoroughly test the general theory. Do these outliers simply point to further nuances in our understanding, or do they call into doubt the explanatory power of the theory? These questions are best addressed by examining some potential clarifying addenda to the book's central argument.

Stipulation 1: the role of homogeneity

Some have suggested that much of the variation in the religiosity of nationalism can be explained by looking at the religious homogeneity or

heterogeneity of a particular nation. To what extent can religious nationalism be explained by the fact that a nation is either largely or entirely alike
with regard to religion? On the other hand, to what extent does religious
variation within the nation exclude religion as a source of nationalism?
These are both complex questions with complicated answers. However, it is
possible to begin addressing them here.

We can begin by dismissing the notion that religious homogeneity causes
religious nationalism. There are simply too many exceptions: France, the
Czech Republic, Austria, the Scandinavian countries, and Iceland, just to
name a few. It is clear that simple homogeneity does not lead to a religiously
based national identity. This does not mean that homogeneity plays no role.
If we look at the issue of homogeneity/heterogeneity not as a causal factor,
but as an inhibitor of sorts, there is some credence to the argument. In other
words, although homogeneity may not lead to religious nationalism, extensive heterogeneity might limit the power of religion in nation building.
Germany, for instance, is an internally divided nation. Approximately half
the population is Catholic and the other half is Protestant. As a result, other
factors may (or may not) be more useful in building a strong unified national
identity. Because religion divides rather than unites, other ethnic, linguistic,
or cultural factors may take the lead in nationalism. Therefore, addendum 1
can best be stated as: religious heterogeneity *may* limit the link between
religion and nationalism in modernity.

This pattern can be seen in two of the European outliers. Albania is a
prime candidate for religious nationalism. Because of its location in the
Balkans, religious frontiers have played a key role in Albanian history.
Primarily a Muslim state, Albania has been surrounded by Orthodox and
Catholic powers for some time, and these other states have proven threatening throughout. In addition, the subjugation of Albania to Communist rule
seemed a prime motivator for religious resistance, as occurred in Poland.
However, Albania is not a religiously homogeneous state. Nearly 30 percent
of Albanians are either Orthodox or Catholic, and the 70 percent who are
Muslim are themselves divided into Sunni and Bektashi subgroups. The
result is an ethnic emphasis in national rhetoric because of the diminished
power of religion in uniting the Albanian people.

The Ukraine displays a similar pattern. Although it is seemingly a perfect
breeding ground for religious nationalism because of its threatening religious
frontiers (with Russia to the east and a number of Catholic states to the
west), the Ukraine is divided internally between Uniate Christians, Orthodox
Christians professing their allegiance to the Ukrainian church, and
Orthodox Christians professing their allegiance to the Russian church. As a
result, religion was useful in the independence movement, but has been more
limited in its ability to create a unitary and strong nation-state.

This limiting power of religious heterogeneity is not constant. There are
examples of heterogeneous nations that adopt a religious concept of
nationalism and then proceed to purge those who no longer belong to the

newly conceptualized nation. Poland provides a good example. In the seventeenth century, Poland was considered to be one of the most tolerant and diverse nations in Europe. A large Jewish population lived in the state and participated in society. However, as Polish power waned and the threat from non-Catholic neighbors increased, the Polish nation became increasingly centered on Catholicism and its role in nationalism. It was from this point onward that the Polish nation became increasingly homogeneous. As a result, the homogeneity was created by religious nationalism and not vice versa.

The point of the above discussion is to clarify two key ideas: (1) the relationship between religious demography and religious nationalism is highly complex; and (2) religious heterogeneity may hinder religious nationalism in certain cases. Some states that experience threatening religious frontiers may not necessarily resort to religious nationalism as there may be other national identifiers that are more useful in national unification.

Stipulation 2: the role of historic religious associations

Another argument that appears in the sociology literature claims that historic shifts in religious identification may play a role in modern nationalism. Specifically, nations that associate their religion with negative outside influences are less likely to turn to that religion for national differentiation and pride. David Martin, in his classic work *A General Theory of Secularization*, lays out this idea as follows: " ... there is ambiguity where domination restores a religion, as the Counter-Reformation restored Catholicism in Hungary and in Czech Lands, yet has to leave the [national] myth in the hands of a beaten minority" (Martin 1978: 108). Martin's argument is best exemplified through the Czech case. He argues that Czech nationalism has strong ties to the story of Jan Hus because of his emphasis on the local language. The Hussite movement led to an initial awakening of Czech identity which quickly swept across the region. However, the Counter-Reformation devastated the new religion. The Holy Roman Empire banned the practice and expelled all non-Catholic clergy from Czech lands. As a result, the people were reconverted to Catholicism, but the national identity still lay in the concept of Hussite Protestantism. In addition, the Catholic Church was now associated with foreign domination by the Germans in spite of the fact that most Czechs were Catholic themselves. Czech identity could not be associated with Catholicism because Catholicism had been oppressive and foreign, nor could Czech identity be associated with Protestantism because the Czechs were largely Catholic.

Martin places the emphasis on the reconversion aspect. However, it is not the reconversion that causes problems for nationalism. Rather, it is the association of religion with an oppressive and foreign power. As a result, a nation does not have to go through a conversion–reconversion process in order to feel historically severed from the Church. Therefore, the second addendum is: a historic association of religion and national oppression will limit the link between religion and nationalism in modernity.

Two more outliers are useful illustrations: both Estonia and Latvia are predominantly Lutheran states. They also have very strong and threatening religious frontiers – most notably with Russia. However, neither demonstrates a strong religious nationalism. This is largely because Lutheranism has been associated with German domination throughout much of their histories. Germanic influences brought Lutheranism to the Baltics, and German nobles remained in a position of power in these states for centuries. The treatment of locals by these nobles led to a great deal of resentment. As a result, although the majority of Latvians and Estonians are Lutheran, the Lutheran church is associated with oppression and therefore loses its power in the mind of the nation.

This relationship between Church and oppression can also be seen in France. Although the circumstances were very different, the strong ties between the Catholic Church and the monarchy meant that religion lost much of its power leading up to the French Revolution. It had become associated with an illegitimate and oppressive regime, as well as a foreign influence (through Marie Antoinette's Austrian ties). Italy also falls into this category in an abstract way. In Italy, the Church itself became the opposition to national unification. The late nineteenth century saw the church lining up against Italian unification for a variety of reasons, and the end result was a weaker link between nation and religion. In the end, it is safe to argue that threatening religious frontiers almost always lead to religious nationalism; however, if the church itself is threatening or associated with a threat, this link is greatly weakened.

Stipulation 3: the role of religiously minded regimes

A third clarification that must be considered examines the role of authoritarian governments. Specifically, what effect does a religiously minded government have in the overall process of secularization? Can a strong government essentially force secularization on an otherwise religious nation? On the other hand, can a strong government force religion on an otherwise secular (or secularizing) nation? In other words, can the broader causal factors discussed in this book be overruled by force? The answer is maybe, but only temporarily.

There are a wide variety of cases that can illustrate the role of a strong state in the secularization or sacralization of the nation. The most obvious ones occurred in Eastern Europe under Communist rule. Communist ideology dictated the repression of religion in general, but the success of this policy varied widely. In many cases, religion was successfully repressed, but the end of Communism in the 1990s led to a near universal surge in religious attitudes, beliefs, and identification. Even in Russia itself, there was a give and take throughout the Soviet years. During World War II, for instance, the

Church was given more freedom when the state needed to rally support for the war effort. In other cases, the state had little success in deflating the power of religion – Poland is probably the best example, although Romania and Bulgaria are also pertinent. In general, force was only successful in secularizing society in those states that were already predisposed to secular nationalism (i.e., they had no religious frontiers or were not threatened). In those countries where threatening religious frontiers were present, force was sometimes successful in repressing religious identity. It was never fully successful in destroying it. Those nations that were most obviously threatened by religious frontiers (Poland, Serbia, Croatia, Bosnia) were also the ones in which religion was the most difficult to suppress.

On the other hand, there are also several examples of states that experienced the opposite situation: an authoritarian government that sought to support religion rather than suppress it. Although this type of regime is not uncommon in European history, it is rare in *modern* European history. The two most obvious examples are Spain and Portugal. In each of these cases, a reactionary government was formed in response to liberalizing and anti-clerical forces in the early twentieth century. In both cases, the forces of secularism had begun to influence society in the nineteenth century. In both cases, leaders who were strongly aligned with the Catholic Church came to power and, in both cases, they used their power to retard the progress of modernization. As was the case in Eastern Europe, this effort was successful in the short term. However, the broader context of Iberia meant that there was no threatening religious frontier to preserve a religious concept of the nation. Both Spain and Portugal are currently in the process of secularizing after the Franco and Salazar regimes came to an end in the late 1960s and early 1970s. Although both are still largely religious, the shift towards secularism has been clear, particularly in Spain.

The third stipulation in this theory is: a powerful government may temporarily impose either secularism or religion from above. However, its long-term success will ultimately be dictated by the broader social conditions at hand (i.e., threatening religious frontiers). David Martin also addresses this stipulation as follows: " ... there is ambiguity where a revolution forces the nation to split into two and an old 'integrisme' confronts a new 'integrisme'. This is most likely to happen in Catholic countries since Catholicism is inherently an 'integriste' and organicist system" (Martin 1978: 108). Martin is only addressing half the equation. The important aspect is the imposition of a particular (religious or secular) mindset on the nation. This falls more in line with Nicolas Demerath's concept of directed versus non-directed secularization and sacralization (Demerath 2001). Forced secularization or sacralization is never as successful as that which occurs in a more organic fashion. As a result, the religiously minded Iberian states and the secular-minded former Communist states are likely to continue to revert back to their natural states as dictated by religious frontiers and threats.

Perhaps the best way to summarize the above stipulations is to say that context matters. In general, the argument that threatening religious frontiers create religious nationalism holds true. However, circumstances are unique in each and every nation, and these unique attributes must always be taken into account. In several cases (Portugal, Spain), it can be argued that their seemingly contrary state will self-correct in the near future. For a few other cases (Latvia, Estonia), we see that unique historical circumstances have dictated that Lutheranism will not likely play a role in national identity even in the presence of religious frontiers. And in others (Albania, Ukraine), internal religious divides weaken the broad mobilizing power of religion, thus severing it from national rhetoric. In each of these cases, the broader argument would have held true had it not been for a number of unique conditions. As a whole, it is quite obvious that threatening religious frontiers play a very important role in determining the level of national secularization.

Alternative theories

In order to be as thorough as possible, it makes sense to take a step back and consider some of the alternative theories that were laid out in Chapter two. Although the argument of this book has been shown to be largely accurate in explaining religious nationalism, the examination of these other potential explanations allows for further clarification. In addition, it reveals whether or not these competing theories can explain as much as the theory presented above.

Alternative 1: economics and modernization

The first theory worth exploring is one that has been held in some esteem in the social sciences for some time. Modernization theory essentially argues that economic development is part of a natural process that carries with it a variety of other social changes – urbanization, rationalization, secularization. The assumption has long been that economically developed states are more secular states. On the surface, this argument makes sense. After all, Europe is both the most secular and the most developed region in the world.

Closer examination reveals the flaw. Some of the most economically developed states in Europe are also some of the most religiously nationalist. Ireland alone is enough to cause a problem for this argument. When one considers that Italy, Spain, Portugal, and Greece are all in the upper half of European economies and are all considered developed by the World Bank, the argument is damaged even further. On the other hand, many of the poorest states in Europe are also the most secular. Albania, Latvia, and Estonia are examples. The United States further complicates the picture: one of the most advanced economies in the world with an undoubtedly high prominence of religion in society.

There is a broad pattern that does seem to hold true. In general, economically advanced countries tend to be more secular than those that are economically underdeveloped. However, this correlation has long been taken for granted, and there has been little scientific explanation for this phenomenon. This study reveals an important causal mechanism behind the relationship between economics and secularism. It seems that economic development is merely one of many ways in which a nation can diminish threats to its existence. A nation that exists at a religious frontier may experience a variety of threats from that frontier. We tend to think of military threats first and foremost. However, economics can play a large role in the susceptibility of a state to military and cultural threats. The chances of an economically developed nation being integrated or subsumed by a neighbor are significantly less than those of a nation that is economically weak.

A few examples from European history will help to demonstrate this process. Poland illustrates how a strong and economically developed state can collapse into a position of economic weakness and vulnerability. During its "Golden Age," Poland was one of the strongest economies in Europe. It thrived on agricultural exports and boasted a powerful military alignment with Lithuania. However, as its economy collapsed in the seventeenth and eighteenth centuries, Poland became an increasingly threatened nation. In addition, it changed from a religiously tolerant state to an exclusive and highly Catholic state. The same transition can be seen in the other direction in many other European states. Britain, for example, demonstrated a strong linkage between Protestantism and national identity until the eighteenth and nineteenth centuries, when Britain established itself as the world's economic leader. As Russia's economy has collapsed over the past two decades, there has been a shift towards insecurity and an increase in the prominence of its religious frontiers, most notably with Islam.

What is important to note in each of these cases is that there was a shift in national threat. As these countries became either more or less economically secure, the importance of their religious frontiers waxed or waned. The religious frontier stayed the same; the threat was altered. Although economics is only one form of security or threat, it does play a role in religious nationalism in this indirect manner. As a result, a state such as Ireland may be very advanced economically and still exhibit the signs of religious nationalism because the threat from Britain has not been adequately calmed by the economic success that the island has experienced in the past decade. Therefore, the level of economic development at which each state secularizes will vary based on its own unique circumstances. Is there a religious frontier? How threatening is it? Will economic development diminish that threat? As a result, economic development does play a role in secularization, but only indirectly through the ability of economics to diminish national threats across religious frontiers.

Alternative 2: cultural defense (Steve Bruce)

The main argument of this book derives partly from Steve Bruce's theory of cultural defense. Thus, there is not a lot of room for disagreement between the two approaches. However, it is worth pointing out the differences that do exist and explaining why this argument improves upon Bruce's own.

Bruce argues that "modernity undermines religion except when it finds some major social role to play other than mediating the natural and supernatural worlds" (Bruce 1996b: 96). This, in turn, occurs when religion takes on the role of "guarantor of group identity" (Bruce 2001: 259). When religiously differentiated groups come into conflict, the result is that "the religious identity of each can acquire a new significance and call forth a new loyalty as religious identity becomes a way of asserting ethnic pride and laying claim to what Max Weber called 'ethnic honor'" (Bruce 1996b: 96). Cultural defense also occurs "when there is a people with a common religion dominated by an external force (either of a different religion or of none at all)" (Bruce 1996b: 96).

Although this appears, at first, to be quite similar to my own theory, there are subtle differences with much larger ramifications. The first difference is found in the depth of Bruce's examination. Bruce spends only a brief time addressing these exceptions to secularization. His larger goal is to understand the social phenomenon of secularization, not the political phenomenon of religious nationalism. Although they fall in the same realm, they are remarkably different.

According to Bruce, the first condition under which secularization is moderated is "conflict" between religious groups. Conflict is sufficiently vague as to leave us with questions regarding exactly what type of conflict is pertinent. Threat, on the other hand, explains the circumstances surrounding religious nationalism more fully. Actual conflict is not required to create a religiously based national identity. The threat of assimilation or destruction, however, is clearly linked. In many cases (i.e., Greece and Turkey), actual direct conflict has not occurred for quite some time. However, the threat has been sufficient to maintain religious ties to national identity.

The second condition under which cultural defense occurs – external domination – is also much more complicated than Bruce allows for. As explained above, there are times when external domination in fact leads to secular identity (Latvia, Estonia, and Czech Republic). In addition, external domination is successful in explaining the independence movement in Greece, but does little to explain why religion has continued to play a key role in Greek nationalism to the present. When foreign domination ceases, religious nationalism does not necessarily follow suit.

Essentially, the point here is that Bruce makes a good argument. However, the lack of detail which Bruce devotes to the subject means that his conclusions are rather vague. This is understandable given the fact that Bruce is not seeking to explain religious nationalism *per se*. Rather, he is investigating the broader trend of secularism in society (i.e., religious practice, attendance, etc.). The depth of the present investigation allows for Bruce's ideas to be refined and built upon. The result is a more comprehensive and parsimonious theory.

Alternative 3: denominational interfaces (John Coakley)

Like Bruce's theory of cultural defense, John Coakley's arguments regarding "interdenominational interfaces" are pertinent to this investigation, but the lack of depth (once again understandable considering Coakley's purpose) means that this study has been able to refine the ideas laid out by Coakley. As a reminder, Coakley argues that "interdenominational interfaces" are crucial to an understanding of why certain states avoid the broader trend of secularism. "It frequently happens that major political borders fail to coincide with lines of religious division, leaving large minorities on the 'wrong' side of a border ... " (Coakley 2002: 216).

As is the case in Bruce's theory of cultural defense, Coakley makes a good argument, but the devil is in the details. Coakley's concept of interdenominational interfaces comes very close to the concept of religious frontiers. The difference can be found in Coakley's emphasis on political borders. As has been explained, the actual political borders are the ultimate goal of religious nationalism; they have only a minor role in its beginnings. Rather, religious frontiers have no concern for actual political borders. This is clear when one examines cases in which the political borders have been corrected, but religious nationalism continues to be strong – Greece, Ireland, Pakistan, and Poland are all good examples. The religious frontier is present regardless of what the political landscape looks like. As a result, the political borders may or may not play a strong role in the creation of religious nationalism.

As with Bruce, the shortcomings in Coakley's argument are few. For the most part, his conception of interdenominational interfaces provides a good beginning for our understanding of religious frontiers and religious nationalism. However, his focus on political conditions rather than social and geographic conditions is problematic. Similar to Bruce's concept of external domination, Coakley's argument is unable to explain the continued religious nationalism of states that have gained their independence. Once again, the religious frontier is persistent, even if the political conditions have changed.

Alternative 4: church–state relations (Jose Casanova)

Jose Casanova puts forth another common argument in his discussion of caesaropapist states. According to Casanova, caesaropapist states (or states with a strong linkage to the church) weaken the ability of the church to respond to societal demands. As a result, the church is much more likely to lose its power over the nation. According to Casanova, "It was the caesaropapist embrace of throne and altar under absolutism that perhaps more

than anything else determined the decline of church religion in Europe"
(Casanova 1994: 29).

The classic example is France, where the church and state were so closely
aligned that the church was no longer representative of the people. At the
time of the French Revolution, an overthrow of the monarchy necessarily
included an overthrow of the church. In contrast, the Irish church has been
historically independent of any central authority and, as a result, has been
much more able to respond to and represent the will of the Irish people.
Therefore, the church has maintained a stronger presence in the national
self-conception.

At first glance (and with these two examples), Casanova's argument seems
to make a lot of sense. In general, there is little doubt that strong usage of
religious symbols and rhetoric by European monarchs over the years has led
to the overall strength of secularism in Europe. However, on a case-by-case
basis, Casanova's theory is problematic. Of particular concern are the
Orthodox states of the former Ottoman Empire. Greece in particular casts
doubt on the premise. The Greek church was used by the Ottoman
Empire to maintain rule over Greek subjects. However, at independence,
the Greek church was not cast aside as in France. Rather, it was heartily
embraced by the Greek people. To this day, there is a strong tie between the
Greek state and the Greek Orthodox Church. Modern Greece is clearly a
caesaropapist state, and yet it is also one of the strongest religious nationalisms in Europe. In addition, one would expect a strong separation of church
and state (i.e., France) to encourage the linkage between nation and religion,
but this has not occurred. Instead, the linkage between religion and national
identity has been shaped by religious frontiers and threats in spite of current
or historic ties between church and state. It so happens that some church–
state linkages prove threatening and others do not. In the end, the general
concept that strong church–state linkages lead to secularism simply does not
hold up.

Alternative 5: rational choice

The final theory worth addressing is rational choice. As discussed in Chapter
two, the basic logic behind rational choice approaches to secularization is
that if " … the demand, desire, or need for religion is more or less stable,
then the manifest variations in the pace and intensity of religious activity,
commitment, and interest must be explained by variation in supply" (Bruce
1999: 44–5). In other words, rational choice " … offers a supply-side
approach to religion, suggesting that a demand for religious activity will
increase if the supply is both sufficiently diverse and sufficiently attractive to
entice the religious consumer" (Davie 2001a: 275).

There are a number of problems with this approach in Europe. At the
most basic level, there are issues with the assumption that demand for religion is constant. The entire point of this study is to argue that varying

conditions lead to varying demands for religion. It is likely that a nation that is threatened by religious frontiers will experience a much higher demand for religion than a safe and isolated nation. In other words, this study takes a demand-side approach, whereas rational choice (in this particular case) takes a supply-side approach.

There are also major concerns with the supply-side aspect of the theory. Simply looking at the countries in Europe shows this assertion to be problematic. Many of the most secular states are religiously diverse – in fact, one of the major stipulations above showed that religious plurality may be detrimental to religious activity in a country. The religious pluralities of Britain and Germany have not created strong religious societies. Nor has the lack of diversity created a secular society in Ireland, Poland, or Greece. It is likely that the equation is actually reversed. Highly religious societies (religious nationalisms) are likely to destroy religious plurality, as was the case in partitioned Poland or post-independence Greece. Similarly, a secularized society is more likely to be tolerant and therefore pluralistic. It is likely that Britain's pluralism in the religious realm is because it is no longer a nation defined by religion. A Muslim or a Catholic is no longer perceived as an outsider.

The basic problem with rational choice explanations of secularism or religiosity (in this case at least) is that they get the process reversed. The demand for religion is not fixed. Rather, demand for religion varies according to a variety of factors, including religious frontiers and threats. Thus, the assumption that supply shapes overall religiosity is faulty. Rather, as is true of most economic situations, supply is driven by demand. In Poland, there was a strong demand for Catholicism due to historical and political circumstances. In Britain, there was a more subdued demand (in general) and a wider demand across the spectrum. In the end, the evidence simply does not support the argument.

Conclusion

As stated previously, the proposition that threatening religious frontiers leads to religious nationalism has been proven remarkably robust. Only a few cases in Europe deviate from the broader pattern, and each of those can be explained through an examination of their particular circumstances. Thus, this approach provides a more comprehensive and thorough understanding of religious nationalism in today's Europe. Social science has been moving away from simplistic understandings of modernization for some time, and this book further clarifies the complexity of the phenomenon. In doing so, the theory laid out successfully integrates several other theories of religious nationalism. It adds not only to our understanding of religious nationalism in Europe today, but our broader understanding of the implications of religion in foreign policy, mass mobilization, economic development, and more. By clarifying the complex relationship between religious frontiers and national identity, a process that was once assumed to be true (secularization as a part of modernization) can now be more fully understood in its complexity. A deeper understanding adds to our ability to understand the world we live in. Although there is much more to be examined (substate identity, impacts on foreign policy, the complexities of how identity shifts occur), this examination will hopefully point us in the right direction.

Bibliography

Acquaviva, S. S. (1979) *The Decline of the Sacred in Industrial Society*, Oxford: Blackwell.

Anderson, B. (1983) *Imagined Communities*, London: Verso.

Anderson, B. (1991) *Imagined Communities: Reflections on the Origin and Spread of Nationalism*, London and New York: Verso.

Ardagh, J. (1995) *Ireland and the Irish: Portrait of a Changing Society*, London: Penguin Books.

Bachman, R. D. (ed.) (1989) *Romania: A Country Study*, Washington, DC: US Library of Congress.

Baldacchino, G. (2002) "A Nationless State?: Malta, National Identity and the E.U." *West European Politics*, 25, 191–207.

Bartlett, T. (1992) *The Fall and Rise of the Irish Nation: The Catholic Question 1690–1830*, Savage, MD: Barnes and Noble.

Berger, P. L. (1973) *The Social Reality of Religion*, Harmondsworth: Penguin.

Berger, P. L. (1974) *Religion in a Revolutionary Society*, Washington, DC: American Enterprise Institute for Public Policy Research.

Berger, P. L. (1998) "Protestantism and the Quest of Certainty" *Christian Century*, 115, 782–84.

Berger, P. L. (1999) "The Desecularization of the World: A Global Overview" in Berger, P. L. (ed.) *The Desecularization of the World: Resurgent Religion and World Politics*, Washington, DC: Ethics and Public Policy Center.

Boatswain, T. and Nicolson, C. (1995) *A Traveller's History of Greece*, New York: Interlink Books.

Brewer, D. (2001) *The Greek War of Independence: The Struggle for Freedom from Ottoman Oppression and the Birth of the Modern Greek Nation*, Woodstock: The Overlook Press.

Bromke, A. (1987) *The Meanings and Uses of Polish History*, New York: Columbia University Press.

Brown, C. G. (1992) "A Revisionist Approach to Religious Change" in Bruce, S. (ed.) *Religion and Modernization: Sociologists and Historians Debate the Secularization Thesis*, Oxford: Clarendon Press.

Bruce, S. (1992) *Religion and Modernization: Sociologists and Historians Debate the Secularization Thesis*, Oxford: Clarendon Press.

Bruce, S. (1996a) *Religion in the Modern World*, Oxford: Oxford University Press.

Bruce, S. (1996b) *Religion in the Modern World: From Cathedrals to Cults*, Oxford: Oxford University Press.

Bruce, S. (1999) *Religion and Choice*, Oxford: Oxford University Press.

Bruce, S. (2001) "The Social Process of Secularization" in Fenn, R. K. (ed.) *The Blackwell Companion to Sociology of Religion*, Oxford: Blackwell.

Burant, S. R. (ed.) (1989) *Hungary: A Country Study*, Washington, DC: US Library of Congress.

Buzan, B., Waever, O. and de Wilde, J. (1998) *Security: A New Framework for Analysis*, Boulder, CO: Lynne Rienner Publishers.

C.I.A. (2004) *C.I.A. World Factbook online*, available from https://www.cia.gov/library/publications/the-world-factbook/ (accessed 13 September 2004).

Carey, J. P. C. and Carey, A. G. (1968) *The Web of Modern Greek Politics*, New York: Columbia University Press.

Carey, M. J. (1983) "Catholicism and Irish National Identity" in Merkl, P. H. and Smart, N. (eds) *Religion and Politics in the Modern World*, New York: New York University Press.

Casanova, J. (1994) *Public Religions in the Modern World*, Chicago, IL: University of Chicago Press.

Chadwick, O. (1990) *The Reformation*, London: Viking Press.

Chrypinski, V. (1984) "Church and Nationality in Postwar Poland" in Ramet, P. (ed.) *Religion and Nationalism in Soviet and East European Politics*, Durham, NC: Duke University Press.

Churchill, W. (1929) *The World Crisis*, London: Thornton Butterworth.

Claydon, T. and McBride, I. (1998) "The Trials of Chosen Peoples: Recent Interpretations of Protestantism and National Identity in Britain and Ireland" in Claydon, T. and McBride, I. (eds) *Protestantism and National Identity: Britain and Ireland, c.1650–c.1850*, Cambridge: Cambridge University Press.

Clogg, R. (2002) *A Concise History of Greece*, Cambridge: Cambridge University Press.

Close, D. H. (2002) *Greece since 1945: Politics, Economy and Society*, London: Longman.

Coakley, J. (2002) "Religion and Nationalism in the First World" in Conversi, D. (ed.) *Ethnonationalism in the Contemporary World: Walker Connor and the Study of Nationalism*, London: Routledge.

Colley, L. (1994) *Britons: Forging the Nation, 1707–1837*, London: Yale University Press.

Collier, D. and Mahoney, J. (1996) "Insights and Pitfalls: Selection Bias in Qualitative Research" *World Politics*, 49, 56–91.

Collier, D., Brady, H. E. and Seawright, J. (2004) "Sources of Leverage in Causal Inference: Toward an Alternative View of Methodology" in Brady, H. E. and Collier, D. (eds) *Rethinking Social Inquiry: Diverse Tools, Shared Standards*, Lanham, MD: Rowman and Littlefield.

Connor, W. (1978) "A Nation is a Nation, is a State, is an Ethnic Group, is a … " *Ethnic and Racial Studies*, 1, 379–88.

Corish, P. J. (1985) *The Irish Catholic Experience: A Historical Survey*, Dublin: Michael Glazier.

Corona, L. (2000) *Poland*, San Diego: Lucent Books.

Couloumbis, T. A., Kariotis, T. and Bellou, F. (2003) "Introduction" in Couloumbis, T. A., Kariotis, T. and Bellou, F. (eds) *Greece in the Twentieth Century*, London: Frank Cass.

Cronin, S. (1980) *Irish Nationalism: A History of its Roots and Ideology*, New York: Continuum.

Curtis, G. E. (ed.) (1990) *Yugoslavia: A Country Study*, Washington, DC: US Library of Congress.

Curtis, G. E. (ed.) (1992) *Bulgaria: A Country Study*, Washington, DC: US Library of Congress.

Curtis, G. E. (ed.) (1994) *Poland: A Country Study*, Washington, DC: US Library of Congress.

Curtis, G. E. (ed.) (1995) *Greece: A Country Study*, Washington, DC: US Library of Congress.

Curtis, G. E. (ed.) (1998) *Russia: A Country Study*, Washington, DC: US Library of Congress.

Cviic, C. (1983) "The Church" in Brumberg, A. (ed.) *Poland: Genesis of a Revolution*, New York: Random House.

Darby, J. (1983) "The Historical Background" in Darby, J. (ed.) *Northern Ireland: The Background to the Conflict*, Belfast: The Appletree Press.

Darby, J. (1997) *Scorpions in a Bottle: Conflicting Cultures in Northern Ireland*, London: Minority Rights Publications.

Davie, G. (2000) *Religion in Modern Europe: A Memory Mutates*, Oxford: Oxford University Press.

Davie, G. (2001a) "Patterns of Religion in Western Europe: An Exceptional Case" in Fenn, R. K. (ed.) *The Blackwell Companion to Sociology of Religion*, Oxford: Blackwell.

Davie, G. (2001b) "The Persistence of Institutional Religion in Modern Europe" in Woodhead, L., Heelas, P. and Martin, D. (eds) *Peter Berger and the Study of Religion*, London and New York: Routledge.

Davies, N. (1982) *God's Playground: A History of Poland*, New York: Columbia University Press.

Davies, N. (1986) *Heart of Europe: A Short History of Poland*, Oxford: Oxford University Press.

Demerath, N. J. I. (2001) "Secularization Extended: From Religious 'Myth' to Cultural Commonplace" in Fenn, R. K. (ed.) *The Blackwell Companion to Sociology of Religion*, Oxford: Blackwell.

Dokos, T. P. (2003) "Greece in a Changing Strategic Setting" in Couloumbis, T. A., Kariotis, T. and Bellou, F. (eds) *Greece in the Twentieth Century*, London: Frank Cass.

Durkheim, E. (1912 [1995]) *The Elementary Forms of Religious Life: The Totemic System in Australia*, New York: Free Press.

Dziewanowski, M. K. (1977) *Poland in the Twentieth Century*, New York: Columbia University Press.

Eriksen, T. H. (2001) "Ethnic Identity, National Identity, and Intergroup Conflict: The Significance of Personal Experiences" in Ashmore, R. D., Jussim, L. and Wilder, D. (eds) *Social Identity, Intergroup Conflict, and Conflict Reduction*, New York: Oxford University Press.

European Values Study (2007) http://www.europeanvalues.nl.

Foster, R. F. (1990) *Modern Ireland, 1600–1972*, London: Penguin Books.

Foster, R. F. (2001) *The Oxford History of Ireland*, Oxford: Oxford University Press.

Freud, S. (1927 [1989]) *Future of an Illusion*, New York: W. W. Norton & Co.

Gage, N. (1986) *Hellas: A Portrait of Greece*, New York: Villard Books.

Gallant, T. W. (2001) *Modern Greece*, London: Arnold Publishers.

Geddes, B. (2003) *Paradigms and Sand Castles: Theory Building and Research Design in Comparative Politics*, Ann Arbor, MI: University of Michigan.

Geertz, C. (1963) "The Integrative Revolution: Primordial Sentiments and Civil Politics in the New States" in Geertz, C. (ed.) *Old Societies and New States: The Quest for Modernity in Asia and Africa*, New York: Free Press.

Gellner, E. (1983) *Nations and Nationalism*, Oxford: Blackwell.

Gellner, E. (1994) "Nationalism and Modernization" in Hutchinson, J. and Smith, A. D. (eds) *Nationalism*, Oxford: Oxford University Press.

George, A. and Bennett, A. (2005) *Case Studies and Theory Development in the Social Sciences*, Boston, MA: MIT Press.

Gilberg, T. (1984) "Religion and Nationalism in Romania" in Ramet, P. (ed.) *Religion and Nationalism in Soviet and East European Politics*, Durham, NC: Duke University Press.

Gill, A. (2001) "Religion and Comparative Politics" *Annual Review of Political Science*, 4, 117–38.

Goertz, G. and Levy, J. S. (2002) *Causal Explanation, Necessary Conditions, and Case Studies: The Causes of World War I*, Paper presented at the Institute for Qualitative Research Methods, Tempe, AZ.

Gottfried, R. (1949) "Spenser's Prose Works" in Greenslaw, E. (ed.) *The Works of Edmund Spenser, A Variorum Edition*, Baltimore, MD: Johns Hopkins Press.

Guelke, A. (2003) "Religion, National Identity and the Conflict in Northern Ireland" in Safran, W. (ed.) *The Secular and the Sacred: Nation, Religion and Politics*, London: Frank Cass.

Gula, J. (1994) "Catholic Poles in the U.S.S.R. during the Second World War" *Religion, State, and Society*, 22(1), 9–35.

Gurr, T. R. (1993) *Minorities at Risk: A Global View of Ethnopolitical Conflicts*, Washington, DC: US Institute of Peace Press.

Hadaway, C. K., Marler, P. L. and Chavez, M. (1996) "What the Polls Don't Show: A Closer Look at U.S. Church Attendance" *American Sociological Review*, 58, 741–52.

Hamilton, M. (1995) *The Sociology of Religion: Theoretical and Comparative Perspectives*, London and New York: Routledge.

Haskins, C. H. and Lord, R. H. (1920) *Some Problems of the Peace Conference*, Cambridge, MA: Harvard University Press.

Hastings, A. (1997) *The Construction of Nationhood: Ethnicity, Religion, and Nationalism*, Cambridge: Cambridge University Press.

Heelas, P. and Woodhead, L. (2001) "Homeless Minds Today?" in Woodhead, L., Heelas, P. and Martin, D. (eds) *Peter Berger and the Study of Religion*, London and New York: Routledge.

Hirschon, R. (1999) "Identity and the Greek State: Some Conceptual Issues and Paradoxes" in Clogg, R. (ed.) *The Greek Diaspora in the Twentieth Century*, London: Macmillan Press.

Horowitz, D. (1985) *Ethnic Groups in Conflict*, Berkeley, CA: University of California Press.

Huntington, S. P. (1996) *The Clash of Civilizations and the Remaking of World Order*, New York: Touchstone.

Inglehart, R., Basanez, M. and Moreno, A. (1997) *Human Values and Beliefs: A Cross Cultural Sourcebook*, Ann Arbor, MI: University of Michigan Press.

ISSP (1998) International Social Survey Program: Religion II, Vol. 200, Zentralarchiv fuer Empirische Sozialforschung.

Iwaskiw, W. R. (ed.) (1995) *Estonia, Latvia, and Lithuania: Country Studies*, Washington, DC: US Library of Congress.

Juergensmeyer, M. (1993) *The New Cold War?: Religious Nationalism Confronts the Secular State*, Berkeley, CA: University of California Press.

Kedourie, E. (1960) *Nationalism*, London: Hutchinson.

Kennedy, M. D. and Simon, M. D. (1983) "Church and Nation in Socialist Poland" in Merkl, P. H. and Smart, N. (eds) *Religion and Politics in the Modern World*, New York: New York University Press.

King, G., Keohane, R. O. and Verba, S. (1994) *Designing Social Inquiry: Scientific Inference in Qualitative Research*, Princeton, NJ: Princeton University Press.

Kohn, H. (1944) *The Idea of Nationalism: A Study in Its Origins and Background*, New York: Macmillan.

Koliopoulos, J. S. and Veremis, T. (2002) *Greece: The Modern Sequel; From 1831 to the Present*, New York: New York University Press.

Kolsto, P. (2000) *Political Construction Sites: Nation-Building in Russia and the Post-Soviet States*, Boulder, CO: Westview Press.

Konidaris, I. M. (2003) "The Legal Parameters of Church and State Relations in Greece" in Couloumbis, T. A., Kariotis, T. and Bellou, F. (eds) *Greece in the Twentieth Century*, London: Frank Cass.

Kourvetaris, Y. A. and Dobratz, B. A. (1987) *A Profile of Modern Greece: In Search of Identity*, Oxford: Clarendon Press.

Laqueur, W. (1992) "Russian Nationalism" *Foreign Affairs*, 71, 103–16.

Larkin, E. (1989) "The Irish Political Tradition" in Hachey, T. E. and McCaffrey, L. (eds) *Perspectives on Irish Nationalism*, Lexington, KY: University of Kentucky Press.

Makrides, V. N. (1997) "Secularization and the Greek Orthodox Church in the Reign of King George I" in Carabott, P. (ed.) *Greek Society in the Making, 1863–1913: Realities, Symbols and Visions*, Aldershot: Variorium.

Markus, V. (1984) "Religion and Nationalism in Ukraine" in Ramet, P. (ed.) *Religion and Nationalism in Soviet and East European Politics*, Durham, NC: Duke University Press.

Martin, D. (1978) *A General Theory of Secularization*, New York: Harper Colophon Books.

Marx, K. (1844 [1970]) *Contribution to the Critique of Hegel's Philosophy of Right*, O'Malley, J. (ed.), Cambridge: Cambridge University Press.

McCaffrey, L. (1989) "Components of Irish Nationalism" in Hachey, T. E. and McCaffrey, L. J. (eds) *Perspectives on Irish Nationalism*, Lexington, KY: University of Kentucky Press.

McGarry, J. and O'Leary, B. (1995) *Explaining Northern Ireland: Broken Images*, Oxford: Blackwell.

McLeod, H. (1999) "Protestantism and British National Identity, 1815–1945" in van der Veer, P. and Lehman, H. (eds) *Nation and Religion: Perspectives on Europe and Asia*, Princeton, NJ: Princeton University Press.

Merriam-Webster *Merriam-Webster Online*, available from http://www.webster.com.

Michel, P. (1991) *Politics and Religion in Eastern Europe*, Cambridge: Polity Press.

Miller, D. (1995) *On Nationality*, Oxford: Oxford University Press.

Moynahan, B. (2002) *The Faith: A History of Christianity*, New York: Doubleday.

Moyser, G. (1991) "Politics and Religion in the Modern World: An Overview" in Moyser, G. (ed.) *Politics and Religion in the Modern World*, London: Routledge.

Neville, P. (2003) *A Traveller's History of Ireland*, New York: Interlink Books.

Nitzova, P. (1997) "Bulgaria: Minorities, Democratization, and National Sentiments" *Nationalities Papers*, 25(4), 729–40.

Nordal, J. and Kristinsson, V. (eds) (1996) *Iceland – The Republic*, Reykjavik: Central Bank of Iceland.

O'Malley, P. (1997) *The Uncivil Wars: Ireland Today*, Boston, MA: Beacon Press.

Panikkar, R. (1983) "Religion or Politics: The Western Dilemma" in Merkl, P. H. and Smart, N. (eds) *Religion and Politics in the Modern World*, New York: New York University Press.

Pollis, A. (2003) "Greece: A Problematic Secular State" in Safran, W. (ed.) *The Secular and the Sacred: Nation, Religion and Politics*, London: Frank Cass.

Ragin, C. C. (2000) *Fuzzy-Set Social Science*, Chicago, IL: University of Chicago Press.

Ramet, P. (1984) "Religion and Nationalism in Yugoslavia" in Ramet, P. (ed.) *Religion and Nationalism in Soviet and East European Politics*, Durham, NC: Duke University Press.

Raun, T. U. (2003) "Nineteenth- and Early Twentieth-Century Estonian Nationalism Revisited" *Nations and Nationalism*, 9, 129–47.

Remeikis, T. (1972) "Self-Immolations and National Protest in Lithuania" *Lithuanian Quarterly Journal of Arts and Sciences*, 18(4), available from http://www.lituanus.org/1972/72_4_04.htm.

Rémond, R. (1999) *Religion and Society in Modern Europe*, Oxford: Blackwell.

Rezsohazy, R., de Groote, J. and Pyle, D. (1990) "Religion, Secularism, and Politics" in Boudart, M., Boudart, M. and Bryssinck, R. (eds) *Modern Belgium*, Palo Alto, CA: The Society for the Promotion of Science and Scholarship.

Rieffer, B.-A. J. (2003) "Religion and Nationalism: Understanding the Consequences of a Complex Relationship" *Ethnicities*, 3, 215–42.

Rokkan, S., Campbell, A., Torsvik, P. and Valen, H. (1970) *Citizens, Elections, Parties: Approached to the Study of Development*, New York: McKay.

Safran, W. (1998) *The French Polity*, New York: Addison Wesley.

Safran, W. (2003) "Introduction" in Safran, W. (ed.) *The Secular and the Sacred: Nation, Religion and Politics*, London: Frank Cass.

Sarafis, M. and Eve, M. (eds) (1990) *Background to Contemporary Greece*, London: Merlin Press.

Scarfe, A. (1984) "National Consciousness and Christianity in Eastern Europe" in Ramet, P. (ed.) *Religion and Nationalism in Soviet and East European Politics*, Durham, NC: Duke University Press.

Shelley, B. L. (1995) *Church History in Plain Language*, Nashville, TN: Thomas Nelson.

Shinn, R. S. (ed.) (1985) *Italy: A Country Study*, Washington, DC: US Library of Congress.

Slovenia, S. O. o. t. R. o. (2002) POPIS 2002, Vol. 2004.

Smith, A. D. (1989) "The Origins of Nations" *Ethnic and Racial Studies*, 12, 349–56.

Smith, A. D. (1998) *Nationalism and Modernism: A Critical Survey of Recent Theories of Nations and Nationalism*, London: Routledge.

Solsten, E. (ed.) (1993) *Cyprus: A Country Study*, Washington, DC: US Library of Congress.

Solsten, E. and McClave, D. E. (eds) (1993) *Austria: A Country Study*, Washington, DC: US Library of Congress.

Solsten, E. and Meditz, S. W. (eds) (1988) *Spain: A Country Study*, Washington, DC: US Library of Congress.

Solsten, E. and Meditz, S. W. (eds) (1990) *Finland: A Country Study*, Washington, DC: US Library of Congress.

Spenser, E. (1596) *A View of the Present State of Ireland*, available from http://www.uoregon.edu/~rbear/veue1.html.

Squires, J. E. (2003) "The Significance of Religion in British Politics" in Safran, W. (ed.) *The Secular and the Sacred: Nation, Religion, and Politics*, London: Frank Cass.

Stachura, P. (1999) *Poland in the Twentieth Century*, New York: St. Martin's Press.

Stark, R. and Bainbridge, W. (1985) *The Future of Religion: Secularization, Revival and Cult Formation*, Berkeley, CA: University of California Press.

Stark, R. and Bainbridge, W. (1987) *A Theory of Religion*, New York: Peter Lang.

Stavrou, T. G. (1995) "The Orthodox Church and Political Culture in Modern Greece" in Constas, D. and Stavrou, T. G. (eds) *Greece Prepares for the Twenty-First Century*, Washington, DC: The Woodrow Wilson Center Press.

Steven, S. (1982) *The Poles*, New York: Macmillan.

Stump, R. W. (2000) *Boundaries of Faith: Geographic Perspectives on Religious Fundamentalism*, Oxford: Rowman and Littlefield.

Szajkowski, B. (1983) *Next to God, Poland: Politics and Religion in Contemporary Poland*, London: Frances Pinter.

Tanner, M. (2001) *Ireland's Holy Wars: The Struggle for a Nation's Soul, 1500–2000*, New Haven, CT: Yale University Press.

Taras, R. (2003) "Poland's Transition to a Democratic Republic: The Taming of the Sacred" in Safran, W. (ed.) *The Secular and the Sacred: Nation, Religion and Politics*, London: Frank Cass.

Taylor, P. J. and Flint, C. (2000) *Political Geography*, London: Prentice Hall.

Theotokis, Y. (1961) *Pnevmatiki Poreia*, Athens: Fexis.

Tomka, M. (1995) "The Changing Social Role of Religion in Eastern and Central Europe: Religion's Revival and its Contradictions" *Social Compass*, 42, 17–26.

Tonge, J. (1998) *Northern Ireland: Conflict and Change*, London: Prentice Hall Europe.

Toynbee, A. (1981) *The Greeks and their Heritages*, Oxford: Oxford University Press.

US Dept of State (2003) International Religious Freedom Report, Vol. 2003, Bureau of Democracy, Human Rights and Labor.

Vacalopoulos, A. E. (1976) *The Greek Nation, 1453–1669: The Cultural and Economic Background of Modern Greek Society*, New Brunswick, NJ: Rutgers University Press.

Vasquez, J. A. (2000) "What Do We Know About War?" in Vasquez, J. A. (ed.) *What Do We Know About War?*, Lanham, MD: Rowman & Littlefield.

Veremis, T. and Koliopoulos, J. (2003) "The Evolving Content of the Greek Nation" in Couloumbis, T. A., Kariotis, T. and Bellou, F. (eds) *Greece in the Twentieth Century*, London: Frank Cass.

Wallis, R. and Bruce, S. (1992) "Secularization: The Orthodox Model" in Bruce, S. (ed.) *Religion and Modernization: Sociologists and Historians Debate the Secularization Thesis*, Oxford: Clarendon Press.

Walt, S. (1987) *The Origins of Alliances*, Ithaca, NY: Cornell University Press.

Walt, S. (1991) "The Renaissance of Security Studies" *International Studies Quarterly*, 35, 211–39.

Waltz, K. (1959) *Man, The State, and War: A Theoretical Analysis*, New York: Columbia University Press.

Waltz, K. (1979) *Theory of International Politics*, New York: McGraw Hill.

Weber, M. (1994) "The Nation" in Hutchinson, J. and Smith, A. D. (eds) *Nationalism*, Oxford: Oxford University Press.

Weclawowicz, G. (1996) *Contemporary Poland: Space and Society*, Boulder, CO: Westview Press.

Weintraub, W. (1971) "Tolerance and Intolerance in Old Poland" *Canadian Slavonic Papers*, 13, 21–43.

White, R. W. (2001) "Social and Role Identities and Political Violence: Identity as a Window on Violence in Northern Ireland" in Ashmore, R. D., Jussim, L. and Wilder, D. (eds) *Social Identity, Intergroup Conflict, and Conflict Reduction*, New York: Oxford University Press.

Wilson, B. R. (1966) *Religion in Secular Society*, London: C. A. Watts.

Wilson, B. R. (1982) *Religion in Sociological Perspective*, Oxford: Oxford University Press.

Woodhouse, C. M. (1991) *Modern Greece: A Short History*, London: Faber and Faber.

Wright, F. (1973) "Protestant Ideology and Politics in Ulster" *European Journal of Sociology*, XIV, 213–80.

Wuthnow, R. (1992) *Rediscovering the Sacred: Perspectives on Religion in Contemporary Society*, Grand Rapids, MI: William B. Eerdmans.

Zickel, R. E. and Iwaskiw, W. R. (eds) (1994) *Albania: A Country Study*, Washington, DC: US Library of Congress.

Index